HEART AND SOLE

HEART AND
SOLE
A RUGBY LIFE

DAVID SOLE
with Derek Douglas

Foreword by
IAN McGEECHAN

MAINSTREAM
PUBLISHING

First published in Great Britain in 1992 by
MAINSTREAM PUBLISHING COMPANY (EDINBURGH) LTD
7 Albany Street
Edinburgh EH1 3UG

ISBN 1 85158 493 5

A catalogue record for this book is available from the British Library

Typeset in 10½/12pt Garamond by Blackpool Typesetting Services Ltd
Printed in Great Britain by Butler & Tanner Ltd, Frome, Somerset

For Jane, Jamie and Gemma

PHOTOGRAPHIC ACKNOWLEDGMENT

The authors are grateful to the *The Herald* newspaper for permission to reproduce many of the photographs which appear in *Heart and Sole*

CONTENTS

FOREWORD

By Ian McGeechan

Scotland coach and coach to the 1989 British Lions

DURING my first game as coach to the Anglo-Scots, against Lancashire in Manchester away back in 1983, a young Exeter University student turned up to play at prop forward. He certainly hadn't the age, shape or the initials (he had three!) that one would normally associate with the archetypal image of a prop. But after 80 minutes I was aware that I had seen someone who was just that bit special and I said as much to Anglos' selector, Iain Laughland, at the time.

This young student had skill, pace and general awareness of the game that was not commonly associated with front-five players. I was convinced then that I had seen a future Scottish Internationalist in the making. Such was my introduction to D. M. B. Sole.

From that moment on it is quite extraordinary how our rugby paths were to remain on a parallel course. These paths became almost too close for comfort (mine at any rate) at Dunfermline in 1983 when we played a District Championship game together as team-mates. The Anglos tend to have a fairly unique selection procedure and it was with some trepidation that after some years in retirement I found myself – supposedly the coach – actually playing, because we had suffered two late call-offs.

Surprisingly, I played in a winning side that day so that was definitely the time to hang up the playing boots for good. What I recall most about that afternoon was the total involvement of David Sole. Playing alongside him made me realise just how often he was involved in the action, whether it was driving or running with the ball or making tackle after tackle. Because he never stops competing this has the effect of putting opponents under almost constant pressure.

A few years ago I called David a prototype player for the Nineties because his overall performance was just so far ahead of any other prop in the world. It could be argued that some of his rivals were better than David at individual skills in the propping armoury but there is not one who can match the breadth of his capabilities. A check-list of propping skills set alongside David's performances would have any other prop left far behind and it is his universal contribution to so many aspects of play which has been of such vital importance to the overall play of recent Scottish teams.

I have to admit, though, that as a prototype player for the Nineties I would like to have seen much more of him in the actual Nineties because he is a player who provides genuine enjoyment for those who watch him.

I have never seen any other player drive forward with such dynamism and pace and yet his innate skill always gave him the balance to remain in total control. He has always been a skilful handler of the ball with the ability to time the pass as well as judging its strength. On the rugby field, things always happened around David simply because his skill brought others into play and he created so many opportunities for others to exploit. As a coach, when you have a player who possesses the ability to achieve things like that from the prop forward position then you really are presented with an additional and highly welcome attacking potential.

One has to bear in mind that David achieved all of this while operating – in International terms – within a relatively lightweight front five. Scrummaging has not always been easy simply because the bulk was not there behind him. Even allowing for this there are still some strong scrummaging images fresh in the memory: the much vaunted Welsh pack of 1987 being accelerated backwards across their line in total disarray and a try resulting; the England pack being hit and lifted in the early moments of the Grand Slam game in 1990; and the Calcutta Cup pushover try of 1992 which was achieved with a relatively inexperienced pack.

In scrummaging terms, though, it was a different matter on the British Lions' Tour of Australia in 1989. It was a delight to see David as part of the Lions' pack which created havoc on that Tour. This was particularly so in the game against Queensland which remains to this day one of the hardest forward battles that I have ever witnessed. And again during the second and third Tests when the forwards exerted growing control.

More recently, in 1992, David captained a World XV side that competed every inch of the way to record a first-rate victory over the

All Blacks in the first Centennial Test in New Zealand. After that game, Australia's Bob Templeton who coached the world side alongside myself, nicknamed David 'Captain Courageous'. Why? Because Bob had pinpointed the other reason which made David genuinely world-class: he leads fearlessly from the front and into the very heart of the physical confrontation. Often he paid the price and after that game he had some very interesting patterns etched on his body and legs!

David always led from the front. As a captain there wasn't a situation into which he would expect others to go and yet not go himself. Captain Courageous indeed.

During training with Scotland much of our contact work is done with the aid of tackle-bags. On the training paddock David's attitude has always been the same; one of total commitment to the task in hand. I remember yet the looks of utter astonishment on the faces of some of the non-Scottish Lions in 1989 as we prepared for the Tour. There was David tearing into the tackle-bags as if there was no tomorrow. So far as they were concerned he took bag-work into another dimension.

Even world-class players get better with the company they keep and David had the ability to create time and space for those around him and that was an aspect of his play that won true appreciation from his team-mates. He has earned the respect of rugby folk all around the world and that is something of which he can have personal pride.

When he is well into his retirement we will all readily recollect the Sole image of the broad white head-band and the look of steely determination that went with it. I have one or two personal memories such as the look of bemused amusement on his face as he made ready for his first scrummage in International rugby against the French in 1986 when the French opted instead to take a snap lineout and Pierre Berbizier ran in for a try which took everybody by surprise. I shall remember, too, the Tour 'Sunday Schools' with the innocent choir-boy face and the unlikely looking 'ministers'.

Other incidents from David's career give me particular pleasure. During the inaugural World Cup competition in 1987 Scotland are playing France and Berbizier rolls the ball into a scrummage. However, such is the pressure the French front row is under that they are unable to strike for the ball and it just lies there in the middle of the tunnel. Scotland win possession and immediately the entire Scottish team is presented with a tremendous psychological boost that leads to an out-standing team performance. Then, outwith the confines of the scrummage, against Wales in 1989, two young half-backs – Gary Armstrong and Craig Chalmers – are fresh on the scene and Gary scores a try in the corner after a demonstration of superbly subtle link-work by David Sole.

Another memory. It is 1989 and the Lions are playing ACT. An injury brings David on as a replacement at wing-forward. He revels in the position and, even at this level, looks not the slightest bit out of place. Then there is 1990, Murrayfield, the Grand Slam and THE WALK. That will remain forever one of the most poignant moments of my sporting life.

The most recurring memory, though, is of David taking a lineout tap and driving straight through the opposition with the rest of the Scottish pack baying in his wake. It was a feat he achieved on innumerable occasions. He did it, and made it look easy, because he was so technically correct. He made it easy, too, for his team-mates to follow because his body-position was so low and so strong that he produced the ideal platform on which others could build. And it was the same with his rucking. He was one of the most technically proficient ruckers of a ball that I have ever seen. Everything that Jim Telfer coached about rucking and body-position were part and parcel of David's game. His style of play and his commitment should be compulsory viewing for any aspiring prop forward. There would be no better role model to emulate.

David has been one of a unique group of individuals on the Scottish International scene and his captaincy has reflected their commitment. I am sure that he would agree that the support he enjoyed from Finlay Calder and John Jeffrey, in particular, meant that the responsibilities of leadership could be shared.

There was a mutual respect among them all which allowed him and them to take Scotland to extended success. To work with David and to talk to him about rugby and other things is always enlightening. Like all good players he was always looking ahead and preparing to take on fresh challenges. The ability to change and adapt kept him and Scotland going forward.

I am sure that in retirement he will do well in business because I have first-hand knowledge of his commitment. In retirement he will merely be exchanging one team for another. However, as part of the team which he has now left I wish him well and I am sure that his own words will give you an intriguing insight into International rugby and beyond. I am sure I speak for all Scots when I say thank-you for the marvellous memories – I only wish there were more to come.

Ian R. McGeechan,
Edinburgh, 1992.

CHAPTER 1

THE FINAL WHISTLE

Farewell in Oz

FIFTY THOUSAND ecstatic Scots applauding Grand Slam victory over the Auld Enemy at Murrayfield with D. M. B. Sole side-stepping his way to a spectacular match-winning try. That would have been the Hollywood dream factory version of the final moments of my International career. The reality was somewhat different. It was Sunday, 21 June, 1992, and we were in Brisbane, 12,000 miles from home. It was the end of the most gruelling rugby Tour that I have ever undertaken. I got the try but there wasn't a side-step in sight and, more importantly, we had just lost 37-13 to the world champion Wallabies.

The high-intensity emotion of the occasion, though, was real enough. Until the final whistle I had not allowed myself to wallow in nostalgia or to ponder on those 44 Caps and all the memories that went with them. There was a job of work to be done at Brisbane's Ballymore Stadium. Beforehand I had thought we could win. Three years previously in the same stadium with the British Lions we had ignored the pundits to record a series-levelling Test victory over Nick Farr-Jones's Wallabies. But on the day we Scots weren't good enough. The referee didn't do us any favours but the bottom line remains thus: the Aussies were better than we were.

It was only when the New Zealander Colin Hawke (of whom more later) blew his whistle for no-side that the reality of retiral finally struck home. This would be the last time that I would wear the Scotland jersey. I looked around and tried to soak up the atmosphere. It would be the last time that I would experience the sights and the sounds, and the smells, of International rugby. Back in the changing-room I looked at the boys who had accompanied me on this most arduous of Tours. Their heads were down. They were disappointed in defeat. Throughout my captaincy it had become my custom – win, lose or draw – to say a few words to the players in the immediate aftermath of the match.

I began steadily enough. I thanked them for the mighty efforts that they had made during the Tour. I urged them, especially the young ones, to salvage something from defeat and to do that by confronting and overcoming whatever weaknesses they perceived in their own games. If they did that then weakness would be transformed into strength and they would each have profited from the afternoon's proceedings.

Thereafter, the emotion of the moment got to me and the eyes misted over. That was it. I would never again sit with fellow players in the combat-closeness of an International dressing-room. A unique relationship exists between members of a team, and not just an International team, and it is a privilege to have been part of such a close-knit community. Rugby has played a major part in my life for over 20 years. For the past decade it has virtually been my life. I shall miss it. But most of all I shall miss playing for Scotland. I shall miss the big occasions. They were what made the daily training grind worthwhile. I have been immensely privileged. But it has not been easy. International rugby never is. Success comes in direct proportion to effort expended.

I've gone at the age of 30 – too early, said some. If it were possible to play for Scotland without the time-consuming drudgery of training then I would have played on until the cows came home. However, it is not, and because for family and business reasons I was no longer able to give the commitment necessary to maintain the levels of fitness that I would have been happy with, the only honest course was for me to retire. I could have gone after the 1992 Five Nations' Championship but that would have been the easy option. I knew that the Australian Tour was going to be a hard one and that we would be going without Fin Calder, John Jeffrey and Derek White who had retired and Paul Burnell who was on the injured list. We were also blooding a number of young players and going with a fresh coaching team in Richie Dixon and David Johnston. The last thing the party needed on top of that, I reckoned, was a new captain as well. In addition, I freely confess that I enjoy touring and also I wanted to play the world champions in order to see how good they really were – and to see how good we were.

But when first I saw the Tour itinerary with its back-to-back crunch games and the appalling distances to be covered, I thought that somebody was having me on. I could not believe that Murrayfield had accepted such a demanding schedule. It was a much harder programme than that finally accepted by the British Lions in 1989 or by the All

Blacks who arrived in Australia just as we were leaving. It was officially a two-Test series but in reality, such is the strength of Queensland and New South Wales, we were effectively in for a four-Test trip. Then, as we discovered when we were actually in Australia, even the notionally 'easy' games turned out to be something other than they appeared. The Austrialians packed the less difficult sides with guest players. It got to the stage that after we had met the scrum-half Anthony Ekert for the fourth time in various guises we were on the point of having him measured for a Tour blazer! I spoke in jest but was making a very serious point when at the end of the trip I remarked that we had met so many 'ringers' that the Tour sponsors should have been Bell's and not Chivas Regal.

Nevertheless, and allowing for all that, I didn't feel that we 'broke par'. With two wins, two draws and four defeats from the eight-match programme I don't feel that we did ourselves justice. 'Par' would have been four wins instead of two. It would have been reasonable to have expected that at least.

We arrived in the steamy, sub-tropical heat of Darwin with only five days to acclimatise before the opening game against a Northern Territories' Invitation XV at the Marrara Sports complex. Theoretically, Darwin was a superb spot in which to get the Tour underway. The Aussies looked after us tremendously well. They took us, for instance, to see the reptilian star of the film *Crocodile Dundee*! We were staying in the same hotel as the Australian women's hockey team who were trying to acclimatise for the Olympics in Barcelona by playing a five-match series against their New Zealand counterparts. The way that they approached their sport was immensely impressive. It was, I think, indicative of the manner in which the Australians look at sport. To them, as an outdoor nation, sport is important and they compete to win. The hockey ladies were accompanied by their own sports psychologists and had a room choc-a-bloc full of video editing equipment which they used to fine-tune their game.

They were staying on the floor beneath us in the hotel. To some of the free-spirits in the Scotland camp this was too much of a challenge. Doddie Weir it was who equipped himself with a fishing rod and, showing great dexterity and not a little skill, managed to snare some 'nether garments' from the balcony below. He then paraded them around the swimming pool asking for their owner to step forward and make herself known. The ladies extracted their revenge when Andy Nicol was told that a journalist wanted to interview him outside where he was greeted by torrents of water cascading from the hockey girls' balconies. At that point an honourable draw was declared.

The game against the Northern Territories was to be played in the evening which meant that the stultifying heat wouldn't be as great a problem as it would have been had we been playing in mid-afternoon. Additionally, on paper at least, it should have been merely a 'loosener' designed to get the Tour off to an acceptable start. Unfortunately, in the words of the old sporting adage, we weren't playing them on paper.

For the sake of setting out on the right note it was crucially important that we got a win. However, when we saw the selection for the Northern Territories side it became immediately apparent that the Aussies were playing a very clever selection game. The Northern Territories' selectors had included five invitation players from New South Wales and Queensland in the side. They had slotted them in very cunningly with one in the front row, one in the middle row, one in the back row, one at scrum half and the fifth guest at inside centre. This meant that they now had class performers in key positions and this was obviously going to be of immense help to the Northern Territories' regulars.

That said, we played poorly. Because the game against Queensland was following on at the weekend we couldn't risk first-string players and so we opted not to pitch our top players into immediate battle. We paid the price with a morale-sapping 17-16 defeat. Peter Dods led the side from fullback and we had Stirling County's immensely promising youngster Ken Logan on the left wing. Additionally we had the Melrose duo of Derek Bain and Graham Shiel paired together in the centre and Gregor Townsend in tandem with David Millard at half-back. These were two very raw combinations. But the only way to introduce youngsters to the rigours of International rugby is to throw them in at the deep-end. You hope that they will have been sufficiently well tutored that they don't go under. In reality, though, there really is no substitute for serious match action.

In a see-saw match the lead changed hands several times and the Aussies kicked the winning penalty goal with about five minutes left to play. Watching from the sidelines I was disappointed that the team never managed to exert any control on the game and that, for the most part, they were unable to adjust to the requirements of International rugby.

The Tour had got off to a bad start. There was no getting away from that. We had lost a game that we had been expecting to win. I was concerned that because we had such an inexperienced party, that defeat might cause lasting hurt deep inside. With Queensland coming up in just a few days' time it was essential that we regrouped and got the show, even at such an early stage, back on the road. I think we managed to do that but there is little doubt that we carried the hurt of that defeat for quite a while and that, at the very least, it adversely affected the mid-week side on their next outing against the Emerging Wallabies.

After the Darwin defeat the cruel nature of the itinerary agreed to by the SRU immediately made itself felt. A five-hour flight saw us travel from the northernmost tip of the continent, where the temperature was well into the 30s celsius, to the more temperate climate of Brisbane where we had but one day before taking on Queensland who are, without a doubt, the strongest provincial side in the world. Thereafter we were back in an aeroplane and bound for Hobart in Tasmania, where the temperature dips below freezing at night, to play the Emerging Wallabies. Therefore, within the space of our first week in Australia, we had disected the continent and experienced three distinct climates.

I don't think that anyone who had ever been touring in Australia had been consulted about the itinerary. Certainly Ian McGeechan wasn't and he had been the coach to the successful 1989 Lions out there and one of those who had declined to accept the original itinerary proposed for that trip. I feel strongly that we should have taken a leaf from the Lions' book and declined to tour on the schedule as provided by the ARFU. Even the Austrialian media referred to the almost impossible nature of the itinerary and, bearing in mind how much stick we had taken from them with the Lions, you begin to realise that when the Aussie press get on your side, you really have been sold a pig in a poke. It was a crazy, crazy itinerary and whoever was responsible for accepting it at Murrayfield certainly didn't do us any favours.

The 'loaded' itinerary, though, didn't mean that on an 'off-field' level the Aussies didn't do everything within their power to make our stay a pleasant one. In fact, one of the most pleasing aspects of the Tour was the huge difference which showed itself between the off-field Aussie attitude to us as Scots compared to that experienced three years earlier when I had been a member of the British Isles' Tour party. Scots seem to bring out the best in their hosts wherever they go. The amount of goodwill shown to us was immense and at marked variance to that displayed to the British Lions.

As a touring party, too, the boys got on well with each other. In a playing sense the going was tough and results were so mediocre that the Tour could quite easily have fallen to pieces. That this didn't happen was due in no small measure to the strength of character shown by the players, the management and the coaches.

When you are 12,000 miles from home, into the third week of a tour and have still to lodge your first win then, in character terms, the men are really sorted out from the boys. It is essential that you adopt a positive attitude and just go for it. The moment that people start moping around and start thinking 'We're never going to win. I wish I'd never come', then you end up in the mess that Wales got themselves into in 1991 when they were hammered out of sight and the Tour disintegrated both on and off the field. Despite the results that we were getting, there was never any danger of this happening to us. Everybody knuckled down and I was proud of them.

The game against Queensland was real make or break stuff for us. Queensland were unbeaten that season having already lifted the scalps of Auckland, Wellington, Fiji and Canterbury. They had just won the Super Six championship involving top provincial sides from New Zealand, Australia and Fiji itself. In 1990 they had seen off France, Wales and England. Their line-up bristles with Wallabies. Imagine a Scottish district side with the likes of Jason Little, Tim Horan, Paul Carozza, Michael Lynagh, Rod McCall, John Eales, Cameron Lillicrap, Tom Lawton, Dan Crowley, Troy Coker, and so on and so on. That was the calibre of the side that we had to play after the (if you'll pardon the rather dire alliteration) devastating defeat in Darwin.

We conceded a soft try early on after a high-ball mix up between Gavin Hastings and Andy Nicol. Timmy Horan, who really is an outstanding player, pounced for the try and Peter Kahl converted. Almost in a trice we were six points down. Thereafter it was hard going. We were conceding more than a stone a man in the scrummage and really had to grit our teeth to avoid being swamped. Peter Wright, the Boroughmuir prop, deserves a mention here. Peter has flattered to deceive in the past and quite often he has been perceived to suffer from an 'attitude' problem. However, he stuck to his guns throughout and the Australian Tour might well have been the making of him in an International sense.

We recovered from that early set-back with a try by Derek Stark which Gavin converted from the touchline. We were back in the game but having to defend like demons. We tackled everything that moved. Really it was a triumph of will. We just refused to be beaten. The Australians with their big pack were winning a lot of ball and we had our hands full with their driving maul tactics.

Sean Lineen put us ahead with a try and once again Gavin converted from the touchline. Kahl had a penalty and a drop goal for Queensland to level terms but Craig Chalmers kicked us back into the lead with a penalty goal. Kahl made it all square once again with his second penalty goal. It was 15-15. It hadn't been a win but against that standard of opposition we had regained our self-respect. Gavin received a knock on the head and he had to have some stitches inserted. Ken Logan came on as a replacement and, once again, impressed with the coolness of his play. Ken has the arrogance of youth but allied to that a willingness to listen and learn. He reminds me so much of the young Hastings boys. I think he is going to be a star.

After the game the Aussie media had a bit of fun and indulged in what, really, was the only example of the propaganda barrage that we had found ourselves under constantly during the Lions' Tour in 1989. Under the headline 'Scots send SoS to McGeechan', the Sydney *Daily Telegraph Mirror* reported that Ian McGeechan, the national coach who had not been able to make the trip, was being asked to fly out in an effort to restore sagging morale. This was, of course, balderdash.

There had been a suggestion before we left home that Geech might have come out as an observer for the two Tests but nothing came of it. From a personal point of view I have to admit that I found it very strange to be touring without the presence of Ian. Geech has been coach to every representative side that I have toured with. In fact before the first Test I received a fax from him which so impressed me that I read it out verbatim to the team just after we had performed the traditional, low-key ceremony of handing over the match jerseys. I said simply that I'd had a fax from a man who meant an awful lot to me. I said he was 12,000 miles away on the other side of the world but he was very much with us in spirit and then I just read out Geech's word of encouragement. It was quite a touching moment.

But the game which most preoccupied us next was that against the Emerging Wallabies in Hobart, Tasmania. Again, we were caught between a rock and a hard place so far as our team selection was concerned. With New South Wales, another formidable provincial hurdle coming up just four days later, we were loath to risk a large input of first-string players. However, as was to become their practice, the Aussie selectors weren't doing us any favours because the Emerging Wallabies weren't any mugs either.

The game began disastrously and then got worse! Rarely have I seen a Scotland side play with as little commitment. I was listed as a replacement and watched from the bench with mounting concern, not to say anger, as the Emerging Wallabies ran all over us. We were 15-0 down and looked set for a real howking when the flanker Stuart Reid went off with a cut nose and I went on in his place. We had wanted to rest Doddie Weir and so I agreed to sit on the bench as cover for the front and back rows – a pretty unusual combination but one which I had already carried out on the Lions tour. There had been no heart to the Scottish play. It had been inept in the extreme. When I went on I was keen not to step too hard on Peter Dods's toes as he was captain for the day. I reckoned that the least I could do, though, was try to get the forwards fired up and, putting it diplomatically, I gave them a piece of my mind!

My sojourn in the back-row was short-lived as I moved to my more usual loose-head berth after Alan Watt was carried off in the most unusual of circumstances. Matt Ryan, the Queensland prop, was lying on the ground injured. Wattie was wandering around waiting to get into a scrum. He accidentally stood on Ryan's hand and the Queensland prop leapt up and smacked Watt on the jaw. Wattie went down like a sack of tatties and Ryan was sent off for his troubles. Kenny Milne came on for Wattie, Ian Corcoran went into the back-row and Peter Jones took over at tighthead allowing me to slot into more customary territory on the other side of the front row.

There had been no fire or aggression and for a while it had looked as if the boys were just going to lie down and be trampled on. Gradually, though, we began to fight back and from 24-4 in arrears we pulled back to 24-all. We had salvaged something and had managed to keep another defeat off the Tour record but, in truth, it had been a pretty gutless performance and not one to go down in the annals of Scottish rugby.

I picked up a knee injury in the game and was, therefore, sidelined for the next match against New South Wales in Sydney. The problem was with a ligament and, in normal circumstances, it might have kept me out for a few games but Tour injuries are much more easily treated than those back home. Because you have a physio in 24-hour attendance you can have four bouts of treatment a day and this makes a huge difference to the speed of recovery. I was hopeful, therefore, that I would be out for only the one game.

Causing more immediate concern on the injury front, however, was Stuart Reid. Before our departure Stuart had been suffering from an Achilles' tendon injury. Frankly, there were suspicions before we had even left the UK that the ankle wasn't as it should have been. After the Emerging Wallabies game it deteriorated and Stuart was out of the Tour and on his way home. We called in Andy Macdonald, the six foot eight inches Scotland 'B' and Heriot's FP lock as cover. Andy flew in via Moscow and London from Siberia where he had been touring with the Barbarians. Gavin Hastings was also giving cause for concern. He had bruised a bone in a leg in the Queensland game and was out of sorts so he couldn't start against NSW either.

At the Waratah Stadium in Sydney we were, quite simply, gubbed. We were taken to the cleaners in the scrums, didn't win a great deal of lineout ball, and their back-row had a field day. We conceded six tries to none and were lucky to get away with a 35-15 defeat. There had been an hour's bus ride from the hotel to the ground and that had the effect of deflating the spirit which had been built up. We had left the hotel in fine fettle but by the time we reached the ground it had all gone flat. Of course that wasn't the reason for our defeat but such a downbeat build-up certainly didn't help.

From Sydney to Tamworth – the 'country capital of Australia' – where we were to take on New South Wales Country at the town's Rugby League ground, Scully Park. Four games down, four to play and still we were looking for our first win. We reckoned it was now or never. Surprisingly, rural Tamworth was one of the high points of the entire trip. As an indication of how arduous the trip had been, it was here – three weeks in – that we had our first purely social, off-duty outing as a squad when we were royally entertained at a barbecue by the locals; we sold the last of our stock of 1,000 Tour T-shirts and, glory be, we won 26-10. What a relief. Damian Cronin was named man of the match which was no less than he deserved. In the past Damian didn't travel well. Bill Cuthbertson, one of Damian's boilerhouse predecessors in a Scotland shirt, was such a bad traveller that he was nicknamed Gulliver. Damian had been to Zimbabwe, Japan and New Zealand with Scotland and he had never really done himself justice. He had moved from Bath to London Scottish and was obviously peeved that his place in the Scotland set-up had been usurped by Doddie Weir. Whatever the reason, he played as well on the Australian Tour as he had done throughout his Scotland career.

That win in Tamworth was a great preparation for the first Test in Sydney. It hadn't been particularly significant in terms of results in the grand scheme of things but as a tonic for the entire party with the first Test looming it couldn't have come at a better time.

Our base in Sydney, the Manly Pacific Park Royal Hotel, also acted as a boost for spirits that could have been flagging. It was just off the beach and we were able to walk in Pacific splendour to the training ground past surfers and the beach-life which the Australian climate allows. I approached the Test in a buoyant frame of mind. I certainly didn't fear the Australians and considered that, all else being equal, we could give them a tough old time.

The Scotland side more or less selected itself. There was some debate about Carl Hogg v Dave McIvor at blind-side wing-forward. What eventually tipped the scales in Carl's favour was the three or four-inch height advantage that he enjoys over Dave. It was hard on Dave, who had come into the side for that year's Five Nations' Championship. He is a genuine 100 per cent player. He never delivers less than his all. But we reckoned that against the Australians' towering lineout presence we would need more height at the tail of the line. There had been some debate in the media about Scott and Sean in the centre. However, within the squad there was little doubt that they would be our first-choice centre partnership. Things hadn't gone particularly well for them in the preceding Five Nations matches or, before that, the World Cup. However, a lot of the problems were not of their making. On the Australian tour the entire back-line worked much better than it had done for a couple of seasons and got back to something resembling what had been on display during the Grand Slam season in 1990. Scott's defence throughout the Tour was of the highest order. His fitness never ceased to amaze me. He would make one tackle, get up and make another and then go on to make a third and win the ball into the bargain. Often, two centres and a fleet-of-foot open-side flanker don't make that kind of impression. Scott doesn't really get the credit that he deserves for his attacking play but in addition to his rock-solid defence he is also pretty quick, with a keen eye for the gap. If he goes on the 1993 Lions' tour to New Zealand – which I am sure he will – then I have a tip for the selectors: pick him as a wing-threequarter and you won't be disappointed.

In the Test itself what let us down was a general lack of concentration. The mental hardness which is necessary for success in Test rugby wasn't there. We actually led 9-7 at the interval and if we had kept our concentration at the level it had been at in the opening period then I remain convinced that we would have won. If – and I'm aware that 'if' is one of the most abused words in the English language – we had got a quick score after the interval we would have had the Wallabies on the ropes. A loose clearance by Gavin allowed David Campese to run the ball straight back at us and Michael Lynagh got a foot to a loose ball for Paul Carozza to get the try which pushed the Aussies in front. That five-minute period just after the interval is one of the most critical in any game of rugby and at the Sydney Football Stadium it was Australia who made the most of it and therefore gained the psychological edge.

The Australians are a very good side. In terms of teams I have played against they are right up there amongst the front-runners. They are the world champions after all. The first Test represented our best opportunity to beat them. It was their first match of the season; they hadn't played together since the World Cup and Michael Lynagh and David Campese were just back from their off-season sojourn in Italy. There are no apparent weaknesses anywhere in the team. They are good scrummagers. They have a good array of lineout talent and a world-class back-row. Willie Ofahengaue invariably lives up to his nickname, the Tongan Torpedo, and Tim Gavin, just back from injury during our visit, is a number eight forward of rare ability.

Behind the scrum, Nick Farr-Jones has a superbly astute tactical brain and he links tremendously well with his back-row. Michael Lynagh is a class act and outside him you have Jason Little and Tim Horan. Little couldn't play against us because he had glandular fever, but when Horan and Little are paired together you have one of the all-time great centre partnerships. There is probably nothing I can say about Campo that he hasn't already said himself! Or even as the Wallaby lock John Eales said: 'David fell in love with himself ten years ago and has remained faithful ever since!' He is, though, quite simply, different class. He has the ability to turn a game by a stroke of sheer genuis and that kind of player comes around only once or twice in a generation.

It had been our intention to keep the ball away from the touch-lines. We aimed to kick long balls down the field and then follow-up, close them down and force them to kick to touch. Also we wanted offensive-defence. The plan was to pressurise them by getting in some big hits. We always reckoned that we would be under pressure in the scrummage but when Kenny Milne had to go off after only 10 minutes with a leg injury that really upset the apple-cart.

Kenny is a very strong scrummager and his throwing-in is pinpoint accurate. Ian Corcoran came on to replace Kenny, and Ian just doesn't have Kenny's scrummaging bulk. As the game wore on we found ourselves under intense pressure in that department and the game just drifted away from us to, eventually, a 27-12 defeat.

It was immediately apparent that Kenny's torn calf muscles weren't going to allow him to take any further active part in the Tour and so an SOS was sent back to Scotland for Dunfermline's Scotland 'B' hooker Martin Scott to join the party. The intention was to give him a run-out against Queensland Country who were our midweek opponents before the second and final Test the following weekend in Brisbane.

Once again, at Toowoomba, the Queensland Country selectors had rung the changes and selected a few ringers! They had included Sam Scott-Young, who is a Queensland regular, Dan Crowley, who played in the front-row for Queensland, plus one or two others who had played good 'rep' rugby. In spite of this we won 29-12 and the general display was an awful lot better. Gregor Townsend, the young Gala stand-off who shows great promise for one so immature in playing terms, had a very good game. Damian Cronin, whose appetite for the game showed how desperate he was to win back his Scotland place, also had a good game and did more than enough to guarantee his selection for the second Test.

Gavin Hastings, though, couldn't make the second Test. He hurt his back at a training session on the Friday and although we had hoped that he would be fit in time it became clear by Saturday night that he wasn't going to be there. However, we saw no reason to alert the Aussies to this fact and we were 'economical with the truth' right up until the final moment when it was announced that Kenny Logan, selected on the wing, would play at fullback and Tony Stanger – or Trevor Strange as Damian Cronin misheard the name on their first meeting – would come back into the side in his usual right wing berth.

So, to Ballymore where I would play out my final, and most frustrating, 80-odd minutes of rugby. I have rarely, if ever, publicly criticised a refereee after a game of rugby. They have their job to do and, like the rest of us, they are only human and subject to the frailties that the human condition dictates. However, I think that as players we have the right to expect that the officials appointed to adjudicate in Test matches – the pinnacle and the showcase for rugby worldwide – are, at the very least, competent. I'm sad to say that Mr Colin Hawke, the New Zealand traffic cop who was in charge of that game at Ballymore, simply wasn't up to it.

He opted out of refereeing the lineout. He simply didn't want to know. There were occasions when Mr Hawke penalised Doddie Weir for allegedly climbing over his opposite number when, at the time of the perceived offence, Doddie was sitting on his backside having been unceremoniously barged out of the proceedings.

Mr Hawke, who wasn't a refereeing debutant at International level, having already taken charge of two big games, had, perhaps, been influenced by the campaign which the Australian media ran in the week before the Test. They had been writing that the only way the Scots were going to win any lineout ball was by cheating. My impression was that Mr Hawke went into the game with the preconceived notion that we were going to be getting up to all kinds of skullduggery and, accordingly, he was only refereeing the one side – us!

When it became apparent that we weren't going to get any help from the referee I got the guys together and told them that if anyone laid a single finger on a Scot at the next lineout then we were all to get stuck in and sort it out ourselves. However, at the next lineout the Aussies once again started their barging and nudging and I got stuck in amongst them, looking around for the rest of the troops to follow. It was the classic case of the guy who shouts 'charge' and then gets up to the enemy trenches to find that there's nobody with him. It would have been laughable had it not been so serious. The intention had been to 'wisen up' the Australians to the fact that if the referee wasn't going to do anything about their tactics then we would. Ahem, what was game-plan two?

However, if his refereeing of the lineout was marginal (and I give him the benefit of the doubt) then his interpretation of the laws covering the playing of the ball on the ground was plain wrong. Scots were penalised time and again for going over the top at the tackle when it was obvious to everyone, even those in the back seats of the stands, that Australian players were transgressing by failing to release the ball. At the interval the penalty tally was 13-7. We, of course, had the 13 against. You simply cannot afford that kind of disparity when the opposition has a goal-kicker of Lynagh's renown although, to our great good fortune, he was only able to goal six from 12 attempts throughout the afternoon. The referee's decisions were a mystery to me. I spoke to him frequently seeking clarification and, eventually I suppose, that became counter-productive. On several occasions I even had a word with David Bishop, one of the touch-judges, almost imploring him to get his colleague in the middle to have a real look at what was going on. But all to no avail. Mr Hawke just wasn't at the races.

Even allowing for the referee's influence, we didn't play well in the first half. After the interval, though, the boys got it together a bit better and, particularly in the last 20 minutes when we got our two tries – one for me and the other for Sean who, although nobody outside of a few close colleagues knew it at the time, was also playing his last match for Scotland. That, then, was it – 37-13 and a thoroughly frustrating manner in which to end a Scotland career.

Immediately after the game I was interviewed by Australian TV and had already decided that I would make a point or three about the referee's performance. I hope that I am not just munching on sour grapes, and I don't think that I am, but it was a genuinely below-standard performance by the referee. When the players have put so much blood, toil and sweat into their preparation then it is absolutely essential that the official is up to International standard and I don't think Mr Hawke is. There is, of course, an unwritten convention that you don't criticise the referee and that he is never more right than when he is wrong. But what had happened at Ballymore that afternoon hadn't just been an isolated incident where the referee had got it wrong. He had been wrong, wrong and wrong again. I found that just unacceptable and I said so. I was criticised by some for doing so, but I make no apologies. I stand by everything I said and had I not been retiring and if the same set of circumstances had presented themselves again then I would have had no hesitation in saying exactly the same things. As a postscript to this affair, I would have to say that I, for one, wasn't in the least surprised when, the following month, Mr Hawke took charge of the England 'B' v All Black XV match in New Zealand and was on the receiving end of a few unflattering comments from the English captain, Stuart Barnes.

After the game we had a great night. In my speech at the official function I said that matches were relatively insignificant and results were relatively insignificant because long after I had forgotten specific matches or particular results I would remember all of the friendships that I had made during my career.

And finally. We might not have beaten the Wallabies but I eventually achieved my life-long ambition of performing a bungee jump. Two years beforehand, while touring in New Zealand, a few of us had been on the verge of jumping but when we turned up at the site at Auckland harbour the operation was closed for the day. I suspect rather more of the party were relieved than were disappointed.

In Australia, though, there was no such excuse. Bungee jumping, for those not acquainted with its eccentric charm, basically involves plummeting headlong from a great height with a giant rubber band attached to the ankles. At Surfers' Paradise the bungee jump was open for business. The jumping platform was atop a crane and well over 100 metres above a river estuary.

Being captain, even a recently retired one, I thought it best for squad morale if I went first. When you are on terra firma with your mates then group bonhomie is the order of the day. Once you are in that hoist, though, and watching as your colleagues become little specks in the downward distance then you begin to wonder if those still back at the hotel might not have made the right decision after all.

You get just a few moments to collect your thoughts at the top and then you are plunging head first for the water. God, does that take your breath away. The earth is rushing upwards at a frightening rate of knots and, believe me, you have more than enough time to wonder if the elastic will hold. When it does and you go rocketing back upwards before coming down and then up again like a yo-yo it is quite the most fun you can have with your clothes still on! I enjoyed it so much that they let me back for a second go. After the 'low' of Ballymore it was the perfect antidote to end the career in style on a bungee jumping 'high'. Not so much a final bow, more of a graceful swallow-dive.

More seriously, I have been particularly fortunate to play for Scotland during a golden era. The blokes that I have played alongside, the 'Bears', Finlay Calder, John Jeffrey, Derek White, Sean and the Hastings boys, have been some of the all-time greats. It's been a privilege to play alongside them and to call them friends. And these are friendships, I am sure, that will last a lifetime. No doubt in 40 years time, when Scotland are winning their umpteenth Grand Slam, the newspapers will seek out the old codgers Fin and JJ and Sole and Co and we'll bore all the young guys with our accounts of how it was in our day. One thing I will be able to tell them, though, is that whatever else we might have done, we had a lot of fun.

CHAPTER 2

THE SAINT, A BEATLE
AND SCHOOLBOY CAPS

The Early Years

WHEN, WITHIN days of each other, The Saint and a Beatle turn up
in your parents' sitting room, then it's clear, even to an innocent eight-
year-old, that something quite out of the ordinary is going on. And it
was. We were on the move. The Sole family was quitting its Hemel
Hempstead homestead for Grandfather James Barclay Milne's estate at
Glenbuchat in Aberdeenshire. Commuter-land was giving way to Scotland and I was delighted. From as early as I could remember I had spent
each summer in Scotland. When it was announced, after the death of
Grandfather Milne, that we were to be moving *en famille* to Glenbuchat
I thought this augured nothing but more of the outdoor life that I loved
and holidays all the year round. About this, I was sadly mistaken.

The first eight years of my life were spent in the south of England.
I was born at Aylesbury General Hospital, on 8 May 1962. My father,
Tommy, was a chartered surveyor in the City. He had picked up a cartilage injury in his late teens so his rugby career was severely curtailed,
but after War service in the Hampshire Regiment he went on to win a
hockey blue, and in fact to captain the side at Cambridge University.

I was very much the baby of the family. My sisters, Jane and Anne,
are 13 and nine years older than I am. They were largely away at school
by the time I was up and about and so very often it was just Mum and
Dad and me around the house.

At that time we stayed at the delightfully sounding Tring which
my mum, Jean, to this day recalls with a certain amount of fondness
because it afforded her the opportunity to attend the trial of the Great
Train Robbers which took place in the local Crown Court. She was an

29

avid spectator. I often wonder if, had she been around at the time of the French Revolution, she would have been one of those ladies who used to bring their knitting to the daily guillotine show on the Place de la Revolution. It all sounds just a bit bloodthirsty to me.

After Tring we moved to a palatial mansion near Hemel Hempstead which is where the Beatle and The Saint come in. It was much, much too big for us and I suspect that Dad must have bought it as part of a property deal that he was involved in. It stood in what seemed to be acres of land. It had a separate stable block, a pond, tennis courts, swimming pool, the whole works. When Mum's dad died, Colonel James Barclay Milne (from whom I inherited one of my middle names and the Scottish blood in my veins), it was decided that we should move north to take up residence on the family estate.

I had already had my first taste of rugby by this time. Like many families we used to settle down of a Saturday afternoon in front of the telly to watch the Five Nations' Championship on *Grandstand*. It really does seem quite strange now that the voice which I remember from those early days when I watched TV was that of Bill McLaren. And here he is today, still commentating in his own splendidly informed style, on games in which I have taken part. But the actual first hands-on taste of the game which was to play such a huge part in my life took place at a prep school called Beechwood near our Hemel Hempstead home. Its real claim to fame, though, is not that it's where the future captain of Scotland first touched a rugby ball but that it is the place where the former Chancellor of the Exchequer Nigel Lawson first learned to do his sums. Maybe it has a lot to answer for!

I played scrum-half at Beechwood which in retrospect seems to have been a serious case of miscasting on somebody's part. The games we took part in weren't particularly serious but I do vividly remember scoring one spectacularly over-the-top try complete with a graceful swallow-dive across the line. It was just like those I'd seen in the international matches on television. I was rather pleased with myself. It went down a treat with my team-mates but not with the rugby masters who considered it just a shade too showy for their tastes. And so it was. I'm ashamed of myself when I think of it now.

But my lasting memory of Beechwood has nothing at all to do with rugby. Rather it has everything to do with the other, Association, code, which rugby folk tend to call soccer. The Beechwood blazer was a glorious red colour. The lining of the sleeves was white and it didn't take us long to realise that if you took off the coat, turned it inside out and did up the buttons then you had, if not a tailor-made then certainly a schoolboy-made, Arsenal strip. We spent our break times and lunch hours charging around the playground taking on all-comers at 'Highbury'.

We eventually moved to Scotland in the summer of 1970. The house at Hemel Hempstead was placed on the market and one of the first of those due to come and look the place over was a gent by the name of McCartney. We had no idea that it was to be the most famous Mr McCartney in the land. His name had just appeared in Dad's appointments book as 'Mr McCartney, 11.30'.

He came up the driveway in a battered old Land Rover. When he jumped out I couldn't believe my eyes. The Beatle Paul McCartney! In our house! And sitting on our settee! I rushed off to get Mum shouting, 'Mum, it's a Beatle, it's a Beatle!' Until she went down to the sitting room to see for herself that there was, indeed, a Beatle perched on our sofa she must have thought that her young son was several sandwiches short of a picnic!

A few days later, in similar circumstances, sister Annie was the victim of a ghostly apparition. The name of the next prospective purchaser in the appointments diary was R. Moore. Sure enough, right on time, Mr Roger Moore turned up on the doorstep. Annie showed him into the same sitting room that only a few days before had played host to 'our' Beatle and rushed off to find Dad.

'Dad! The Saint's in the sitting room,' she announced. Once again, our parents were flummoxed and only when they came through to meet the would-be buyer did they see that Annie was indeed correct as at the time Roger Moore was starring in the famous TV series based on the Leslie Charteris books.

Sadly, neither the Saint nor the Beatle bought the property and eventually it was sold for conversion to office accommodation. Nevertheless, the house now disposed of, the Soles upped sticks and took off lock, stock and barrel for rural Aberdeenshire.

The 16,000-acre Glenbuchat estate, in the glen of the same name, stands on the banks of the River Don about 40 miles west of Aberdeen. It is now given over predominantly to forestry but it is still marvellous grouse shooting territory where it is possible to go out on to the moors and work a different beat virtually every day of the week.

So far as I was concerned, as an eight-year-old fresh from the delights of Hemel Hempstead, it was sheer heaven. I had loved my time at Glenbuchat during the summer holidays so to be able to go out on the hills whenever I wanted was just bliss. I naïvely imagined my days from now on as being nothing more than being out on the moor from dawn until dusk. I could have asked for nothing more.

But that wasn't quite how it worked out. Mum and Dad had other ideas and the one which headed that list was school. I must admit I had thought that, at the age of eight, my school days were behind me. Think again, young Sole. Within months of our removal to Aberdeenshire I was enrolled as a boarder at Blairmore School just over the hills, but 27 miles by road, from the estate. My freedom had been short-lived indeed.

I was heartbroken. Not only would I have to leave behind Mum and Dad and the moors that I loved. I also had to bid farewell to my faithful Jack Rusell terrier, Patch. I was finding out early that life isn't all a bowl of cherries.

Blairmore School, six or so miles from Huntly, stands in 40 acres of wooded grounds, 700 feet above sea level. It gets cold there in the winter! It sounds like a dreadful old cliché but I can indeed remember, just as if it were yesterday, my first day at the school. Mum and Dad drove me around the twisting, narrow roads from Glenbuchat and were then gently ushered away as I got my kit and belongings organised into a dormitory. Mum was as upset as I was and she cried all the way home. I was in tears for all of my first night and for most of the rest of the first week.

They say that it's character-building, and I suppose that in a way it is, but the lonely horror of that first night at Blairmore is burned into my soul.

My parents, though, really didn't have that much of an option. Having decided to return to the remote family home there weren't any schools on the doorstep and boarding was the most sensible solution. They also reckoned that was where I would get the best education. That's not, I must say, how it seemed to me at the time.

After my folks had motored off down the long driveway which leads up to Blairmore I felt absolutely wretched. I was very tearful at dinner that night. It was bacon and eggs. I've never forgotten it. It's like a piece of music or a particular aroma which immediately conjures up a memory, or an incident or a specific place or time. Bacon and eggs, for me, always means that first tearful day at my new boarding school.

After dinner it was off to the dormitories and bed. That was even worse. They say the darkest hour comes just before dawn and I can vouch for that. That kind of experience marks you for life. I think scar is just too strong a word to use in this context but there's no doubt that for an eight-year-old, especially one who had led the kind of sheltered life that I had, being pitched into that kind of environment does have a major effect. Nothing can prepare you for it. However, once you do get over the initial shock then there's little doubt that it does make you mentally more strong. They say that ex-public schoolboys take quite easily to prison life. Well, I've no wish to sample Her Majesty's hospitality but I can see what people mean by that.

Being isolated and separated from your loved ones at such a tender age prepares you for just about anything. It develops an amazing self-reliance. You learn to live with it. Later, when I was at university, I used to find classmates who became extremely homesick and these were people 18 and 19 years of age. To somebody who has been stuck away in a school since eight their attitude at relatively mature years was totally incomprehensible.

After that first night, and the bacon and egg dinner, I was still dreadfully upset. I disgraced myself by bursting into tears at a French lesson and had to dash off to the loo, where I was physically sick. But the up-side of that kind of adversity means that you very quickly strike up a rapport with other boys who are in the same boat.

I struck up a binding friendship with a young lad by the name of Andrew Campbell. His folks lived in Zambia. That was a damned sight further away than Glenbuchat on the other side of the hill so, if anything, Andrew was in a more isolated position. Being an expat, even at the tender age of eight, he seemed to be more conditioned to being away from home than I was and we became bosom buddies. We arrived at Blairmore on the same day and got along famously. Because his parents were in Africa he couldn't dash off home at half-term and short holidays and so he used to come back to Glenbuchat with me.

The headmaster of the school during my time was a gent by the name of Dan Latham. To us youngsters he seemed like a giant in the Wade Dooley mould. He was very intimidating. He had a fearsome reputation, not always deserved, and once we came to know him we respected him enormously. But the real character of the school was a master called Colonel Collard. To this day I have absolutely no idea what his first name was. Maybe he didn't have one. He certainly didn't have one so far as the school community was concerned. He was simply known to all and sundry as Colonel Collard. Maybe his first name was Colonel! He always wore the kilt and a tweed jacket. No matter what the weather was, sweltering sun, torrential rain or driving snow, his attire was always the same, tweed jacket and kilt.

He taught all manner of subjects in an amusing and anecdotal kind of way. Invariably, the lesson of the day would be prefaced by the words, 'When I was in India . . .'. It mattered not to the Colonel whether he was supposed to be teaching history or geography or English, his opening gambit was always the same, 'When I was in India . . .'. His great *tour de force*, though, took place each summer during the school sports day. Colonel Collard was always alloted the role of official starter. But the regulation .22 starting pistol which fits neatly in the palm of a hand wasn't his style at all. He would have the boys line up for the 100-yard dash and then send them on their way by means of an enormous Webley service revolver. Even after all these years, every time I picture the scene it brings a smile to my face. The boys would be 'on their marks' and there would be the rotund figure of the Colonel, resplendent in the summer heat with his kilt and tweed jacket, and brandishing in his right hand this howitzer-sized pistol. It was like something straight out of Monty Python. 'On your marks. Get set. BLAAM!' The sound of that gun going off was like the clap of doom and half a dozen eight-year-olds would rocket off down the track like a pack of startled rabbits.

Colonel Collard – now sadly no longer with us – may have been the most endearingly eccentric of the staff at Blairmore but my particular favourite was Madame Cavalier, the French mistress. She had close-cropped hair, was very French and we had what might be termed a love-hate relationship. I think we each pushed the other to the limit. Certainly French lessons were more than usually fraught. Actually, I was quite good at the subject but I don't know whether this came as a source of pleasure or distress to Madame Cavalier. Languages were a bit of a forte of mine in my early years at school and I was a bit of a whizz at Latin too, although that kind of admission is just the type of thing to have you drummed out of the Front Row union. Just after Scotland had won the Grand Slam in 1990 I was asked to go back to the school to make a speech. I agreed, on one condition. I had to be given a seat of honour next to Madame Cavalier. The ceremony was taking place on a Saturday and Madame Cavalier came in on her day off and spent the afternoon sitting next to me. I think we both thoroughly enjoyed the experience. I know I did and I hope she did too.

Sheila Latham, the wife of the headmaster, was another teacher with whom I did not always see eye to eye. She did her level best to inculcate in me some basic musical principles. I took up piano but never practised so gradually fell more and more into arrears as each lesson came around. The whole thing turned into a bit of a nightmare. Mrs Latham also organised the school plays and musicals. I recall one year we were doing Gilbert and Sullivan's *Trial by Jury*. I hated it. A friend and myself were getting such a hard time, as we saw it, from Mrs Latham that we decided upon a spot of revenge.

At the time they were building a new dining-block at the school so, late one night under cover of darkness, this accomplice and I sneaked across to the partly constructed dining-hall and buried what we called a 'time capsule' deep in the foundations. Inside the 'capsule' – actually it was a tobacco tin – we wrote the most appalling notes for posterity declaring what an awful person this Mrs Latham was. Dreadful behaviour. Now, as these things tend to work out, I get on extremely well with Mrs Latham and quite often after an International match a note would arrive from her at my home in Edinburgh. We have met several times since I left Blairmore and at one of those meetings my conscience got the better of me and I confessed all about the dining-hall time capsule. Thankfully, she took it in good stead.

As the first term wore on I wasn't yet entirely convinced about Blairmore and was still feeling a bit sore about being left on my own. Really, it wasn't until my last couple of years there that I began to find it more to my liking. There was, however, one further incident which led to a certain amount of notoriety and some 'frank discussions' with the staff.

As boarders we were allowed to keep personal pets, but sadly not dogs like Patch, at the school. Most of the other boys kept the usual standard schoolboy fare like rabbits or guinea pigs or hamsters. I kept a ferret. Flip and I used to go out rabbiting when we were at home in Glenbuchat. I was delighted when I was allowed to have her with me at Blairmore. One time, though, Flip escaped from her cage and treated herself to a rather tasty nocturnal meal of her more docile companions in the school menagerie. Flip may have enjoyed herself. I'm sure she did. But the incident left rather a nasty taste in the mouths of the school authorities, not to mention my fellow pupils whose pets had been devoured.

School life went on and I made the most of it. But so far as I was concerned, Blairmore's saving grace was its sporting facilities. Even at the age of eight or nine I was getting heavily into sport and deriving a great deal of pleasure from taking part. Blairmore was the only prep school in Scotland which boasted its own ski tow, so that gives an indication of the kind of priority that they placed on sport and outdoor pursuits. We had all-weather cricket nets, good rugby pitches, cricket pitches and so on. The surroundings were absolutely second to none. It was a very beautiful place in which to be educated. That is the kind of thing that you don't actually appreciate until you are older and have left.

It was at Blairmore, too, that my rugby education began in earnest. True, I had played the game at Beechwood when I was still down south but at Blairmore the game took on an altogether more serious aspect. It was at Blairmore, also, that I was introduced to the position that I was to occupy for virtually the rest of my rugby life. One of the masters, I can't recall exactly which but I suspect that it may have been the

Colonel because in addition to all of his other duties he also took rugby, said: 'Young David Sole. You have the look of a loose-head prop to me. I think we'll give you a try out in the front row.'

Loose-head prop? I'd never heard the expression before. What did it mean, I wondered to my eight-year-old self. Did my head look as if it was about to drop off? It was a complete mystery to me. It was explained that I would pack down on the left of the front row of the scrummage and that my head would be exposed to the left of the opposition prop forward whose head could not be seen from outside the scrummage and hence he was called the tight-head. Simple? Not to an eight-year-old débutant it wasn't. Luckily, I found playing in the position much more to my taste than attempting to absorb all the descriptions of why it was called what it was. I took to it like a duck to water and during that first term in 1970 I was picked, aged eight, to play in the under-11 side, so I must have had some ability or affinity for the game.

We played a few games with me at loose-head before the first real outing of the season. It was a game against Lathallan, another Scottish prep school situated south of Stonehaven. We were absolutely stuffed. We lost by 30-odd points. It was total humiliation and we all began to wonder if this rugby lark was all that it was cracked up to be.

On a sartorial note, the Blairmore strip was blue which was quite obviously a portent of things to come. With just a couple of exceptions, every team I've ever played for has had blue in the colour scheme somewhere. We played in blue when I went to Glenalmond. It was blue, white and black at Bath, blue and white stripes at Edinburgh Academicals, blue for Edinburgh and blue for Scotland. The only exceptions have been the British Lions, the Barbarians and Exeter University where we turned out in green and white.

I soon got over that first time out drubbing against Lathallan and looked forward more and more to our regular games against other schools. I was promoted to the first XV but as a hooker, not as a loose-head prop. I was destined to play three years in the first XV at Blairmore and in my final year there we actually began to get quite good at the game. From memory, I don't think we were beaten. We always seemed to be playing bigger, older boys but we always gave a good account of ourselves.

I enjoyed my last couple of years at Blairmore. Academically things were popping along nicely and I was revelling in the sport. I was made captain of cricket which was in fact a minor bone of contention because the rugby captain was a chap by the name of David McCorquodale. The pair of us always felt that I was a better rugby player than he was and that he was the better cricketer.

I always considered rugby to be my first love but during the summer my time was given over more and more to cricket. I had a good eye for the ball and a good pair of hands but I don't think I could ever term myself a great stylist. This was a fact well known to my father who was a bit of a cricketer in his own right. Every summer we would have a Sons v Fathers match at the school. I was captain of the school side so my old man skippered the Fathers' XI.

He knew exactly what kind of batsman I was. I used to come in at number three and try to knock off a few runs as quickly as I could. I suppose 'cultured slogger' would be as good a description of my style as any. I used to be an extremely bad loser. I wasn't exactly in the John McEnroe curled and petted lip class but I didn't like to be beaten at anything and didn't much mind who knew it.

One afternoon I got out stupidly and went into a real tantrum, bat petulantly thrown to the ground, that kind of thing. My old man was at the match and he was not best pleased. What a ticking off he gave me! I still don't like losing but I would hope that at least some of my old man's advice on the nature of Kipling's twin impostors – victory and defeat – has stuck with me down the years, and particularly so into my International rugby when sometimes winning did seem to be the be-all-and-end-all. I always reckon that if you have done your best, and maybe a wee bit more, then you really shouldn't be too down-hearted if you end up losing. If you and your side have done everything that you could possibly do, tried your darnedest and you still lose then the better side has won and that is probably how it should be. I still don't like it though!

Anyhow, back to the Fathers v Sons match. I came in at number three and had made a few runs when my old man positioned a fielder at mid-wicket and told his bowler to send down a juicy long-hop. True to form I couldn't resist the lure of a couple of tantalisingly easy runs. I gave the ball an almighty swipe and promptly holed out to the fielder so judiciously positioned at mid-wicket by my old man. Had it been tennis it would have been game, set and match to Dad. He knew only too well that I would not be able to resist falling into his trap.

That cricket match more or less brought my Blairmore days to an end. After the summer it was time to be on the move again. Another school beckoned. I was bound for Glenalmond in Perthshire.

Glenalmond was the alma mater of the distinguished TV journalist and newscaster Sandy Gall. It also educated the recent Hong Kong Governor Sir David Wilson, and the Scottish Conservative politicians Lord Sanderson of Bowden and the late Alick Buchanan-Smith. More interestingly from my point of view, on the year that I arrived another former pupil was winning his first Cap for Scotland. David Leslie would become one of the great Scottish flankers and a member of the 1984 Grand Slam-winning side. Of course I had no way of knowing it at the time but the events of 17 March 1990 at Murrayfield would provide the school with a unique double.

Glenalmond College, ten miles west of Perth, was founded as Trinity College in 1841 by the Liberal statesman and three-times Prime Minister William Ewart Gladstone. He intended it to be a purveyor of the muscular brand of Christianity. The college itself is set in 250 acres of gardens and playing fields. The main buildings are grouped around two quadrangles and from the very first time I laid eyes on the place I loved it.

I was 13 years old and I took to the place immediately. There was none of the homesickness I had experienced at Blairmore. Maybe that was because I was growing older or just because I had become used to it. Whatever the reason I can honestly say that I look back on my five years at Glenalmond as one of the most enjoyable periods of my life.

For a start rugby was compulsory and that suited me down to the ground. Nevertheless, my Glenalmond rugby career got off to a decidedly unpromising start. Our introduction to College rugby took the form of fitness and speed tests. Once the results had been evaluated they then announced the personnel for the various teams. I was hopeful of getting into one of the top XVs for my age-group but when they read out the names of the forwards my name wasn't there. I was mortified. I wondered what could have gone wrong. I thought that I'd done quite well at the various speed tests. I had. Too well in fact. I wasn't in the forwards but I found myself listed as a centre-threequarter, so for the first few weeks of term I was stationed out there in the wide open prairie looking very much like the archetypal front-row forward who has lost his way.

In one school trial match I recall marking Sandy Thompson who went on to play for Kelso and the South of Scotland. He was a big sturdy lad and when he ran he was all arms and legs. His running style resembled that of a wounded antelope, as someone once said about the Ireland wing Simon Geoghegan. Sandy got the ball and I shaped up to tackle him but he ran right over the top of me and into the wide blue yonder. Thankfully the powers-that-be soon recognised that I had a limited future at centre and recalled me to the security and anonymity of the scrummage. I didn't return to hooker, though, where I had spent my time latterly at Blairmore. Instead I found myself back at loose-head prop, the position that Blairmore's Colonel Collard had manfully tried to spell out for me five years previously.

Rugby at Glenalmond was taken very seriously indeed. The master in charge of the under-14s was Jim Wainright, who had won a Cambridge blue and whose son Rob, a Scotland Cap, played alongside me at Edinburgh Academicals in later years. Whenever we were playing big rivals like Fettes College or Edinburgh Academy the whole school would turn out to watch. That's a big crowd for youngsters to play in front of and it does you good. In my first few years at the school, whenever I had finished playing in one of the younger XVs we would all sprint across to the main pitch to see how Big – as the first XV was called – were getting on. It was the ambition of all the small boys, of which I was one, to turn out one day for Big. When you watched them playing you thought that it looked so good and so professional (with a small 'p' of course!) that although you dreamt that you might play for them some day you wondered whether you would ever be able to be that good.

I suppose that by the time I was 16 or so I began to realise that I had a bit of a talent for the game. We had a very good under-16 side at Glenalmond and in our last season we won all of our matches by the proverbial country mile. We averaged 44 points a game. That was a very useful side indeed.

My breakthrough into Big came as I was playing for that under-16 XV. As so often happens, it came about through injury to an established player. The first XV prop was hurt and his natural replacement in the seconds was also injured. I was called up as a 15-year-old from the under-16 side. I did a few scrummaging sessions with Big and that seemed to go OK and then I was told that I was going to be playing at loose-head against Edinburgh Academy on the Saturday. That was a real heart-thumper. This was it! I was 15 years old and I was going to play for Big. It necessitated an immediate visit to the sports shop which the school cricket professional's wife ran under the pavilion.

The school first XV was the only team permitted to wear white shorts. The whole school wore blue jerseys but, with the exception of Big, all the other teams wore matching blue shorts. So far as I was concerned, a blue shirt and white shorts equalled only one thing – Scotland. I got a real buzz from dashing across to the sports shop and buying my first pair of white shorts. I was well known at the shop. In fact, I was one of Mrs Dennis's best customers. I was forever popping in to snap up the latest boots or a new bat, or batting gloves or whatever. As if the school fees weren't high enough, it must have caused my old man's eyebrows to zoom skyward whenever he was sent the bill for his son's habitual presence in the sports shop.

My Big-time début passed off without any great disasters. Despite the fact that I was playing against boys who were, in the main, three years older than myself I don't recall the experience as being particularly demanding in a physical sense. Tactically, though, the whole experience was a real eye-opener. I was just a wide-eyed kid playing alongside all those heroes from Big and that game was my first real experience of getting really psyched up for a match. In the lower XVs we just turned up, warmed up and played. Before that first match for Big, there was a tactical talk about who was going to do this and who would do that. The captain of Big at that time was Graham Gordon, whose brother Rick was capped against Australia in 1982. Graham was a centre and some years later we played together for the Anglo-Scots. However, this initial outing with Big was my first experience of the captain telling the team what was expected of us and then the coach, Malcolm Jack, coming into the dressing-room and saying look after this guy and that guy and so on.

Sad to relate, my new-found star status in Big was short-lived. The chap I had replaced got fit again and within weeks I was back down to the under-16 side. But, if nothing else, my appetite had been whetted. I really loved the game and was determined that I would do everything I could to get better at it.

This even stretched to training out of season. Even at rugby-mad Glenalmond, that was above and beyond the call of duty. I used to go training by running over the moors in the summer. Such devotion, though, does have its pitfalls. When we were in the Upper Sixth I and a good friend, Mike Boyd, who was dead keen to get into Big, decided to go for a run. He had been staying with us at Glenbuchat and we decided we'd go for a spot of training after Sunday lunch. We'd been out the night before and Mum had cooked us a nice lunch. We stormed out and did a couple of miles at a fair old pace. We were on the final lap, panting back up the hill towards the house when Mike and lunch parted company. Mum's best home-cooking was deposited all over the driveway.

Much more to my liking was a method of keeping fit whereby you could earn some money at the same time. I liked the financial symmetry of it. I used to go out grouse-beating on a neighbouring estate. You could earn £6.50 a day and, so far as I was concerned, that was big money. It was pretty hard work trekking over the moors from dawn until dusk but I enjoyed it. I earned my pocket money and got fit at the same time.

During the summer term at school I played cricket. I had been in two minds as to whether or not to continue with the cricket or to take up golf, which was also on offer. I was persuaded to persevere with the cricket and spent three years in the first XI. I'm naturally fairly quick and had good hands so I was usually positioned out at cover where they tend to put the better fielders. There is a dipping bank on the far-outfield of the cricket ground at Glenalmond and one of my little japes was to run after a ball, sweep it back so that it didn't go over the boundary and then duck down into the dip just beyond the boundary rope. I'd then suddenly reappear and try to take the batsman by surprise with the throw in to the stumps. I don't think you'll find such a ploy in any of the coaching manuals and I'm sure that the MCC would frown upon it but I thought it was a bit of fun.

Later, I got a trial for the Scotland under-16 side – about which the least said the better – and played regularly for Scottish Wayfarers, including matches against Scotland under-19, but really cricket was only a summer distraction. I couldn't wait for the autumn term to come around each year so that I could get the rugby boots out of hibernation and get on with the game which was my first love.

When I finally made a permanent breakthrough into Big I was in my element. In any closed community such as a boarding school, a pecking order very quickly establishes itself and at Glenalmond the first rugby XV, so far as I was concerned, was about as high in the pecking order as you could go. In my first couple of years there I used to look upon the members of Big as being virtual gods. Members of Big who had won their colours were allowed to wear a blue and white striped scarf and they stood out a mile.

It was a great thrill to play in front of the entire school at home games. If you are a bit of a showman, which I suppose I was, it's a great bonus to play in front of big crowds. It wasn't all sweetness and light, though. Depending on how the crowd felt about you they weren't slow in voicing their displeasure if one of their 'villains' had the ball. They would deliver all sorts of verbal abuse if they didn't particularly like one individual or another. It made the kind of reception that some teams get at Stirling County or down in the Borders positively benign by comparison.

During my first term at Glenalmond I was walking in one of the quadrangles and coming the other way was an older boy called Pete Wise. He played later in the second row for West of Scotland and even in those days he must have been over six feet in height. Pete was slouching along with his hands in his pockets when suddenly out from one of the doorways that lead on to the cloisters appeared a master by the name of Bill Crow. Bill had had a Trial at loose-head prop for Scotland and had a truly fearsome reputation. He didn't suffer fools, gladly or otherwise.

Bill fixed his eyes on Pete slouching along and blew his top. 'What kind of an example is that to set for younger boys?' he demanded, taking Pete by the lapels and pinning him to a notice board. Whether in feigned fury or not Bill made the point very strongly that if you were a member of Big then you had to set certain standards and slouching around with your hands in your pockets wasn't the kind of example he wanted set. I've never forgotten that. Bill used to coach the under-16 side and later on, when Malcolm Jack left to go to Loretto, he took over as the first XV coach. Bill is still at Glenalmond and he's a very nice guy with a marvellously dry sense of humour but when he was in charge of the teams that I was in I was absolutely terrified of him.

I remember one occasion, when I was vice-captain of the first XV, and the skipper, vice-captain and secretary of rugby would be invited along to discuss team selection with the coach. We were mulling over the respective merits of a couple of fly-halves when Bill said, with regard to one of the contenders, 'I'd have him in the side. He's got a big boot on him.'

Stupidly, and out of sheer wickedness, I replied: 'Well, he might have a big boot but can he kick the ball a long way?'

For a moment I thought my number was up. Bill fixed me with the kind of death-ray stare I'd seen him use on poor Pete Wise six years earlier and I looked around the room to see which notice board I was liable to be pinned against. He said nothing but that look made it perfectly plain that he considered rugby to be a serious business and that now was not the time for levity. I came to know that look extremely well indeed in the years ahead as I became involved with the incomparable Jim Telfer in the Scotland set-up. Bill and Jim were cast in the same mould.

As one grew older and went deeper and deeper into the game of rugby, one began to realise what might be possible. Ever since I had seen the senior Glenalmond boys coming back from Schools' International matches, and wearing for training the French, English and Welsh jerseys they had swapped with their opponents, I had thought that I would dearly love to gain a Schoolboy Cap. The possibilities were further brought home to me when Jamie Chalmers, the injured boy whom I had replaced for my first outing in Big, won his place in the Scottish Schoolboys' side.

My chance came via the annual schoolboy SRU President's XV game against one of the schoolboy district sides. These were, and are, a regular feature of schools' rugby in Scotland and the selectors used them very much as an additional Trial.

The President's XV is made up of boys from Glenalmond, Loretto, Edinburgh Academy, Fettes College, Merchiston and Strathallan. The six schools are asked to supply a list of the names of their best players and the team is selected from that. I was on the bench for my first involvement with the President's XV in 1978 but the following year I made it to the team proper when we took on the South of Scotland at the Stewart's-Melville ground in Inverleith, Edinburgh.

As luck would have it, with the Scottish Schools' selectors in attendance, I scored one of those flashy, headline grabbing tries. I took a pass from our centre on the South ten-metre line. It was one of those Gobi Desert jobs with all the space you didn't want and only the winger to beat. Really, it was just a case of pinning back the lugs and going hell for leather for the line. But lest I should make it sound too much like a formality I have to confess that to my eternal shame, and at the risk, again, of being drummed out of the Front Row union, I produced from somewhere the most splendidly cultured sidestep to leave the winger stranded as I crossed over for the try.

The selectors must have been impressed because just a few days later the teams were announced for the Scottish Schoolboys' Trial and my name was there. To say I was chuffed would be the understatement of the millenium. I was, as they say in the round ball game, Absolutely Over the Moon, Brian. What was more, I had been picked in the senior Blues side.

The Trial took place on the Edinburgh Wanderers' pitch behind the West Stand at Murrayfield. The Whites' tight-head prop was an Edinburgh Academy boy whom I had played against several times in the past so I knew what I was up against. Being a Trial match the selectors, and not the referee, were calling the shots and instead of two 40-minute halves we played three periods, each half an hour long. I was absolutely knackered by the end. Most of the other boys had been switched or substituted but I had to play the entire one and a half hours without a breather.

I was quite happy with the way that I had played and on the way back to Glenalmond from Edinburgh the master accompanying me said that he thought I had done not too badly. Just keep your fingers crossed, he said. Keep my fingers crossed! I kept everything crossed until the team to play France was announced about a week later and my name was there. Absolute bliss! All the training and the knocks suddenly seemed worthwhile.

The team gathered at Craigiehall, the Army's Scottish HQ on the outskirts of Edinburgh. This was the real big time. We had Scotland tracksuits and the Press and TV cameras turned up to watch us training. We were given Scottish Schools' RU badges to sew on to our new tracksuits. Being at boarding school I had to sew mine on myself but I made such a botch of it that I took it off again and did without.

The game was at Braidholm, the Clarkston RFC ground in Glasgow. To be honest I don't remember too much about it. We lost 10-6 which in those days was a pretty respectable scoreline. That French side contained future stars such as Eric Champ and Philippe Sella. They were a pretty useful outfit. The Scottish Schools side that day was: Gavin Hastings (George Watson's College); Graham Gaston (Hawick High School), Derek Buglass (Haddington), Ralph Lynch (Kelvinside Academy), Dougie Anderson (Jedburgh Grammar School), who sadly died later of leukaemia; Julian Scott (Daniel Stewart's and Melville College, who was captain), Norman Kerr (Jedburgh Grammar School); David Sole, Neil Small (George Watson's College), Kenny Muir (Clarkston), Graham Burton (Marr College), Neil Clark (Leith Academy), Ally Haggart (George Watson's College), Russell McIntyre (Portobello High School) and Simon Frame (Daniel Stewart's and Melville College).

Andrew Gavin Hastings, at 18 years of age, was exactly the same as he is now. Totally imperturbable, immensely talented, imbued with great self-confidence and the life and soul of any party. Since then we have played together for Edinburgh, the Barbarians, Scotland, the British Lions and a World XV and he hasn't changed one iota from the very first day that I met him.

An added reward for making the team to play the French was that after the game we were allowed to buy the Scottish jerseys – at a fiver a time. That was a white jersey, of course, the Scottish Schools turning out in the 'change' strip as we were playing the French at home. I swopped it for a French jersey with my opposite number because what I really wanted was a real Scottish blue jersey. To achieve this goal I would need to keep my place in the side until after the final game of the season. Only when the jerseys had done a season's duty did the schools' hierarchy put them up for sale. I was determined to have one. It would go down well at training sessions back at Glenalmond.

I must have done OK against the French because I was re-selected for the following weekend's game against Welsh Schools. This one was at Murrayfield, on the big pitch, and that was a major thrill. The game was played as a curtain-raiser for the senior Scottish Trial and I can remember coming in after our game and going for a pee. There, in the team toilets under the stand, was no less a personage than John Rutherford, the Scotland fly-half. Wow! This is what it's all about. I had just played for Scottish Schools on the main Murrayfield pitch and now there I was having a pee in the team toilets next to John Young Rutherford. It's strange the kind of thing that registers in the mind when you're 18 years old and eager to soak up all the atmosphere that's going – even in the loo!

Murrayfield was virtually empty when we played. As Derrick Grant, the former Scotland coach, once remarked, there's more atmosphere in many a graveyard than in a less than full Murrayfield, but it didn't matter to me. I was just delighted to be there and to be playing on the big pitch. Once again our opponents held the physical advantage and they won 13-6. Virtually every Scottish team that I've ever been involved with has had to face up to this problem of bigger and heavier opponents.

Stuart Barnes, who went on to play for England, was in that Welsh Schools team and a chap called Mike Pincock, who actually shares the same birthday as me, was on the bench. Mike and I met up a couple of years later when we both ended up at Exeter University and he played tight-head prop with me on the loose-head. It really is quite amazing how people you have opposed or played alongside from schoolboy level right up to the British Lions keep on popping up. It is a small world in rugby terms.

The next outing for Scottish Schools was against England and this was the match after which I would finally get my hands on a Scottish jersey of my own. Only it almost didn't happen. To this day the Scottish Schools' selectors don't know what took place but I had to indulge in the telling of a wee white lie in order to excuse my absence from the Trial match held before the side to meet the Auld Enemy was picked.

I'm afraid it is a tale of youthful over-exuberance and of a brush with the demon liquor in which I came off decidedly second best. The day before the Trial was due to take place I had been a member of the Glenalmond side which played in the George Heriot's School seven-a-sides at Goldenacre. As it happens we were beaten by Daniel Stewart's in the final but that was just the start of my evening of woe. I was staying with sister Annie in her flat in The Meadows district of Edinburgh. So far as we were concerned it was a night out from school and we determined to make the most of it. Make the most of it I did. I was up for most of the night being violently ill. Come the morn' I was in no fit state to stand let alone turn out in a Scottish Schools' Trial match. I thought I had blown it. All those years of hard graft looked as if they were going to be for nought and I wasn't going to get my hands on the Scottish jersey that I had so set my heart on.

I was in a real quandary. What was I to do? Playing was out of the question. I was liable to be sick all over my poor opponent at the first scrummage. Luckily my old man had motored down to watch the game and he came to the rescue. He took it upon himself to dash across to Murrayfield to announce to the selectors that poor David had been stricken by food poisoning and that he was 'indisposed'. Bad seafood.

Nothing serious but unfortunately he would be unable to put more than a few yards between himself and the nearest loo. Dad pulled it off. I was excused Trial duty and my bacon had been saved.

Nevertheless, I sweated buckets until the team to play England was eventually announced. When it was and I was in the side my sense of relief was enormous. And I'm delighted to be able to relate that we beat England. We played them under the floodlights at Nuneaton and it was the first time that Scottish Schools had beaten their English counterparts away from home.

That was quite a notable victory for Scottish Schools as the England side we faced that evening contained a number of future stars. Fran Clough, David Pegler, Dave Egerton and Mark Rose were all in the side. My immediate opponent was a tight-head prop called Martin Witcombe who went on to play for Leicester, Sale and the RAF. The England hooker was Keiron Rabbit who later played for Sale and Liverpool St Helens. When Liverpool came down to play Bath at a time when I was with the West Country club, Keiron was the Liverpool skipper and we were able to renew our acquaintanceship. Once again, as with all of the players I've named from that England Schools side, our paths would cross time and again in the years ahead. As I observed earlier, it really is a small world in this game of ours.

After that victory over England, and with my much cherished Scottish Schools' jersey safely in the bag, I was more or less finished with schoolboy rugby.

I went back to Glenalmond to the Upper Sixth to do some hard academic graft for Oxbridge entrance. I achieved the necessary qualification and applied to Magdalene College, Cambridge, to read Land Economy. Just my luck. On the very week that I was due to attend for an admissions interview there were headlines all over the national Press to the effect that Magdalene had appointed a new admissions tutor and that he was determined to clamp down on the practice, as he saw it, of dimwits being enrolled to read Land Economy simply in order to bolster the College and University rugby sides.

I have to admit I had hoped that, all else being equal, my sporting background might have tipped the scales in my favour with the University authorities. Obviously that wasn't going to be the case now. Initially, it was my intention to study natural sciences – Chemistry, Biology and Maths – and then do a couple of years Land Economy. My interview was with the science tutor and despite having got the necessary 'A' Levels I have to concede that I was way out of my depth. During the interview I was inwardly praying that he would ask me about rugby but all he wanted to speak about was the DNA double-helix molecule and technical stuff like that. I had been expecting a cosy wee chat. I hadn't dreamt that he would want to ask me serious questions. The interview did not go well! Next, I saw the outgoing admissions tutor and I told him that I was desperately keen to come to Cambridge and that I had a bit of a sporting background as well. He cleared his throat in an embarrassed kind of way and asked if I had seen the headlines in the newspapers that week. It appeared that a sporting background in the current climate would be a positive hindrance to admission. I knew then that my luck was well and truly out and that I wouldn't be going to Cambridge.

After my unsuccessful flirtation with Cambridge, and an even briefer dalliance with the Army at Sandhurst (not at all to my liking), I decided to go the whole hog and choose my university strictly on its sporting reputation. I got out the UCCA handbook and listed those universities offering top-grade rugby facilities. I opted for Exeter on the basis of its recent amalgamation with St Luke's, the renowned PE establishment. I enrolled to read Economics and Agricultural Economics but, more importantly from my point of view, rugby was as high on the university's agenda as it was on mine.

Because I already had my 'A' Levels, I received an unconditional acceptance from Exeter but then found myself with the better part of a year on my hands before I would actually start there. Glenalmond ran an exchange scheme with a Canadian school, St Andrew's College, Aurora, about 40 miles north of Toronto, and I jumped at the chance to go out there and teach remedial maths and English and some PE.

The kids at the school were pretty well-off. The Prime Minister of Jamaica's son was a student as was the, soon to be, Hollywood actor Kiefer Sutherland. It must be some kind of claim to fame that I actually initiated Kiefer into the intricacies of rugby union football. The school paid the return air fare and gave me 250 dollars a month, which was basically beer money. The added attraction from my point of view was that my arrival coincided with the start of the Canadian rugby season. I got in touch with Toronto Scottish and played a few games in the seconds and thirds before breaking through into the first XV. And my enrolment with Toronto Scottish provided me with my first experience of rugby tours.

You didn't require the forensic abilities of a Sherlock Holmes to realise pretty sharpish that the social side of the weekend was going to play as big a part in the itinerary, if not bigger, than the on-field activities. We travelled in one of those big, yellow North American school buses. The rear seats were given over entirely to copious stocks of beer. Further down the bus there was a huge barrel in which the tour barman was mixing a particularly potent and noxious mixture. He swore it was tequila sunrise.

Another feature of the tour was a toy pig attached to a set of handcuffs which were snapped on to any member of our party who was seen chatting up a particularly unglamorous female. There was also a strait-jacket into which anybody who stepped out of line would be strapped. Generally this meant anyone who dared to snatch a bit of shut-eye or who broke the tour rules on sobriety, i.e. anyone who remained sober. It was that kind of tour!

We booked half a dozen hotel rooms in Montreal and Ottowa and 26 of us sneaked in under cover of darkness. We had also been tasked to bring back to base a series of useless items. I was wending my way back to the hotel with an assortment of building site scaffolding and traffic cones when I was accosted by a French-speaking Quebec policeman. I speak the language fairly well but not at 4.30 in the morning and through a beer and tequila induced alcoholic haze. Discretion became the better part of valour and the items were returned with alacrity as the cop made it clear that if they weren't I would be spending the rest of the night in the local nick.

We did play some rugby in the midst of all this mayhem. We beat a team of French-speaking Canadians in Montreal 16-13. It was a particularly rough game, as I recall. We then moved on to Ottowa, and the reason we had included the Canadian capital on our itinerary was that the secretaries who worked in the Government offices were acknowledged to be among the best lookers in the whole of Canada. Also, Ottowa straddles the states of Quebec and Ontario and because of the differing licensing laws it was possible to drink right through until the early hours of the morning. On Sunday we played an Ottowa side but by that time the excesses of the previous two days and nights had taken their toll and we were in no fit state to play tiddliwinks let alone a game of rugby. We lost by a barrel-load of points and the expression is most appropriate.

After my four-month Canadian sojourn it was time to return to Scotland but I still had the summer to kill before starting at Exeter. With three Glenalmond friends, Mike Boyd, Rod Mitchell, who went on to play wing-forward with me in the Edinburgh Accies side, and Paddy Walker, who was later to be my best man, we decided to motor to the south of France. I had a tiny Fiat 127 and the four of us plus all our camping gear set off down the west coast of France, ending up at Bordeaux. Cash was a bit of a problem and we slept rough in vineyards and sneaked into camp-sites after dark, departing again before the sun and the warden were up in the morning.

In the 'seventies my sister Janie had taken a cooking job with Princess Antoinette, sister of Prince Ranier of Monaco. I used to send the princess postcards whenever I was on holiday and developed a bit of a 'pen-pal' relationship with her. She always said – as people do – that if ever I was in her neck of the woods then I should pop in and see her. Well, we were. And we did. She lived in an imposing villa set on the hillside overlooking the Mediterranean. The driveway was barred by a wrought-iron gate and there was a security intercom linking the gateway with the mansion.

I pressed the button and when the female voice answered I said: 'Could I speak to the Princess please? It's David.'

'David who?' replied the obviously puzzled and disembodied voice.

'David Sole from Scotland,' I said hopefully, by now realising that the princess, who was on the other end of the intercom, hadn't a clue who I was.

'Ah, David,' she said, obviously racking her memory in an effort to determine who the hell this 'David Sole' was. Suddenly, it must have clicked. The gateway opened and we made our way up the driveway. By this time we had been living rough for quite some time and were unshaven, probably a bit smelly, and dressed in shorts and T-shirts.

The princess was gracious to a fault. 'Tea? Coffee?' she said. 'Or from the look of you, probably beer.' She rustled up four beers and we chatted for a while before she offered to fix us up with some complimentary passes for the sights of Monaco. We had a splendid time, all courtesy of the House of Grimaldi.

Dundee United were playing Monaco in a UEFA Cup match while we were there and so we took in the game. We also pooled our rapidly diminishing supply of cash to buy tickets for a Santana concert which was taking place in a Roman amphitheatre at Fréjus, just along the coast from Monte Carlo. It was one of those glorious evenings that you just couldn't have planned to go any better. The setting was superb. The Mediterranean sun was dipping beneath the horizon and the huge crowd packed into the amphitheatre had obviously been experimenting with exotic substances for several hours in advance of Santana appearing. The air was heavy with the sweet smell of waccy baccy. We threw a rugby ball around as Santana played on and the crowd got stoned. It was a magical finale to our French holiday.

Back home in Scotland, all that remained to be done was a final appearance at Glenalmond for the Old Boys game and then it was down to Exeter for pre-season training with the university side. My relationship with West Country rugby was about to get under way.

CHAPTER 3

THEM'S ONLY BOYS!

Exeter University

EXETER UNIVERSITY provided me with my initial introduction to the world of grown-up rugby. I can tell you that it came as quite a shock. Schools' rugby – even at International level – is the purest form of the game. It is largely devoid of the cynicism which bedevils senior rugby. The players have not yet been around long enough to become well versed in the blacker arts of the game. I am constantly reminded of this whenever I play in the annual Glenalmond Old Boys' game. After so many years of playing top-level rugby some of its ruder aspects – like jersey pulling and all-in wrestling at the lineout – have, I'm ashamed to admit, become accepted as part and parcel of the game. In a recent Old Boys v Glenalmond 1st XV game, one of the youngsters was tugging away at my jersey and, momentarily forgetting where I was and almost as a reflex action, I was just about to turn around and skelp him. But before I could do so he apologised. That, for me, summed up the difference between schoolboy and senior rugby. He genuinely hadn't meant to hold me back. In the senior game the intention would have been the exact opposite.

The year before my arrival at Exeter, the University had won the Devon Cup and thus had the opportunity to gain entry into the first round of the John Player Cup competition. The University took its rugby very seriously and the 'freshers' list was closely scrutinised by club officials for potential recruits. The University was due to play the Gloucestershire side Lydney in a John Player Cup first-round tie and I was one of those asked to report early for pre-season training and selection.

The only other new face asked to go down for pre-season training was a full-back from Nottingham University by the name of Robert Baillie who intended doing postgraduate physical education work at St Luke's. Basher, as he was known, and myself, were instructed to rendezvous at a pub in Exeter where the rugby club would be holding a meeting. Basher, who was over six feet in height and of impressive build, made me look like a seven-stone weakling. When the other Exeter guys arrived they were under the impression that the big bruiser Baillie must be Sole the prop and the wee guy with him must be the full-back. I suppose in those days I must have tipped the scales at a sylph-like 14½-stone. Obviously, I thought, the Exeter types like their props built in Neanderthal mould. It wasn't an auspicious introduction to my new team-mates.

After a couple of days' training, though, I was included in the University side to play a Tuesday evening game against the fishermen of Brixham. What an eye-opener that was. There I was, fresh-faced and innocent from Glenalmond and the Scottish Schools' side, being pitched into what was up until then the dirtiest game that I had played in. A couple of years later the Brixham side became the subject of a *Sunday Times* profile, not on account of their superlative playing abilities but because of their somewhat cavalier attitude towards the niceties and finer aspects of the game.

Their attitude towards the callow youths from Exeter University – and it was one repeated time and again during my three years there – was 'Get stuck in. Them's only boys.' To appreciate the full effect, it has to be spoken with a broad Cornish burr. The West Country teams that we met on a regular basis made it a virtual point of honour to attempt to give the Exeter students a right good seeing to. 'Them's only boys,' they would snarl and generally the observation would be smartly followed by a powerful right-hook. It really was a hard, hard school in which to learn your rugby.

During that game against Brixham I found myself being impeded in the lineout by a huge, hairy-arsed Brixham fisherman. I said to Colin Pinnegar, one of our locks who later went on to play for Wasps: 'Colin, this chap's holding on to me.'

Colin gave me an old-fashioned look and replied: 'Well bloody well smack him then.' That wasn't quite what we had been taught at Glenalmond or Scottish Schools. I bopped the big fisherman and the further-education part of my rugby schooling was underway with a vengeance.

The standard of rugby at Exeter University was of a very mixed bag. All of it, though, was very physical in nature. As students, we were mostly in our late teens and early twenties and we were invariably at a physical disadvantage against the rough and tough farmers and fishermen who made up the bulk of the clubs we played against. In those days before the Divisional Championship in England, County rugby was still a big thing and many of the County players in the West Country – Devon, Cornwall, Somerset, Gloucestershire – came from the likes of Plymouth Albion and Exeter and so on. All of these teams appeared on our fixture list and so we regularly found ourselves ranged against wily old campaigners from the County scene.

After that midweek opener against Brixham I was selected to play for the University against Lydney in the Cup game. They were a tough old bunch, including many older players who had turned out to a high standard with Gloucester. We were narrowly beaten, 13–12, and so didn't make it into the rounds of the Cup. Nevertheless, on a personal level I had won my spurs and had established myself in the University first XV.

We had a fair old team. It comprised University students like myself who were nicknamed Jiffs for a reason I have yet to discover. During my first season there were only two Jiffs in the side, the remainder being PE students from St Luke's College. The ex-England scrumhalf Richard Hill was a team-mate in my second year when he actually captained the side. In addition to Richard and Colin Pinnegar, other team members who went on to make their names in high-grade rugby were Mark Lynch who played for Llanelli and South Wales Police, Pete Thornley who played for Nottingham and Leicester, Simon Hogg who went on to play for Bristol and Gloucestershire and Nick Marment, a very gifted footballer who could play virtually anywhere in the backs, and who is now a Gloucester regular.

In addition to our games against West Country opposition, we also played in the Universities' Athletic Union Championship. In 1982 and 1983 we reached the finals which were played at Twickenham. On both occasions we lost by narrow margins to Durham University. The experiences did, though, serve as an introduction to RFU headquarters which was a venue I was to come to know well in the years ahead.

The University rugby club was held in pretty low esteem by those not connected with it or interested in the game. We were, I think, looked upon very much as party animals. Bearing in mind that most of the club members were PE students that's probably a generally fair comment! Being a University student I really had the best of both worlds. I spent a fair deal of my time on the main campus with people who had little or nothing to do with rugby, so I had two distinct social lives.

There's no doubt that we lived life to the limit. I was having a ball. I had as much rugby as I wanted, plus all the social distractions that student life offers. I was breaking through into representative rugby playing for Southern Universities. I also played for England Universities in a Trial match against England Under-23. This was the occasion, as I recount elsewhere, when I wrote to Murrayfield asking if selection for England Under-23 would have burned my boats so far as my cherished wish of playing for Scotland was concerned.

I also struck up a relationship with Bristol University's rugby side and was twice invited to accompany them on summer tours, the most notable of which was a trip to the States when we were centred upon the University of North Carolina. We were all amazed at the quite magnificent sporting facilities on offer to our American counterparts. The University basketball stadium alone seated 10,000 but it was considered to be too small and another, seating 20,000, was under construction. While we were being shown around there were half a dozen students working out on the court. Our guide pointed out one guy in particular who, he said, was so talented that a bright future was in prospect. He told us that his name was Michael Jordan. He has now gone on to become one of the top basketball stars in the USA and to have a range of sports shoes named after him.

We also called in at a college gridiron game. Again, it was a 55,000 sell-out. The Americans take their sport so seriously that if ever they decide to get really interested in rugby then I think we would all have to watch out.

But we also saw the other side of American life on the homeward leg of our tour. We were due to fly from Washington to Newark in order to catch our flight back to the UK. Due to electrical storms our aeroplane couldn't take off and we were marooned at the airport. We were in a bit of a quandary as we had very little money left and nowhere to stay. After much to-ing and fro-ing we got ourselves booked into a Washington youth hostel. The Ritz it wasn't. There was a small park outside and a video surveillance camera on the front wall which was trained on a bench outside.

The reason for this, apparently, was that a number of people who had lain down on the bench had never woken up again. They had been murdered as they slept. It was a rough neighbourhood. We were told not to venture out unless in groups of half a dozen or more and that under no circumstances should we try to go across the park after dark. We told our hostel warden that we were big, strong rugby players and that we didn't scare easily. He looked at us more in pity than anything else and said that no matter how big we were we wouldn't be able to hold our own against bullets. Point taken. We had to eat, though, and as there was a McDonald's Restaurant on the other side of the park we decided that we would risk all for a Big Mac. The entire party of 30 strapping rugby players formed themselves into a defensive phalanx and marched into the dark and across the grassland. There was an armed guard on the McDonald's door and signs inside warning the local ladies of the night against soliciting.

No sooner were we inside than a couple of the local hookers joined us at the counter and started touting for business. By this time the guard on the door was getting an itchy trigger finger and we were feeling decidedly uncomfortable. We bought our Big Macs and beat a hasty and watchful retreat back across the park to the relative safety of our hostel.

Back in Exeter I was still living the good life. With a couple of chums I had moved into a farmhouse on Crealy Barton Farm. It was situated slap in the middle of acres and acres of beautiful and unspoilt countryside. It was an idyllic life. In the summer we would hold starlit, black-tie 'balls'. We would get in barrels of beer and secrete bottles of booze as our strategic reserve at various points around the house and garden. A disco would be set up in the large garage and we would dance and drink the night away before descending *en masse* on a nearby motorway service station where we would each order a restorative fry-up for breakfast. Happy days.

The old farmhouse was idyllic in the summer but it tended to get dreadfully cold inside in the depths of winter. It had a large open fireplace and the bane of our lives was going outside in the rain, snow or frost to collect firewood. This inconvenience was largely negated when we hit upon the simple strategy of systematic demolition of the wooden summer-house to use as kindling. I'm afraid to say that the condition of the summer-house deteriorated in direct relation to the plummeting temperature. Dreadful behaviour.

One of the most popular student haunts in Exeter was the Ship Inn public house. It served authentic Cornish cider. It was the genuine article and about as potent a brew as it would ever be your misfortune to consume. It was mean. Consumption of Ship Inn scrumpy became a regular experience with the University rugby chaps. There existed an almost mythical number 'N' which represented eight pints of scrumpy. In the unlikely event that you had drunk ten pints of the stuff then you could claim to have quaffed 'N + 2'. Students suffering from hangovers would regularly claim to have downed 'N' or any configuration thereof. The record, apparently, was 'N + 4'. Whether the record-holder actually lived to boast of his prowess, however, is not immediately known.

At the start of the 1984 season my rugby education continued when I was selected to play for the Anglo-Scots against Lancashire at Vale of Lune. The match was staged as a kind of Trial and I was delighted that I was being noticed in the right quarters. Those early Anglo games represented the first time that I actually played in the same company as Scottish Internationalists. It was an experience that I relished.

During my last year at Exeter I became involved in the organisation of a rugby tour to Portugal. I rather fear that I spent too much time on the fund-raising and one thousand and one other things that go into the organisation of a rugby tour. I was undeterred by the fact that much of the running around coincided with my Finals when I should have been deeply engrossed in my studies. This no doubt contributed to the Third Class Honours degree which I was eventually awarded. Nevertheless, the tour was a rip-roaring success.

The only previous experience of touring which Exeter had had were two nights of Bacchanalian bliss on the island of Guernsey. As unofficial tour manager and general factotum I threw myself into the fund-raising aspect of the Portuguese expedition, even to the extent of going on a sponsored, alcohol-free month. Eventually we got enough money together to set out for Portugal. It was an ideal place to go because the food and accommodation were cheap and the beer was even cheaper.

We got the tour underway in Lisbon against a Portugal Under-23 side. They were supposed to be quite a handy outfit and we were desperately keen to get the show off on a winning note. We were in the dressing-room getting ready and two of the guys were warming up when they appeared to clash heads. I looked up and blood was spewing from their mouths. I was flabbergasted that they seemed to have done so much damage to each other. I rushed across the dressing-room to find out what had happened. It was a wind-up. They had chewed on joke blood capsules. It was that kind of a tour.

We ran up a cricket score against the Portuguese and we thought that we were on to a easy number. From Lisbon we motored to Estoril where we beat a University side by something like 74–6. We were just soaking up the sun and enjoying the rugby despite our disappointment at what appeared to be the generally low standard of the game in Portugal.

For our third and final match in Oporto we decided to ring the changes. Oporto was meant to be the weakest side on the tour itinerary and so we switched some of the positions around. We had something like six props in the team and so we played three of them in the front row and three in the back row. The centres were put into the second row and the flankers were displaced to the centre. After six minutes we were 12 points down and we began to wonder if this had been entirely prudent!

To make matters worse the referee hadn't turned up and so we had to 'volunteer' one of our PE students, who hopefully knew the rules. Sadly for the ref it turned out to be an appallingly bad-tempered game. Punches, late tackles, it was all going on. It was an absolute shocker. Then one of our wingers was laid out after a straight-arm tackle and all hell broke loose. One of our flankers turned centre went absolutely bananas and waded in to exact retribution on the bloke who had laid out the winger. Within seconds there was a pitched battle and 'our' referee was quite obviously in two minds as to whether he should join in or try to establish something resembling order. Eventually, though, sanity was restored and we ran out winners 28–12.

The Battle of Oporto, however, didn't detract from our enjoyment of the tour. It had been splendid fun from start to finish and brought the curtain down on my student days and University rugby in a magnificent manner. I had already been introduced to the Bath club and my rugby education would continue at the Recreation Ground. As a rugby finishing school par excellence it had few rivals.

CHAPTER 4

THE FASTEST MILK-CART IN
THE WEST COUNTRY

The Bath Experience

BATH IS ONE of the longest established and most successful rugby clubs in the country. It has a proud history dating back to 1865 and regularly attracts the size of crowd which would gladden the heart of many a League football club treasurer. The Recreation Ground on a big-match Saturday is about as close as you will come to a soccer-like atmosphere outside of Wales or, in terms of social mix if not sheer size, the Scottish Borders. West Country rugby attracts players and supporters right across the social spectrum and when I first arrived at the Recreation Ground the club was very much the centre of the Bath social scene. We took to heart that old saying about working hard and playing hard – although in our case it was very much a case of playing hard on the pitch and then playing even harder in the clubhouse afterwards.

The rugby was entertaining to watch and, more importantly from the players' point of view, it was fun to take part in. Jack Rowell was the Bath coach throughout my three and a half years with the club but in the early days John Horton, England's 1980 Grand Slam fly-half, very much called the shots behind the scrum. With players of the calibre of John Palmer, Simon Halliday, Alan Rees, David Trick, Barry Trevaskis and Chris Martin, Bath might not have had the star-studded galaxy of international talent that it can call on today but we were still equipped with guys who could put on some dazzling displays of threequarter play.

We weren't that badly off up front either. We had Richard Hill, still to break into the England side, at scrum-half, while in the forwards, apart from myself, we had Greg Bess, Richard Lee, Gareth

Chilcott, Nigel Gaymond, the ex-Irish international lock Ronnie Hakin, Nigel Redman, John Hall, Paul Simpson, and in charge of the show from open-side wing-forward was one of the hardest and most courageous men I have ever played rugby with, Roger Spurrell.

Roger, who gave up the Parachute Regiment for the more pastoral pleasures of a shepherd's life, wasn't a man who suffered fools gladly and he didn't much mind whether they were opposition flankers and fly-halves or Bath committee-men. He made sure that everybody was aware of his belief that his players were the most important people in the club and that they should be treated accordingly.

I had some great times at Bath. I first met my wife, Jane, there. I won my first Cap out of the club and I picked up a coveted John Player Cup winners' medal but, with Roger's retiral and the growing pressure that accompanied increasing success, the atmosphere began to change. The backs weren't allowed to exhibit their flair and the Bath game became one of attrition and of grinding down the opposition. Rarely was the ball put out beyond the fly-half. The Bath pack became feared and respected the length and breadth of the land, but the flair had disappeared on the way to success and the club began to take some media stick for its inhibited style. There's more to rugby than just two packs of forwards slugging it out until one side gains the upper hand. Suddenly rugby wasn't as much fun as it had been. Bath have gone on to unprecedented success in the English game and I genuinely wish them well. I can't help feeling, though, that I was lucky to have been with them during a particularly golden spell, before winning became the overpowering priority and when we still won but did so in style. Somewhere along the way, it seems to me, those elusive commodities, fun and entertainment, were sacrificed in pursuit of continued success.

But I get ahead of myself. My initial introduction to the club came while I was still at Exeter University. Bath were having a fantastic season and we went up to play them in a midweek game at the Recreation Ground. We drew 6-6 and so far as we were concerned that was as good as a win. It was the best result we had ever had against the first-class sides in the West Country. That game also served as an introduction to a Bath player who was to become a very good friend over the years, although our first meeting was in the most inauspicious of circumstances.

Chris Lilley was playing in the Bath front row. During a lineout he caught me with a splendid right hook. Once the stars inside my skull had stopped spinning I looked around to see who the perpetrator had been. There was Chris smiling away, obviously pleased with his handiwork. I didn't know it at the time but Chris has a rather pronounced squint in one of his eyes. I was somewhat taken aback because I didn't know whether he was looking at me or not and the thought crossed my mind that it would, perhaps, be slightly unethical to skelp a man who was looking the other way.

I thought, 'What the hell.' I decided to give him a bit of a poke and drew back my fist. At this point it suddenly became clear that Chris was, indeed, looking at me and in his broad West Country burr he said: 'If you 'it me, oi'll bite your nose off!' I almost burst out laughing but decided also that discretion might be the better part of valour and we got on with the game. That was typical Lil. Once I'd joined Bath we became good friends and we stayed in the same small village of Colerne. Jane and I were simple villagers but that larger than life character Lil was known to all and sundry as the Lord Mayor of Colerne.

I must have made some sort of impression on the Bath hierarchy despite my not having slugged it out with his Lordship because a short while later I was asked by coaches David Robson and Jack Rowell if I'd care to throw in my lot with them.

Richard Hill had already made the connection with Bath. He was playing in a floodlit game against Exeter, the town not the university, and I travelled down to watch the game. Gareth Chilcott was sent off. It represented an unenviable hat-trick for Cooch. He had already been sent off a couple of times and a substantial ban was on the cards. That was going to leave the club seriously short of front-row cover and David and Jack invited me to come along with Richard to training sessions.

I played in a midweek game against the Royal Navy and sat on the bench for the John Player Cup quarter-final tie at Nottingham. I was in my final year at university and Jack Rowell asked what I was going to be doing the following year. He said: 'Why don't you come and join us permanently and we'll see what we can do about fixing you up with a job?'

I really had no idea what I was going to do career-wise. I was just drifting along having a good time and playing rugby. That was the summer of 1984 and I was invited to go on the club tour to Canada. I was delighted to be asked and determined that I should go but I had also been asked to tour with Bristol University who were going that summer to North Carolina. I had been on tour with Bristol University the previous year and they had invited me back as a guest player. I didn't want to let them down but neither did I want to give up the chance of going to Canada with Bath. I solved the problem by doing both tours. I went first to Canada with Bath and then spent a week or so in the States waiting to link up with the Bristol students in North Carolina. Oh, what it is to be young, keen, footloose and fancy free.

That Nottingham Cup tie, which was cancelled because the Ireland Avenue ground was waterlogged, served as my introduction to the hard school of Bath 'hospitality'. Once the game had been called off we all adjourned to the bar to make ready for our journey back down the motorway in the team bus. Rum coolers were the chosen tipple for away game consumption. We would stop off at an off-licence and load up with Bacardi, orange juice and lemonade. It was a dreadful, sickly sweet concoction but it had the desired effect.

It's a long, long way from Nottingham to Bath and as the new boy I was expected to 'make it a double' every time the rum coolers came around. By the time we were back in home territory I was absolutely legless. I stumbled off the bus at the Recreation Ground and went into Greta Garbo mode. I wanted to be alone.

The following season, and after the summer tours, I joined the club full-time. Two characters in particular leap from the memories of my initial season with the club. One was the skipper Roger Spurrell who, as I've already indicated, was a man apart. A Cornishman, he had a fearsome (and deserved) reputation in the West Country and Wales. He was as tough as old boots. His party-piece was the consumption of live goldfish. Roger was one of the best players I've encountered never to have been capped for his country. He was a superb player, a first-rate captain and good bloke into the bargain. The three do not always go together.

Roger was in his element whenever we crossed over into Wales. Like most West Country clubs, Bath had a long-standing fixture relationship with a lot of the top Welsh clubs. The games were always keenly contested with more than a little needle on both sides. Roger was one of the game's great talkers. He used to taunt the opposition mercilessly. Accordingly, and particularly against the Welsh, he would take some dreadful kickings. They would focus all of their aggro on him and, invariably, Roger would be found raked to pieces at the bottom of a ruck, still with a smile on his face and demanding of his assailants: 'Surely you can do better than that?'

He liked a good time after the game as well and as skipper he always made sure that the boys had their beer money and that they were, generally, well looked after. When Roger was in charge the Recreation Ground bar would go like a fair from the end of a game until closing time. It was a great atmosphere both on and off the pitch.

As I've said, it was thanks to Gareth Chilcott's early propensity to let his fists do the talking that I was invited into the Bath fold. With his Convict 99 hairstyle and his general 'no prisoners' demeanour Cooch looks like one of the most fearsome individuals ever to have donned a rugby jersey. True, in his early days he was a tearaway on the pitch and his reputation as a bit of a bad bugger was undoubtedly deserved. Early in his career Cooch was banned for a full year for stamping on Bob Hesford of Bristol and then, of course, he and my former Bath clubmates Graham Dawe and Richard Hill were all shown the door after that notorious flare-up between the English and the Welsh at Cardiff Arms Park in 1987.

But, at the risk of severely denting his bad boy image, I have to say that, at heart, Cooch is a big softie with a heart of gold. He is one of the most genuine blokes that I have ever met and he would move heaven and earth to help out a mate. He will tell you himself that Bedminster, where he was reared, is not exactly leafy suburbia and that, in truth, it's the kind of place where you have to stand in a queue to be mugged. In fact he will tell you that himself, because it is one of the lines he uses in his new-found calling as an after-dinner speaker.

Cooch won the first of his 14 caps against Australia at Twickenham in 1984. True to what was then his form he earned a hefty black mark for biffing the Aussie scrum-half Nick Farr-Jones when the ref wasn't looking. Everybody else in the ground and those watching on TV had seen it but the ref hadn't. The England committee obviously had, though, because Gareth didn't play for his country for another 18 months.

It was just after his international début that I introduced him to the art of after-dinner speaking. Cooch is now an acknowledged raconteur and, as millions of TV viewers saw for themselves when he was a member of ITV's panel of experts during the 1991 World Cup, a fine ambassador for the game. But back in 1984 when I asked him to be the main speaker at the Exeter University rugby club dinner he was a novice at the game. In fact he had never spoken publicly in his life before. The invitation was made at the Recreation Ground bar. It must have been late because Cooch accepted without demur. We told him that we would write the speech, collect him and take him down to the university and all that he would have to do would be to stand up and deliver the lines we had written for him.

Come the appointed night we picked Coochie up and were on our way to Exeter when he said: 'Where's the speech then? I'd better have a look at it before we get there.'

I didn't have the heart to tell him that I'd not had time to write it. As we got nearer and nearer to the university clubrooms Cooch was getting more and more nervous. 'Where's my speech?' he said in a voice which indicated an imminent panic attack.

'Look,' I said, 'just stand up and tell a few stories. You're an England internationalist. The boys'll just be glad that you're there.

Crack a few jokes and then finish up with something like it's always a great pleasure to play Exeter University. Simple. Nothing could be easier.'

Cooch wasn't convinced. By the time we got into the clubrooms he had the look of a condemned man about him. He was sitting at the top table and all the university blokes were buying him drinks. He was so nervous he couldn't touch a drop. There must have been half a dozen pints lined up in front of him. I was watching him out of the corner of my eye and by this time feeling appallingly guilty at having let him down by not providing him with the promised script. His meal was left untouched – a sure indication in Cooch's case that something was badly amiss.

Then, to compound it all, the university captain, Ian Osborne, got up and delivered the most outrageously witty speech – completely in rhyme. I glanced at Cooch and he was sitting with his head sunk in his hands. By now I was almost as nervous as he was. Sole, I thought, you are in deep trouble. Very soon Mr Chilcott will be wanting to see you alone and outside and he won't be wanting to admire the moon.

By the time it was Coochie's turn to speak I had resigned myself to the prospect of a real seeing-to. When he stood up he was shaking like a leaf. He began by telling a few tales about his misspent youth in Bedminster. Then he moved on to recount the occasion when he was arrested for 'air-piracy' on a Thai Air jumbo-jet and ended up in a Karachi prison cell. I'll not spoil the story because I'm sure it still forms part of Gareth's repertoire. By now Cooch had them eating out of his hand. He is a natural story-teller and as he saw that his audience was hanging on his every word he really began to enjoy it.

Gareth has turned into a first-rate ambassador for the game and for the Bath club. Despite his 14 Caps and a British Lions' tour he is still the same old Cooch.

When we were together at the club we had a fair old rivalry. Cooch was in the fortunate position that he is one of those rare individuals who can play on the loose-head or tight-head almost without giving it a second thought. During my time at Bath we had something like 56 fixtures to fulfil in a season. The club played high-grade rugby Saturday and Wednesday virtually throughout the season. When the League and the Cup plus County and Divisional commitments were taken into account this placed a tremendous strain on player resources. Richard Lee was the other prop on the books and the coaches worked a kind of rota among myself, Cooch and Richard. It wasn't ideal because it meant that one of us had to be rested on a regular basis. What it did do, though, was to make for some fairly interesting training sessions with

Murrayfield for me? Surely some mistake. Aged two

The Hemel Hempstead mansion which attracted a Beatle and The Saint

Flip, the homicidal Blairmore ferret

At Glenbuchat. Mum used to break in horses

The Blairmore cricket XI. I'm second from the left in the back row

The Blairmore first XV. That's me seated to the right of the skipper

Blairmore line-out action

The Glenalmond first XV, 1980

Heave! Tug-of-war at Glenalmond

A Scottish Schoolboys' Cap. 29 December 1979. We played the French and I was desperate to get a second Cap in order to secure a 'proper' Scottish blue jersey.

Back row: K. Wallace (Knox Academy), R. A. Young (Merchiston), M. Campbell (Buckhaven High), D. J. Murray (Dollar Academy), D. J. Kennedy (Ardrossan Academy), I. G. Ross (Dollar Academy)

Middle row: R. McIntyre (Portobello High), N. R. Small (George Watson's College), N. Clarke (Leith Academy), A. G. Hagart (George Watson's College), G. D. Burton (Marr College), A. G. Hastings (George Watson's College), R. Lynch (Kelvinside Academy), N. T. Kerr (Jedburgh Grammar)

Front row: K. W. Muir (Eastwood High), G. A. Gaston (Hawick High), J. M. Scott, capt. (Stewart's-Melville College), D. Anderson (Jedburgh Grammar), S. Frame (Stewart's-Melville College), D. Buglass (Knox Academy)

In action during that Scottish Schools v French Schools match at Braidholm. Eric Champ and Philippe Sella were in the French side

Making Finlay Calder's acquaintance. It was the Middlesex Sevens at Twickenham in 1982. Finlay was propping for Stewart's-Melville and I was doing likewise for Exeter University

With Exeter University for the final of the UAU championship in 1982. Our scrumhalf Richard Hill, seated on the left, seems somewhat distracted

On the moor at Glenbuchat with my father, Tommy, and one of the dogs. August 1981

On parade with the Lonach Highlanders in 1982. No prizes for the most apposite caption!

With Bath clubmate Richard Hill during the club's 1984 Canadian tour

Bath's 1985 John Player Cup Final squad at Twickenham before the kick off.
Back Row: *referee Fred Howard, me, Paul Simpson, Chris Stanley, Alan Rees, Richard Lee, Jerry Guscott, John Hall, Nigel Gaymond, Dave Egerton, Nigel Redman, Chris Martin, Simon Halliday, fitness adviser Tom Hudson, Gareth Chilcott, coach Jack Rowell, physio Gareth George, spongeman Pete Pothecary, coach Dave Robson*
Front row: *Barry Trevaskis, Greg Bess, John Horton, Richard Hill, Roger Spurrell, president Jack Simkins, John Palmer, David Trick, Jimmy Deane*

each of us endeavouring to make our mark in order to ensure that it would be somebody else's turn to be rested on the coming Wednesday or Saturday.

My years with Bath gave me, within reason, the opportunity to devote virtually as much time as I wanted to rugby. My whole life revolved around the club. Even my domestic arrangements were woven around club connections and friendships. After my return from the North American tour, David Trick said that he had a spare room at his house in the splendidly named village of Thickwood. Eventually, we would be joined there by fullback Roy Palmer who was one of the Rec's great personalities in the mid-Eighties.

Roy was an Ulsterman who had played for Ireland 'B' during my 'B' team début at Melrose in 1984. However, the next time I laid eyes on him in the Bath dressing-room I had no idea that our paths had crossed at The Greenyards. We were playing for United, the Bath second XV. It was the first match after the transatlantic tour and there was a lot of catching-up and badinage going on among the blokes who had been on the trip. Sitting in the corner was this figure who looked as if he was a refugee from the world of soccer. He had a full head of spectacularly coiffured hair. The way that he was preening himself indicated that he was obviously pretty keen on the way he looked. 'Bloody hell,' I said to one of the guys I knew from the tour, 'who the hell is that?'

'That's our fullback,' was the reply.

I shook my head and thought: 'What a poof. I'll be surprised if he can play much rugby.'

We were playing a Bristol Combination side and we lost. Roy had dropped a couple of high balls and so far as I was concerned my fears about his rugby-playing abilities had been confirmed. Back in the dressing-room we got showered and changed and Roy climbed into a pair of mustard-coloured leather trousers. That clinched it. He was definitely to be filed under 's' for suspect.

However, my initial reaction to Roy proved to be miles wide of the mark and a powerful reminder not to be taken in by first appearances.

My initial diagnosis as to Roy's sexual preferences turned out to be wrong too. Down at the night-club which Roger Spurrell now ran in place of his shepherding stint, Roy was a big hit with the ladies of Bath. He was also, as it turned out, no mean rugby player. Roy and I made our first-team débuts together. It was a floodlit game against Bristol at the Memorial Ground. It was a really important grudge match. Roy played an absolute stormer. He was like the Rock of Gibraltar under the high balls which Bristol rained down on him. Time and again the ball would be popped up in the air and Roy would stand his ground while Bristol's 15½-stone centre John Carr – a crash-ball specialist out of the Ray Gravell or Alistair Cranston mould – came thundering down at him like a runaway express train. Bristol never got any change out of Roy. He was a model of courageous consistency. To cap it all he slotted home the conversion which assured us of a two-point victory. It was a dream début and Roy was a hero.

He was the toast of Bath that night and he loved it. The celebrations went on into the wee small hours. I was working on a milk round with a 3 a.m. rise and, to my chagrin, would invariably have to bail out early from these regular after-match celebrations. It was a regular occurrence for our paths to cross as I was leaving to start the milk round and the other occupants of our Thickwood cottage were returning from a night on the town.

Eventually the kindred spirits within the club formed an élite band (at least we thought it was élite) which became known as The Comancheros. The membership was very select. It included myself, hooker Greg Bess, Roy Palmer and Tony Gunner, a very talented musician who played on the wing and who in another existence had, I am sure, been a Hell's Angel. He was a real hard case.

Whenever we went across to Wales with the second XV we would invariably select an outlandish 'uniform' to go with the club blazer. We have wowed them in the valleys of Wales with bow-ties of various hues and designs, hats of varying description, shorts and braces or Groucho Marx moustaches, glasses and noses. The tough old miners that we used to play against on these trips across the Severn Bridge undoubtedly thought we were stark raving mad.

But the Comancheros met their match on an outing to Exeter during the Grand Slam Wallabies' 1984 tour. There were quite a number of Bath lads playing in the South and South West side and so the Comancheros decided that it would make an interesting away fixture.

We determined that we mustn't become separated from each other and so we took along a pair of braces to which each of us had to be attached at all times. We gate-crashed the official reception being given in honour of the Wallabies. The Bath coach Jack Rowell, who was in charge of the South and South West XV, took one look at us and said: 'God, what are you lot doing here? Just behave, will you?'

We had a great night out on the town. Roger Spurrell, who had been playing, said to me that I should go down and crash out in his hotel room. It was all bought and paid for. At two o'clock in the morning we turned up at the hotel reception desk and I announced: 'I'm Roger

Spurrell and these are my friends. We would all like to stay the night in my room and also to use the room booked in the name of Mr Gareth Chilcott.'

Trusting souls that they were they gave us the keys and 'Messrs Spurrell, Chilcott and Co' were soon fast asleep. A few hours later I woke up and drew my arm out of the bedclothes to look at the time. My watch had gone. I wandered along to where Roy and Tony were sharing Gareth's room and discovered that they had had their trousers taken. There was something very strange going on. I rushed downstairs to report the thefts. However, it transpired that the management hadn't been so daft after all. The manager had come into my room while I was sound asleep and had whipped my watch as security and had decided, for good measure, to take Roy and Tony's trousers as collateral as well.

The manager explained that whoever I was I wasn't Roger Spurrell and none of the others was Mr Chilcott and we would have to pay for the rooms. I was completely broke. I hadn't a penny left on me. Luckily, I did have some travellers' cheques left over in my wallet from the North American tour.

Trying, and no doubt failing, to adopt an air of nonchalant unconcern I asked the manager if he would accept travellers' cheques. He said that he would. I breathed a sigh of relief, signed on the dotted line and beat as hasty and dignified a retreat as I could. The message was simple. In the West Country, even if you have their permission, it doesn't pay to impersonate Roger Spurrell or Gareth Chilcott. The Comancheros had, indeed, met their match.

Bath's Cup campaign of 1984 had been my introduction to the club when I was called in as front-row cover during Cooch's suspension. The club got to the final that year and although I wasn't needed I was invited to go with the team to Twickenham. I didn't go but the following year I sat on the bench when the club once again reached the final and in 1986, when I was established in the loose-head position, I reckoned that, as our Cup run continued with rip-roaring success, this season, finally, I might actually get to take part in a Twickenham final.

Once again, though, my hopes were to be dashed. This time the reason was a contretemps between myself and the Moseley lock Steve Boyle in which my nose came off decidely second-best. I had played for Scotland against Wales in Cardiff and the following weekend Bath were playing a Cup quarter-final tie against Moseley at The Reddings. The incident occurred as I was innocently watching a peel around the front of a line-out. Then, bang! Boyle, who had gone on the British Lions' tour to New Zealand in 1983, walloped me with his elbow on the nose and just below the left eye. There was a horrible cracking sound and I knew right away that it hadn't been a run-of-the-mill bump. I put my hands up to my face and within seconds my nose was streaming blood. Of more immediate concern, however, was the fact that the nose now seemed to be about an inch out of alignment. Hello. That's surely not right, I thought, as I took my nose in both hands and manoeuvred it back to something resembling its normal position approximately between the eyes and above the mouth.

Our skipper John Palmer came across and inquired after my health. By this time the nose was back in position and, I suppose, apart from the blood, it didn't look too bad. I told John that I reckoned it was pretty serious and that I would have to go off.

'Just get the blood wiped away and it'll be OK,' he said.

'I don't think so. It feels as if there's been a bit of real damage done,' I told him. John gave me a rather old-fashioned sort of look but I decided to go off anyway. As I was on my way to the sidelines David Trick came across, somewhat quizzically, and asked: 'You alright, Soley?' I told David, too, that I was retiring. I think he, like John, reckoned that I was maybe over-reacting.

By the time I had showered and generally got myself cleaned up the whole face had swollen alarmingly and even before the guys came back into the dressing-room after the game I looked like the Elephant Man might have after a dozen rounds with Mike Tyson.

'Bloody hell,' they all said as they trooped in. 'You weren't kidding then.'

A visit to the hospital casualty department and several X-rays later it was established that Boyle's elbow had caught me on the orbit of the eye. The medics said I looked as if I'd been in a traffic accident. There was splintered bone all over the place and a sliver of bone from the eye socket was pointing backwards into the eye. In addition the nose was shattered with not much of the bone left to speak of. Two things occurred to me right away. Firstly I was supposed to be playing for Scotland in the Calcutta Cup match the following weekend. Thanks to Steve Boyle and his elbow that was now out of the question. Secondly, how would Jane – whom I was then going out with – react? Once I was back in Bath I went around to see her. There was now even more swelling and I was almost unrecognisable as she came to the door to let me in. In addition to the swelling, the bruising had started to come out and I looked like a malformed panda with a black and blue streak across my eyes and nose.

The following week, once the swelling had started to subside, a couple of eye surgeons at Bath got to work and rebuilt the orbit and cheekbone so that it resembled something like its old self. Then an ear-nose-and-throat man took a look at the nose. He shook his head in that grave way that medics have and declared: 'Frankly there's not a lot left to work on but we'll try and push what there is back into the middle and just hope that it works out OK.'

He was as good as his word. He did a first-rate job and Jane, for one, reckons that the reconstructed nose looks a damn sight better than the original one. And to think that people spend thousands of pounds on getting their nose jobs done. I had mine courtesy of Steve Boyle and a top-notch ENT man.

The injury has left a legacy, though. One of the sinuses is completely blocked. I never bothered to have it corrected while I was still playing because, you never know, I might have come across another Steve Boyle. But now that I've retired a visit to an ear-nose-and-throat man comes near the top of my list of 'things to be done'.

I eventually got my Cup winners' medal in 1987 and I wish I was able to say that it was a wonderful experience which will live with me for the rest of my life. I've no doubt that it was just that but, unfortunately, I don't remember a thing about it.

We were again playing Wasps and the final was the first of the many occasions that I would come up against my old adversary Jeff Probyn. Early in the game I received a knock on the head. I can't remember who, what, when or why but I think it was just one of those things and not the result of anything untoward. From that point onwards the events of the afternoon are just a haze. I was obviously concussed. Early in the second half, as we were getting ready to go down for a scrum I put out my right arm to bind on to the hooker. I looked around and saw that Greg Bess, our reserve hooker, was taking up position. Even in my somewhat detached state I was relatively sure that we had started the match with Graham Dawe!

I said in some bewilderment to my new hooker: 'Greg? What the hell are you doing here?'

Greg said that Dawesie had gone off hurt before the interval. It was very definitely a case of the lights being on but there being nobody at home. I hadn't a clue what was going on and, in retrospect, I suppose I should have gone off. It's still a matter of regret that the memory of what should have been one of the highlights of my rugby career – playing in a Cup final at Twickenham – is lost somewhere in the battered old memory bank.

By the time we went up to collect our medals things were returning to something resembling normality. At least now I knew where I was! I was left, though, with dreadful nausea and the headache to end all headaches. The next day I was due to travel to Scotland for a World Cup squad session at Murrayfield. There had been a cut-off point for players involved in the 1987 World Cup campaign after which they were supposed to have finished playing for the season.

This was the famous occasion when three of my Scotland colleagues, John Rutherford, Iain Paxton and Iwan Tukalo, had gone on an unsanctioned trip to play rugby in the sun of Bermuda. They would have got away with it but for John suffering a horrendous knee ligament injury. It was the injury which cut short his World Cup campaign and which finally ended his fine career. The Tour hierarchy were, to put it mildly, not best pleased. After some debate they had given me special dispensation to take part in the Twickenham final and it was with some trepidation that I flew up to Murrayfield to inform Tour Manager Bob Munro and skipper Colin Deans that I wouldn't be able to play a part in the session because I had been concussed the day before. They were very good about it and just pleased that nothing more serious had taken place. I suppose they were operating on the basis that, so far as a prop forward is concerned, any injury to the old 'brain box' isn't really a matter for serious concern. Bob should know. He was once a prop forward too!

I had graduated from Exeter with a degree in Economics and Agricultural Economics. What this equipped me for in the big wide world of business and commerce I had no idea. Rugby was the central theme of my life and, I'm afraid to say, everything else came a very poor second.

When I joined Bath I was introduced to one of the club's most dedicated supporters, Malcolm Pearce. Malcolm, who wasn't exactly short of a bob or two, was an absolute rugby fanatic and it was agreed that he should fix me up with a job. Among his many commercial interests he ran a wholesale newsagent's business in the West Country. He also ran a couple of farms and Lordswood Daisy, a large dairy company.

I had a degree which touched on agriculture and so Malcolm put me to work in the dairy business. My title was to be 'marketing and management trainee' which basically meant that I would work my way around the multifarious strands of Malcolm's business empire. My first three months were spent as a farm labourer mucking out the byres and bedding down the cattle. At the same time I was working on the milk-round, collecting milk from the farm and delivering it to the dairy. The hours suited me to a tee. I was staying in a bachelor pad in Bath with David Trick and Roy Palmer. I would be up at three o'clock in the morning to deliver the milk and then would get home to snatch a few hours' sleep which still left me plenty of time to train, play rugby and generally have a good time.

I then graduated to the farm office where Malcolm utilised me, for want of a better description, as his project development man. He would have, on average, about an idea a week. He wanted to start a maize-fed guinea fowl operation. The thinking behind this was that the maize turns the fat yellow, which is a great selling point in the food trade. I ran a feasibility study on this but, in the end, it came to nothing. Then Malcolm hit upon a scheme to produce a Roman Beefy Sausage. Bath being a great ancient Roman centre he reckoned that this would be a great money-spinner. We had an ancient Roman recipe but the results were less than inspiring so I had to go around sausage mixture manufacturers trying to develop a twentieth-century Roman Beefy Sausage. Again, the ploy came unstuck but, if nothing else, it kept the bachelor pad well supplied with sausages for a considerable time.

Next, Malcolm wanted to turn one of his fields over to cider apples and run geese underneath so that the geese would eat the fallen apples. I was charged with the task of checking out the feasibility of this latest epoch-making idea. Again it fell by the wayside.

After three months of abortive project development I next went to a restaurant which Malcolm owned just opposite the Pump Rooms in Bath. He wanted to set up an ice-cream parlour there and reckoned that I was just the man for the job. We had to develop an amazingly rich ice-cream and serve it with waffles. Malcolm said that I would have to look the part and I was kitted out with a striped apron and a ridiculous bow-tie.

Very soon, I became known around the Club as Mr Whippy. It was at this point that I decided that this wasn't quite what I'd slaved three years at university for and so, with much regret, I bade Malcolm farewell.

That commercial interlude did, though, have one positive outcome. It was while in milk-man guise that I first met Jane. I had been at a Scotland 'B' training session in Edinburgh and had travelled back down to Bath, reaching the club-house around six o'clock in the evening. There had been a wine and cheese party that afternoon and by the time I got there everybody was somewhat the worse for wear. I spent all the money I had just catching up on the others and then we went off to the pub. Jane, who stayed in Bristol, was in the company. We were all running short of cash and so I persuaded Jane to spend her train-fare on the last round. I told her that I would pick her up in the morning and drive her down to Bristol in plenty of time for work.

However, I didn't tell her what the mode of transport would be. I was up at four the next morning and had to drive to the dairy in my glorified milk-float to collect 1,500 pints of milk for delivery to Keynsham. The milk van was a temperamental beast and much given to an out-and-out refusal to start. Eventually I got it going and set out to collect Jane. When I drove up in a milk-float Jane remained splendidly stoical and said not a word. Then the bloody thing packed in again. With Jane becoming progressively later and later for work I had to telephone for assistance to get someone to come out to use jump-leads on the van before we could get it underway again.

Then we were off to the farm to pick up the milk. You could have cut the atmosphere in the cab with a knife. I was trying and failing to make polite conversation and getting nowhere fast. We arrived at the farm and I backed the van up to the refrigerated store so that I could collect the milk. I had to ask Jane to slide across to the driver's seat so that she could keep her foot on the accelerator pedal to prevent the engine from expiring again. Fifteen hundred pints of milk later we were off to the cash-and-carry where I lugged the milk out of the back of the van. Again Jane valiantly kept her foot on the pedal to keep the thing from stalling.

By now the atmosphere was as frosty as the dairy deep-freeze. It was obvious to anyone that I had absolutely blown my chances. At least, I thought, things can't get any worse. I was wrong.

We set off for Bristol and immediately hit the morning rush-hour. We were in a three-mile tail-back. Then the van packed in again. What a disaster. Jane was late for work. She would more than likely never speak to me again and I was ten miles off my authorised route. Jane had spent all of her money on buying beer for me the night before and I rummaged frantically in my pockets to see if I had any cash so that she could get a taxi to work. I came up with £5 and as I went in search of a telephone to explain to my boss how I came to be in Bristol Jane went off – I reckoned never to be seen again – in the opposite direction in search of a taxi.

However, our paths crossed again just the following week. Jane was 'best mates' with Philippa Jones, whose brother Simon played for Bath and who had got an England Trial in 1980. We were in the Recreation Ground bar after a game and Jane was there. Some remedial action was called for and so my flatmate David Trick went across and told Jane that I had been sacked.

'David sacked? What for?' asked Jane.

'He got the heave for giving you a lift to Bristol,' Trick lied.

That melted the ice, but it was months before I reckoned that the thaw had developed sufficiently for me to ask Jane out and when I did, much to my relief, the fraught circumstances of our first meeting had been relegated to the level of a good laugh.

After leaving Malcolm's employ I next moved into forestry. By which I mean that I was chopping down trees. I worked at felling trees and sawing logs on the Cannon's Country Club development outside Bath. Jerry Guscott, the England and British Lions' centre, worked alongside me. Jerry wasn't then the rugby superstar and male model that he is nowadays. At that time he was playing for the Spartans, Bath's third XV. I have to confess that if ever anyone had to climb a tree in order to lop off difficult branches then, invariably, it was Jerry who was 'volunteered' for the job.

When the forestry job came to an end I decided to mix some business with pleasure and organise a wine-buying holiday in France. I had always been moderately interested in wine – mainly in its consumption – and my old man was a bit of a buff in his own right. So, having swotted up on the subject by means of the *World Atlas of Wine*, Jane and I set off in my Jeep for a tour of the French vineyards.

We had a trailer hitched to the back of the Jeep and a tent for accommodation. The actual business of buying represented a very steep learning curve. We went around dozens of yards and when the price was right we would buy up cases of Chablis and Beaujolais from picture-postcard French farmers complete with berets, string-vests and the obligatory Gauloise dangling from the lower lip. It was great fun and quite an education. Once they realised that we were buying by the caseful and not just by the bottle they would treat us like long-lost cousins and invite us down to the cellar for a vigorous tasting of that season's vintage.

We were living in our tent and employing the tactics that myself and the Glenalmond chums had used to such good effect when we toured the South of France just before going to university, i.e. we arrived late at campsites and were invariably gone before the attendant arrived to gather his fees first thing in the morning.

We had made tentative plans before setting off to sell our stock of wine to friends at the rugby club. As we made our way back to Bath with the trailer groaning under the weight of two dozen cases of wine I hoped that my sales acumen would match what I considered to have been a job pretty well done on the purchasing front. If it hadn't then we would have drunk very well for a very long time indeed.

However, we needn't have worried. Our Bath friends proved not to need much persuading. Once the sums had been done we discovered that we had paid for the holiday and the wine. I had a few quid in my pocket and sufficient bottles set aside for a rainy day. In fact, as I had enjoyed the whole adventure so much and as I was then not exactly in steady employment, I decided to enter the wine-trade full-time and to set myself up as a wholesale wine merchant.

I got in touch with a UK supplier and negotiated sufficient discount to allow me to start supplying the restaurant trade in and around Bath. For the princely sum of one pound I bought a West Country wine distribution franchise from a chap I was introduced to at the Kensington Wine Fair in London. My intention had always been to get some money into the kitty and then to fund my own wine-buying trips to France. Dealing directly with the producers in France was the part of the whole operation that really appealed to me. However, my Kensington Wine Fair man ran into financial difficulties. He ceased trading and that, at a stroke, cut off my only channel of supply. In short, I was sunk. With only one source of supply I had, of course, been a real greenhorn at the business. Still, it had been interesting and rewarding work while it had lasted but now I was back to square one – no job and no income.

It was decision time in the Sole household. Jane and I were recently married. I had no job and was becoming disillusioned with the rugby set-up at Bath. As I recounted at the beginning of this chapter, the club had changed, in my opinion for the worse, during my three and a half years there. Continued success had meant that it acted like a magnet for quality players who wanted to be noticed on the national scene. Anyone who aspires to play International rugby really has to go to a club where they will be seen by the selectors, and the England selectors beat a fairly regular path to the Recreation Ground. Players arrived from all over and this had a detrimental effect on the social side. Guys would just come and train or play and have a couple of beers and then depart. Nowadays, with a young family of my own, I realise that there are competing demands on your time and commitments and I have to admit that at Edinburgh Accies, for this reason, I haven't been a great social member. But in those days at Bath we were mostly young with no family commitments and, as a result of the Roger Spurrell legacy, the club had always boasted a very healthy social side, with a good Saturday night virtually guaranteed.

In addition I was now established in the Scotland side and the continual travelling between Edinburgh and Bath was beginning to wear me down. Throughout the International season I would play for Bath on the Saturday afternoon and then drive to Heathrow Airport, catch the Edinburgh shuttle, eat, sleep, train and then get the shuttle back to Heathrow, drive to Bath and get home early Sunday evening absolutely knackered. This was 1987 and World Cup training commitments virtually followed on from the Five Nations championship.

Jane and I talked it over and we came to the obvious solution. We would move to Scotland. So far as I was concerned it meant going home. We resolved that as soon as the World Cup competition was over we would be Edinburgh-bound. Next stop Edinburgh Academicals and Raeburn Place.

CHAPTER 5

CHASING THE THISTLE

Dr Smith's Diagnosis

DESPITE THE FACT that I was born in England and spent the first eight years of my life deep within Sassenach territory, my overriding rugby ambition was always to follow up my Scottish Schools' Caps by pulling on that superb blue shirt with the white thistle at senior level as well. And it is a superb shirt. Only the All Black top with the silver fern comes close to matching the Scotland strip in terms of being 'just right', in both sartorial and emotional senses.

It has always given me an immense emotional thrill to pull that Scotland jersey over my head. Even when, at times, the going got a little rough, I always considered it to be a great privilege to represent my country at a sport which I loved. From the first to the last of my 44 Caps, and especially so in my 25 times as captain, that almost overwhelming sense of duty, honour and responsibility never palled. At Murrayfield especially I never forgot that there were thousands of blokes out there in the stands and terracings who would have given their eye teeth to have traded places with me. It simply isn't possible to become blasé about playing for your country. It is an honour every single time and it should be looked upon as such by every person who has the good fortune to have his hard work rewarded by a Scotland Cap.

To digress for just a moment, though, and to return to the Scotland and New Zealand strips, I must say that both were much to be preferred with just the simple, unfettered emblem on the left breast. The Kiwi fern is now underscored with the words 'New Zealand All Blacks' while, since 1991, our new, stylised and copyrighted thistle has come with the words 'Scottish Rugby Union'. It's a sign of the times. The

Unions and the kit manufacturers want to make money out of the game by quite literally selling the shirts. But if, as I'm told, for copyright reasons some form of wording had to go beneath the re-designed thistle then wouldn't it have been much better to have had 'Scotland' rather than 'Scottish Rugby Union'? We don't play for the SRU. We play for the team, for the shirt and for Scotland as a whole. However, I write in 1992 and with my international career behind me. My quest in earnest for the Scottish Thistle had begun almost a decade earlier and, I daresay, at that point I wouldn't have much cared even if the Scotland shirts had come complete with the word 'Brigadoon' beneath the thistle.

In 1983, while I was still at Exeter University, I played for English Students against England Under-23s. The game, played on the Wasps' ground at Sudbury, was being viewed as a Trial for the England Under-23s who had an overseas tour coming up. I was very keen to get as much rugby experience at as high a level as I possibly could but, at the same time, I didn't want to burn my boats so far as Scotland were concerned. In retrospect I suppose that it was maybe a wee bit presumptious on my part but after this match I wrote to the then SRU secretary, the redoubtable John Law, pointing out that I was playing at student representative level in England; that there was a chance that I might be picked for England Under-23s and could he tell me, please, at which point might I be considered to have ruled myself out for selection by Scotland?

I have no doubt at all that John Law had never heard of me. Not many people had in Scotland at that time. Nevertheless he was kind enough to write back telling me that if I was picked for England Under-23s then the verdict from Murrayfield was that I would have ruled myself out of contention so far as possible future selection for Scotland was concerned. While I was awaiting John Law's reply I received a letter from Twickenham asking whether, if selected, I would be available for their forthcoming tour. I've no idea whether or not I would have been chosen because within days I had received the word from Murrayfield and had fired off a 'thanks but no thanks' note to Twickenham.

My first step-up on to the senior Scottish representative ladder came with selection for the Anglo-Scots. At Exeter University I was playing well off the beaten track so far as district selection was concerned but the Anglos' selectors had been discussing recent Scottish Schools' sides and, more pertinently from their point of view, Scottish schoolboy Caps who had subsequently gone South for domestic or education reasons. Aparrently, someone said: 'Whatever happened to that chap Sole who used to prop for Scottish Schools?'

The former Scotland centre-threequarter Iain Laughland, who was one of the Anglos' selectors, said: 'Sole? That name rings a bell.' It turned out that he was married to a cousin of my mother's and he went down to watch me in action for Exeter University. You can't beat a spot of good old-fashioned nepotism! Seriously, Iain must have been marginally impressed with what he had seen because I was summoned by the Anglos to take part in a match against Lancashire in September 1983. I got through that alright and next played for the Exiles against Glasgow and Edinburgh where, as I recount elsewhere, I experienced for the first time the fearsome scrummaging power of Iain Milne.

By this time there was talk that I might be in line for a 'B' Cap. I still wasn't well known in Scotland and when I was, indeed, selected for the 'B' side to play Ireland at the Greenyards in Melrose the general reaction north of the Border was 'David who?'

Naturally, I was delighted to have been awarded a first 'B' Cap and, to make matters even better, we won 22-13. But, so far as many of the Press pundits were concerned, that old biblical proverb about the 'first being last' had a ring of truth about it. I had come up against one Des Fitzgerald, a tight-head prop who was to become a good friend and a respected opponent over the years. Dessie and I had a rare old scrap. He has an awkward scrummaging style. He drops his right shoulder on the Irish put-in and there's very little you can do about moving him. I didn't consider that I had been stuffed out of sight by Dessie but some of the media commentators obviously did. Not for the last time in my International career the general cry went up: 'This boy Sole can't scrummage.' To put it crudely, I was slagged rotten in the Press. A retreating scrum or a scrum which hits the deck always looks much worse from the touchline than it does from the front-row but there's no escaping the fact that my newspaper reviews were not good.

I was only 21 years old at the time but many in the media wrote me off. They said I had no future. I didn't think I had played as badly as they obviously thought. I hadn't found Dessie as demanding an opponent as Iain Milne. We never conceded our scrummage ball and, in fact, took two strikes against the head. I had still been able to run around and put in what I thought had been some pretty good work in the loose. Nevertheless I was pretty discouraged by the media reaction. Since that Saturday afternoon at Melrose, Dessie and I have locked horns on many occasions. In the seasons which followed one incident in particular always brings a wry smile to my lips.

In a game at Murrayfield I had skelped Des and he had looked up with a pained expression on his face to say: 'Jees, David. That was a good one. I'm going to get you back for that.' However, in the course of the game Des either never had the opportunity or he simply forgot about it. Either way he never did get his own back and every time we met subsequently at the first scrummage he would invariably promise: 'Look out now, David. Today's the day I get my own back.' In fact he never did – and it's too late now, Dessie! – but the nature of our first meeting at the Greenyards, and the media reaction to it, almost qualified – in the memorable words of one of his countrymen – as a case of getting your retaliation in first.

I was quite despondent, not so much by the afternoon's events but more so by what had been written about them. I didn't think that my International career was over almost before it had begun but a lot of the pundits obviously did.

I was still playing for the Anglos and therefore still had the kind of selectorial stage in which to redress any balance that needed redressing and I knew that I was still in with a shout when I was named to sit on the bench for the International Trial match at Murrayfield in January 1984. The loose-head props that afternoon were my fellow Blairmore 'old boy' Gregor Mackenzie and Gala's Jim Aitken, still with that season's Grand Slam glory to come. Gregor had been on the bench for the Greenyards 'B' game so he had leapfrogged me to become the second choice loose-head, after Jim Aitken, for the Trial.

By the time of the next 'B' International, against the French at Albi, our relative standings had switched again. I was in the side and Gregor was on the bench. Again we won, by the narrow margin of 13-10, but the game was most memorable for the fact that, to this day, it remains the dirtiest that I have ever played in. The French were up to all kinds of cynical thuggery. We never really stood toe-to-toe with them and slugged it out as maybe we should have done but at the final whistle we were ahead, so all of their skullduggery – as it has done on so many occasions at the highest level – came to nought. Scottish rugby really was on a bit of a high. In the 'B' side we had won two out of two and at the same time the senior side was on its way to winning only the second Grand Slam in our history.

The following, 1984-85, season I was back on 'B' team duty against Ireland and France. The Ireland match, played in Galway and which we lost 23-20, was notable not so much for the result nor for the fact that I scored a try, but for the reason that Gavin Hastings (I'm sure he won't mind my saying so) topped off one of his worst ever displays in a Scotland jersey by missing the team bus the following morning. As one of my team-mates who will remain nameless observed: 'Gav missed so much yesterday that it's only fitting that he should miss the bus today.'

For reasons which I am not at liberty to divulge, Gavin hadn't made it back to our hotel headquarters on the Saturday night. We were leaving at the crack of dawn so that the senior squad members could get back for a session at Murrayfield in the afternoon. Gav's 'crime' was compounded by the fact that he was one of the squad members whom we were accommodating by our early start. I would love to have heard his plea in mitigation to Jim Telfer.

The Ireland game was a particularly tense one for me because I reckoned that if I had a good afternoon then I would be in with a shout to play the 1984 Australians who, we now know, went on to complete a Grand Slam against the Home Unions. Jim Aitken, Grand Slam skipper only the season before, had been arbitrarily discarded by the selectors and the loose-head prop berth was up for grabs. However, Gregor, who by now was playing for Selkirk, had a particularly fine game against the Australians for the South of Scotland and he was selected to play against the Wallabies at Murrayfield.

By the start of the 1985 Five Nations' campaign it was soon clear that I was still not finding favour with the national selectors as Gerry McGuinness got into the side ahead of me and that summer Alex Brewster was taken as the only specialist loose-head prop on a Canadian Tour. I was more disappointed about missing out on that Canadian Tour than just about anything else in my rugby career. Alex is a tough, resilient character with a genuine never-say-die attitude. I would come to respect him enormously five years later as he led the mid-week side on our Tour to New Zealand. But in the summer of 1985 I considered that I was ready to make my breakthrough into the senior side.

Another 'B' Cap against the French at Murrayfield when again we won and then, at the start of the 1986 season, my fifth 'B' outing, against the Italians at Old Anniesland in Glasgow, had me genuinely concerned that I was going to break the record for the highest number of 'B' Caps. I was thankful that I was still being seen in high-grade rugby but, by now, pretty desperate to break through into the senior side.

I wasn't alone. There were quite a few players who felt that given the opportunity they would be able to perform at the highest level. Our chance came at the International Trial match in January 1986. I was in the junior Reds XV. We were skippered by Gary Callander, the Kelso hooker who had been understudy so many times to Colin Deans. Colin captained the Blues and was being strongly tipped to take over the Scotland captaincy as well. There were quite a number of points to be made. The Reds team was: Gavin Hastings, Stuart McAslan, Simon Scott, Scott Hastings, Roger Baird, Douglas Wyllie, Stuart Johnston, David Sole, Gary Callander, Norrie Rowan, Alister Campbell, Jerry

Campbell-Lamerton, Derek White, Johnnie Beattie and Fin Calder. The senior Blues side read: Peter Dods, Matt Duncan, Keith Robertson, David Johnston, Iwan Tukalo, John Rutherford, Roy Laidlaw, Alex Brewster, Colin Deans, Iain Milne, Hugh Parker, Alan Tomes, Jim Calder, Iain Paxton, John Jeffrey.

We played hellish well. We won 41-10 and in the process gave the senior side a real howking. The story goes that when Iain Paxton, the Blues' number eight, went off hurt at half-time the selectors told David Leslie, who was a replacement, to take over Packie's duties in the Blues. However, the wily Leslie (maybe it's his Glenalmond upbringing) told Johnnie Beattie that the selectors wanted him to switch to the Blues and that Derek White would take over at number eight with himself, Leslie, filling in for Derek. Even if the story isn't true it indicates that the wily campaigner David Leslie had seen the writing on the wall and that the Reds were very definitely the team to be in.

The Trial result came as a real shock to most people involved with Scottish rugby. It had been a genuine upset. The jubilation in our dressing-room was countered by the downcast feeling in that of the Blues. We then had an anxious three-day wait while the selectors made up their minds. The team to play France in the opening game of the Five Nations' championship was to be picked on the Tuesday night and announced the following day. I was reasonably confident. I felt I had played well but the big question was whether or not the selectors were going to believe the evidence of their own eyes and make the number of changes that the Trial result was crying out for.

At home on the Tuesday evening the telephone rang. It was Dr Doug Smith, the SRU vice-president who had managed the 1971 British Lions and whom I knew because of the Anglo connection. I recognised immediately who it was and, in all probability, why he was calling.

'David,' he said.

'Yes.'

'I have some bad news for you.'

I felt my heart sink. Trying, but not succeeding, to sound as matter-of-fact as I could I replied: 'Oh, what's that, Doug?'

He said: 'I'm afraid . . .' As soon as he had got those words out I felt the sky had fallen in. I couldn't believe that I had missed out on a Cap again.

It was a second or two before it had registered that what Doug had gone on to say was: '. . . you'll never play for the "B" team again.' The bugger had been at it. I was relieved, proud, overjoyed. There were a host of competing emotions. But most of all there was a sense of immense satisfaction. It had been a long and hard road since those days at Beechwood School when, as a six-year-old, I had first laid my hands on a rugby ball. It was a route that had taken me via Blairmore, Glenalmond, Scottish Schools, Exeter University, English Universities, the Anglos, Bath, and Scotland 'B'. I had now arrived at my destination and had achieved a life-long ambition. I had been chosen to play for Scotland. I'm not an emotional person but the surge of pride which overtakes you on first being selected for your country is second to none. For me it was a moment to savour and a moment to treasure for the rest of my life.

Once the make-up of the team had been announced there was general surprise that the selectors had indeed digested the lessons of the Trial. Bravely, they had created six new Caps. In addition to myself, Fin and Jeremy Campbell-Lamerton were included in the pack while Gavin and Scott Hastings and Matt Duncan were introduced as fresh faces behind the scrum. The selectors, though, had been quite canny. Beside virtually every débutant there was an old campaigner. Colin Deans and Iain Milne would ensure that I was looked after; Alister Campbell would pack down alongside Jeremy. The Watsonian David Johnston was alongside his clubmate Scott Hastings and he would also be able to keep an eye on Matt. In any case the Hastings boys have never exactly been found wanting in the confidence stakes. There was little doubt that they, of all of us, would come through with nerves intact.

The build-up to the game was more or less what I had expected and followed the 'B' team pattern. I was pleasantly surprised at the public training session at Murrayfield on the Friday at just how many Press, radio and TV people turned up to watch. They constitute quite a crowd. In fact, it's as big a crowd as is attracted to many club games in Scotland of a Saturday afternoon. The extent of the media interest still takes many new Caps by surprise.

I knew the coaches, Derrick Grant and Ian McGeechan, from 'B' and Anglo rugby. In fact, I played in Geech's last representative game. It was an Anglos' match at Dunfermline in 1983. Our fly-half had called off and Ian deputised at the last moment. He still had all of the touches. Geech has had a profound influence on my rugby career in one way and another. He began coaching with the Anglos at just about the time I was starting with them. Since then we have come up together through Scotland 'B', Scotland and the British Lions.

I'm a fairly phlegmatic character and despite the fact that I was as proud as punch at getting my first Cap I approached the game itself in a fairly low-key manner. I was sharing a room at the Braid Hills Hotel in the Morningside district of Edinburgh with our scrum-half Roy Laidlaw. From about 48 hours before kick-off Roy would give me a regular countdown.

'Forty-eight hours to go. Nervous yet?' he would mischievously inquire.

This went on at regular intervals throughout Thursday and Friday. 'Eighteen hours to go. Nervous yet?' Roy would say.

Eventually, on the morning of the match he had to concede that he had never seen anybody winning their first Cap remaining so calm. It wasn't just a front for Roy's sake. Unbelievably in view of what I know now I had managed to convince myself that it was just another game of rugby and that if I survived it and went on to win more Caps then well and good, but if I didn't then I would have achieved my ambition and I would have one more Cap than most people who had ever pulled on a pair of rugby boots. Such a proposition is of course arrant nonsense. I was desperate to get an extended run in the Scotland team and equally desperate to avoid the tag of 'one Cap wonder'. Nevertheless, when I look back on my first International I do so in wonder at the amount of self-deception I was able to employ.

I was drinking in the atmosphere though. When I'd played for Scottish Schools I had been chuffed just to be able to use the same Murrayfield loo as John Rutherford. Now here I was actually in the same team. By the same token, just a few years beforehand, I and a Glenalmond chum had hung around the Scottish team bus after a Murrayfield game and had slapped each of the players on the back as they had got on board. I remember telling John Beattie that he had played out of his skin and that he was a dead cert for the 1980 Lions' Tour. Again, here I was actually playing in the same team as these heroes.

It's absolutely true what people say about your first International experience. It passes in a blur. At one moment you are in the dressing-room getting ready to come out and then, hey presto, it's all over and you're back in the dressing-room again.

However, even by the standards of International rugby, I and the other five new Caps had a pretty bizarre introduction to the game at the highest level. We were all pretty keyed-up in the moments before kick-off. I couldn't wait to get out and get to grips with Jean-Pierre Garuet, who was to be my immediate opponent for the afternoon. He had a reputation for being a bit of a bruiser. He had been sent off the previous season for gouging and I was visualising the first scrummage and getting it clear in my own mind that if he hit me then he was going to come off decidedly second best.

Colin Deans had won the toss and elected to kick-off. We lined up playing towards the North Terrace and Gavin, with his first touch in International rugby, put the ball out on the full. Through force of habit, we began the trudge to the centre spot where we expected to have to scrummage.

'Thanks, Gav,' I thought as I made my way to the centre along with the other forwards. I would have preferred to have had Garuet running around a bit before the first scrum.

The almost panic-stricken roar of the home crowd was the first indication I had that there was something amiss. Instead of going back to the centre for the scrummage, as everyone had expected, Pierre Berbizier, the French scrum-half, had thrown the ball in from touch to Daniel Dubroca. Berbizier had accepted the return pass to run in for a virtually unopposed try. There were 19 seconds on the clock. I made a mental note: never trust the French! And they have the affrontery to call us Perfidious Albion!

We were all stunned. I'm sure all of the new boys were thinking to themselves that if that was International rugby then you could keep it. However, once we had gathered our thoughts it was clear that we would just have to get on with it on the basis that the score had never happened. True, it was on the board but from the viewpoint of the psychology of the game it was such a freak try that it didn't really count.

We were able to put the false start behind us and, despite being behind at the interval, we really got in amongst the French and ran out worthy winners by 18-17. It mattered little to us that all of our points had come from the boot of A. G. Hastings. What a début for Gavin! Nevertheless, it had been, as the Duke of Wellington said of another tussle with the French, a damned close-run thing. But with six newcomers in the side we had shown we had the character to overcome a nightmare start and to get ourselves in front when it mattered most, at the final whistle.

With that first International under my belt the big worry was whether or not I'd done enough to merit selection for my second Cap in the game against Wales. They always say that the second Cap is tougher than the first and 'they' are right. In fact, in terms of nervous tension, I've never been able to regain the composure that I felt before that first outing. It really was a case of ignorance being bliss. Once you know what to expect it becomes so much harder to treat the coming match with the nonchalance of a first-timer. The added strains of captaincy and the enhanced expectations which attach themselves to the side's 'senior pros' also add to the tension. Now that I have retired there are many, many things that I will miss about International rugby but the incredible tension and almost uncontrollable nerves which permeate the Saturday morning of a big game are certainly not among them. The waiting is the hardest part. Many players are physically sick on the morning of a game. Alister Campbell, the rugged 1984 Grand Slam lock, would be sick before the game and sick at half-time too. It's at such a time that all of the players ask themselves what they are doing there and why they voluntarily subject themselves to such torture again and again.

Despite all of that, though, the last thing you want to be is a one Cap wonder. I waited in absolute desperation to see whether I would be in the side to play Wales at Cardiff in a fortnight's time.

There was only the one change. Jeremy Campbell-Lamerton could count himself unlucky to lose out to Iain Paxton but the British Lion, a genuine world-class player, had come back from injury and was just too good to leave out.

At half-time we led 12-9 but by the end we had slipped behind and went down 22-15. The game was memorable for me primarily for two tries which I scored but had chalked off. Twice, just a couple of yards from the try line, I had taken tapped penalties and twice I had driven over and grounded for fair tries. Both times they were refused and I shall go to my grave convinced that I scored. The other notable incident in the game was even more galling from a Scottish point of view. It was the occasion of Paul Thorburn's 70-yard penalty kick. It was a truly majestic effort. Wind-assisted, it hung in the air for what seemed an age before passing between the uprights. Psychologically, that was a tremendous blow.

Despite our defeat, and despite the rather anti-social quirk the Welsh spectators have of spitting at the opposition team as they run out of the tunnel, I had found my first game at the National Stadium if not, perhaps, enjoyable then certainly interesting. I was no stranger to Wales, having regularly played Welsh opposition during my time with Bath. I thought on that first visit as a player to the Arms Park that the Welsh crowd, although knowledgeable, is the most one-sided in the world. It is a feeling which has been underlined many times since. The Welsh crowd rarely applauds the good things produced by the opposition and Cardiff is without doubt the worst place in the world to lose.

I didn't know it at the time but that Welsh game would be my last for the time being. For me, there endeth the first International season. The following weekend I went to Moseley with Bath and found myself on the wrong end of Steve Boyle's elbow. The fractured cheek and nose which resulted meant that I would miss the next three Internationals.

I missed the record 33-6 victory over England in which Alex Brewster took part. I was also sidelined for the Ireland game and for the match against Romania and the summer tour to France. Alex had done a good job and I was worried that I might not win back my place. Over the summer, with my facial injuries on the mend, I trained very hard in order to be fit for the start of the next season. Scotland had a game early on against the Japanese and I was extremely relieved to get the call.

For Scotland, the 1987 Five Nations' championship got off to a false start as the weather intervened and forced cancellation of our Calcutta Cup game with England. By the time we did eventually get around to playing them at the end of the season we had already seen off Wales and Ireland and went to Twickenham with the Triple Crown in prospect. But there were to be no such honours for us that season. Murphy's Law, which dictates that anything which can go wrong will go wrong, was in operation with a vengeance throughout that entire Twickenham weekend. In short, Twickenham 1987 ranks as my worst ever weekend in Scotland's colours.

From the outset the omens weren't good. Scott Hastings had fractured his cheek-bone and had to call off. We stayed in a hotel in the centre of Weybridge which seemed to be going for some kind of seismic record with its discotheque. On the Thursday night, after a hard day's training, we were all keen to get some good-quality shut-eye. Throughout the night and into the early hours the whole building seemed to reverberate to the disco beat. Half the boys were kept awake by the din – not exactly the ideal way to prepare for an International match in 36 hours' time.

If things were bad on the audio front then the video situation wasn't much better. As part of our tactical preparation we had planned to watch a recording of England's game against Ireland. The whole squad sat in the team room as the video cassette was loaded into the video player. We were all expecting to hear the dulcet tones of the BBC's Bill McLaren, but when the screen flickered into life all we got was the equally distinctive signature tune to the *Dr Who* TV series. Obviously there had been a problem on the video front and so our wish to see England performing in their last outing was denied.

We had half an hour or so before coach Derrick Grant was due to come to the team room for a tactics talk and so we moved on to Game Plan Two: our umpteenth viewing of the steamy video *9½ Weeks*. It had become something of a team favourite over the past few days and we had got it down to such a fine art that we were able to 'fast-forward' to all the 'best' bits. It was just getting interesting when one of the old dears from the hotel bar came into the team room to clear away some glasses. When she saw what was on the TV screen her domestic chores were soon forgotten and, to the great amusement of the team, she settled down to watch the movie with us.

We had been watching for ten minutes or so when Derrick came into the room and, in readiness for the serious business of the day, switched off the TV set. The old biddy from the bar didn't take kindly to this at all. She said to Derrick: 'Oh, do leave it on. It's just getting interesting.'

Derrick, never a man to call a spade a garden implement utilised in the process of digging, exploded: 'We're here to play bloody England, not to watch bloody films. This is supposed to be a serious bloody meeting.'

The lady from the bar beat a hasty retreat and we all contemplated our toes as Derrick launched into a tactical dissertation of what was supposed to unfold on the morrow.

Saturday dawned dismal and dreich. The wind howled and the rain lashed down. We had been playing five number eights in the pack. Derek White, Iain Paxton, John Jeffrey, Fin Calder and Johnnie Beattie all played number eight for their clubs. We didn't really have a genuine middle-of-the-line jumper. By chopping and changing and shifting the lineout target we had managed to cover our deficiency quite well in our victories against the Welsh and the Irish but against the English that day at Twickenham we were well and truly found out. Steve Bainbridge and Nigel Redman had a field day. We were more or less wiped out on the touchline. It was a disaster.

Things weren't going too well for the backs either. Despite the truly atrocious conditions, our threequarters were trying to reproduce all of the intricate manoeuvres that they had put together on the training paddock. They were doing dummy scissors and fancy miss-moves but they were invariably going horribly wrong. Then England were awarded a penalty try when Mike Harrison kicked through and Matt Duncan impeded him. The absolute low point was reached when John Beattie did in his knee. Johnnie gathered in a high ball and, in sheer frustration, ran straight at the English prop Gary Pearce. You could see straight away that the injury was a bad one. The knee just buckled and John had to go off with the ligaments in shreds. The injury was so serious that it ended John's career. That was a real blow to Scotland. John was a complete player. He was fast, athletic and very, very abrasive. He was just the kind of guy you would want in your corner when the going got tough. His departure more or less summed up our afternoon. We lost 21-12 and the entire expedition was a perfect example of something beginning badly and getting gradually worse.

As might be imagined we were pretty disconsolate in the dressing-room afterwards. However, the postscript to the weekend was written not by us but by three Scottish fans who waited in the Twickenham drizzle for the team bus to leave the ground. They were soaked to the skin, their kilts and yellow lion rampant banners hanging rather forlornly in the rain. The first of the trio managed a rather wan smile and raised his arm in a none-too-convincing wave of recognition; the second supporter just shook his head and turned away; the third executed an up-and-down motion with his right hand. His intention was clear. The word he had in mind rhymes with banker and that was what we had played like: a bunch of (soundalike) bankers. The fan was perfectly within his rights to make his feelings known but we didn't need our inadequacies pointed out to us. We knew that we had blown it. That afternoon at Twickenham was the nadir of my Scotland career. There would be other lowpoints to balance out the many highs but that 1987 defeat at the hands of the English when a Triple Crown was on the cards was just about as frustrating as anything I have ever experienced in a Scotland jersey.

Those were my first two International seasons. Since then, I've played 44 times for my country. I don't want to inflict on the reader a blow by blow account of each of those matches. The significant games and seasons are dealt with separately in chapters of their own. I do, however, want to give a feel for what it's like to pull on that coveted blue jersey and to represent your country.

Until my retirement I had my own peg in the Murrayfield changing-room. It was in the corner by the window at the rear of the West Stand. I used this peg every time we played at Murrayfield for the simple and unromantic reason that this is where my shirt was hanging before my first International against the French in 1986. In those days that was how the shirts were made available; you just went into the dressing-room and your shirt would be hanging on a clothes peg. Call me an old romantic if you like but I think that an International jersey is worth more than that. It is a symbol endowed with almost mystical powers and since 1986 the form has changed quite significantly. Now, the jerseys are handed out in a symbolic and often emotional ceremony. There is nothing official about it but the jersey ceremony has become very much an integral part of the build-up to the game.

Usually the jerseys will be handed over at the hotel before we leave for the ground. The team will be formed up in a circle and the jerseys will be folded neatly on the floor. The coaches will also be present and, depending on the circumstances, the players will either walk into the centre of the circle and each individual will pick up his own jersey or, sometimes, the players will give each other their jerseys or the coach will hand them over. If someone is winning his first Cap then often the captain will present the jersey with a few well-chosen words. This is what happened when Rob Wainright won his first Cap against the French in 1992 and I made the presentation. The entire 'ceremony' is underplayed yet highly charged emotionally. It is strictly for the team and coaches and there's seldom a dry eye in the house. It is a very private thing and, taking place as it does just before we leave the hotel for the ground on the morning of the match, it serves the dual purpose of further strengthening the bond within the team and of focusing the players' minds on the business ahead.

Now that the jerseys are presented in such a fitting manner, I just wish that the authorities would make the award of the actual International Cap a much more significant moment in the players' lives. Currently, the Cap arrives totally without ceremony or romance by means of the Royal Mail. It just arrives unspectacularly on the door-mat, courtesy of the postman. There surely has to be a better way than that.

The player simply fills in a form provided by the Scottish Rugby Union on which is entered the required size of cap. This is then sent off by the SRU. I received my Cap from the grand old Edinburgh outfitters R.W. Forsyth, who are now, sadly, no longer with us. On the evening after an International début a player will be presented with his official players' tie at the President's reception but how much more fitting it would surely be if a time and a place could be found for the actual Cap to be awarded in circumstances more appropriate than with the bills and the junk-mail on your door-mat at home.

The arrival on the scene in 1989 of The Corries' anthem *Flower of Scotland* was, I feel, a significant point in the development of the absolutely superb relationship which exists between the team and the Murrayfield crowd. There had been a lot of debate about the advisability of a truly Scottish anthem which could be sung and played home and away and which would provide the Scottish team and supporters with a separate identity as other nations sang their anthems prior to kick-off. The anthem situation at Murrayfield had been brought into sharp focus by the raucous and, to my mind, extremely ill-mannered booing of *God Save the Queen*. This was particularly inappropriate whenever a member of the Royal Family was present or, more specifically, when our superb Patron, the Princess Royal, was in attendance. I can understand the reasons for the crowd wishing to give vent to their displeasure at the playing of the National Anthem which has, in recent years, been more or less usurped by England as its own anthem.

Additionally, some of the verses of *God Save the Queen* that are no longer sung are particularly unflattering from a Scottish point of view. Nevertheless, I felt that the jeering was churlish and reflected badly on the otherwise superb Murrayfield crowd.

Flower of Scotland, which was written by the late Roy Williamson, one half of the Corries singing duo, had always been the Scottish team's private anthem. The song's rugby association, though, went back even further than that because it had been the unofficial tour song of the 1974 British Lions in South Africa. When the debate as to whether or not there should be a Scottish anthem was raging, a few of the senior players got together and informed the SRU that, in our opinion, we should indeed have an anthem and that it should be *Flower of Scotland*. The SRU agreed and wrote off to the Corries asking if they would mind if their song was used for this purpose. The Corries said that they had absolutely no qualms about its use and it was sung for the first time before the Fiji game in 1989. It was during the following season, however, that it came of age and particularly so on 17 March 1990, at Murrayfield when, with the words printed in the programme for the first time, it gave the team an enormous emotional fillip before the Grand Slam decider against England. That is another story, for another chapter, but I think it would be appropriate here to mention just how much the song meant to us, on a day made even more poignant because its composer, Roy Williamson, was terminally ill and couldn't be there to hear it in person. Roy's partner, Ronnie Browne, has said that that day was the proudest in Roy's life. Shortly before he died Roy wrote to me in those terms. Little, of course, can soften the grief of family and friends when a life is cut so tragically short but for so long as the Murrayfield crowd continues to give voice to *Flower of Scotland* then a little of Roy's genius will live on.

I am fortunate to have been associated with Scotland and Scottish rugby during a period which has been, arguably, the most successful in its long and proud history. Two Grand Slams and a share of the championship within a decade plus fourth place in the 1991 World Cup are not achievements to be taken lightly. But those triumphs have been double-edged. At times we have become victims of our own success. The expectations of the Scottish rugby public have been heightened as a result. No longer are we expected just to give a good account of ourselves and, at the final whistle, to be good losers. So far as I'm concerned, these heightened expectations have been a positive force. I've never been interested in just making up the numbers. I have always played to win. At International level there is no other way. Winners make commitments and losers make promises; and throughout my time with the Scotland team I have rarely come across a more committed bunch of individuals.

On the wider political front the successes of the rugby team have run in parallel with an upsurge in national optimism and identity. The team's success on the International stage has given many Scots something to be proud of. That was particularly evident after the 1990 Grand Slam. Rugby success has given Scots all over the world an increased sense of national pride. Without being jingoistic or nationalistic (with a capital N) I think our success has had a spin-off on the political front. During the 1992 General Election campaign I was approached by two parties who asked if I would give them a public endorsement. My politics are my own business and I declined to become involved with either party but I am happy that our achievements on the rugby field appear to have focused attention on Scotland and our Scottish heritage.

I have enjoyed every second of my time as a Scottish inter-nationalist. Over the years, and particularly since my appointment as captain in 1989, I've found that my perspective has changed. At the start of my International career I was just glad to have made it into the team. I enjoyed playing in front of huge Five Nations' crowds and got a buzz from our games being on the telly. As you gather more Caps you begin to get to know your team-mates as friends as well as playing colleagues. You begin to enjoy the social side of the weekend, the 'crack', the blether and the banter. Then, as captain, I enjoyed the added responsibility that went with the job. The enjoyment moves beyond that of personal fulfilment to that of seeing other members of the team succeeding and of seeing the hard work that we might have put in on a particular move rewarded when it comes off on the day and a try is the result.

I have found the mental challenge of captaincy stimulating: getting the best out of individuals, making sure that from the Wednesday to the Sunday the whole International package struck the right note and that the preparation reached its optimum peak on the Saturday after-noon. I have enjoyed working with the coaches and acting, if you like, as their representative on the field of play. My immersion and total enjoyment in all of these things meant that right up until I had taken the decision to retire I was still enjoying International rugby. However, it's simply not possible to play Internationals and Internationals alone. I have to admit that latterly I had found the club game and the training a dreadful bind. And training for an International player these days really is a seven-day week proposition. You would be out on your own every night running, swimming or doing weights; that would be in addition to twice-weekly club training sessions, a match on a Saturday and a national squad session on the Sunday. That is a huge commitment to expect from a young man probably at the start of both family life and career.

I'm not complaining. Nobody forced me to do it and I just cannot imagine what my life would have been like without rugby. But because it won't be possible to turn back the clock to the days when International players just met on the Saturday morning, played, had dinner and then went home, I'm sure that the commitments demanded of anybody who wants to make it to the top flight in rugby are going to become greater and not less. For all of those reasons I decided that I had given as much as I could give without other aspects of my life – family and career – suffering as a result.

The announcement of my decision to retire took a lot of people by surprise but Ian McGeechan and some of the 'senior pros' in the side had known since before the start of the 1992 Five Nations' championship. I had taken them into my confidence because not to have done so would have been hypocritical. Geech, therefore, knew that I wasn't going to continue beyond the Tour to Australia that summer. I hadn't intended making a public announcement until the tour was over but, halfway through our championship campaign and a week or so before we were due to face the French at Murrayfield, I was giving an interview to BBC Radio Scotland reporter David Nisbet when, out of the blue, he asked me if the French match would represent my farewell appearance at Murrayfield.

I suppose I could have lied or fudged the issue but perhaps in a way I was glad that I had been given the opportunity to let the rugby world in on my 'secret'. The intention had been to make a public anouncement after the Australian tour. I had told Derek Douglas of *The Herald* newspaper, my collaborator on this book, that I would give him advance warning if my retirement decision was to be made public and so David Nisbet agreed to delay the broadcast of our interview until the following day. I was genuinely touched by the media and public reaction to the news, even if at times the valedictory newspaper prose read just a bit too much like an obituary for comfort. There were one or two speculative stories which sought to conjure up headline-grabbing reasons for my departure, the most outlandish of which was the theory that I was quitting because Will Carling and not David Sole was to get the 1993 British Lions' captaincy. Frankly, that scenario is too pathetic to dignify with comment.

I was 29 when I decided to pack it all in. People have said that front-row forwards are just reaching their prime at this age. However, in my case it wasn't the registration number that was the problem, it was the mileage on the old body-clock. I had been playing top-grade rugby for virtually a decade. As I've said, that amount of commitment had exacted a tremendous toll on other aspects of my life. There's no doubt that career and family life suffer. At International level a rugby player is, in all but name, a professional sportsman. The commitment is as great and the hours spent in training are as great, only the rugby 'amateur' invariably has to hold down a full-time job as well. I have calculated that in the seven years I was involved with the national squad I have taken off what amounts to a full year for rugby-related activities. My employers, United Distillers, have been absolutely first-rate and I would hope that the other side of the coin is that they have benefited from the PR profile that my activities have given them. However, at the end of the day if one is intent upon advancing in business then it is not feasible or fair to expect an employer to furnish an employee with that amount of time off and still to regard him as a suitable candidate for serious promotion.

We had already played England and Ireland by the time news of my retirement was out in the open. But the International season had begun with me taking stick in some quarters for going on a family ski-ing holiday to France rather than taking part in the Trial match at the beginning of January. We were accompanied by Sean Lineen, who was also in need of a break, and his girlfriend Lynne.

I needed the break. I felt as though I had been playing almost constant rugby virtually since the summer of 1990 when we returned from the Scotland tour of New Zealand. We had had the 1991 Five Nations' championship and then had to maintain fitness throughout the summer for the World Cup in October. I felt quite drained by the time the 1992 Five Nations came around and I had to get away to recharge the batteries. It worked a treat. I came back refreshed and raring to go.

I had considered retiring along with Fin Calder and John Jeffrey but perhaps that would have been too many old heads going at the one time and so I decided to delay my departure. There were, though, off-pitch problems, which I expand upon elsewhere, which played a crucial part in my medium-term decision making. Then, before the International season was even under way, Gary Armstrong – a key player if ever there was one – suffered a serious knee injury in a club match, which meant that we would have to start our campaign without him as well. Chris Gray and Graham Marshall were also on the injured list and so we were having to re-cast the side in quite an extensive fashion.

When we played England in our opening championship match at Murrayfield only a few of the senior players knew that it was to be my last Calcutta Cup match. My Edinburgh Academical clubmate Dave McIvor was in the side for his first Cap at blindside wing-forward, while on the other flank, making his début, was Gloucester's Ian Smith. Ian's elevation to the full Scotland side meant that for the first time in a long while we were playing genuine open-side and blind-side wing-forwards. Fin and JJ had played right and left at the scrum with Fin playing off the lineout tail. Into the second row came that street-wise Harlequin Neil Edwards and taking over from Gary at scrum-half was Dundee HSFP's Andy Nicol, and what a revelation he would turn out to be!

The team had been chosen on the Sunday following the Trial from which I had absented myself. On my return I had spoken to Geech on the telephone and had managed to wheedle its composition out of him. Geech had sworn me to secrecy but I had promised Sean that if I found out what the team was then I would give him a ring to let him know whether he was in or out. Sean, who qualified to wear the Thistle on the basis of a Hebridean grandfather and who had been a permanent fixture in the side since 1989, was concerned for his place.

I reached Sean on the telephone: 'Sean, I'm very sorry.'

'Ah, shit, mate,' he said in a splendidly despairing reply before I could get any further.

'I'm sorry,' I continued, 'it looks as if you'll have to play against England at Murrayfield.'

'Shit, David. Don't do that to me,' said Sean.

It turned out that my call had been the second that Sean had received. Despite the fact that the selectors had been intent on keeping the make-up of the team a secret until the official announcement, it's a small world and, most mysteriously, Craig Chalmers had been quoted the team verbatim by a Melrose team-mate. Craig had then called Sean to tell him that he was in. Sean had, of course, been delighted and relieved by Craig's news. However, when I had called with what had sounded initially like 'the chop' Sean had been more inclined to believe me than the second-hand version from Melrose.

As for the game itself, we played well for the first 40 minutes but then England forced their way into the proceedings and ended up winning 25-7. The scoreline flattered them but they made more of their chances and they deserved to win. The game was notable from my point of view because I felt that I had redressed the balance in my personal duel with Jeff Probyn. Jeff had taken the edge in our World Cup scrummage battle the previous year but we more than held our own in that department in the Calcutta Cup match. We even scored a pushover try which went down with the England pack very much like a lead balloon.

It was notable, too, in a more negative sense, for a vicious blow from behind by Wade Dooley on Doddie Weir. Doddie suffered a perforated ear-drum as a result but he should look upon it as a compliment as he had really out-jumped Dooley and I'm sure big Wade acted out of frustration. More worryingly, Tim Rodber had to go off with what was eventually diagnosed as spinal concussion. The England number eight lay for a long while on the ground and when I went across he said he was experiencing pins and needles in his hands and feet. Spinal damage is the rugby player's greatest fear and I really did anticipate the worst as young Tim, winning his first Cap, lay there on the Murrayfield turf.

There's a kind of convention that is followed when the skipper goes across to enquire after the health of an injured opposition player. Sometimes, if it doesn't look too serious, I'll just ask them how they are and suggest to the ref that we might get on with the game. On other occasions, if it's to our advantage, I'll suggest that they don't look at all well and that, maybe, the best thing to do would be for them to go off. However, as soon as I went over to see Tim, it was clear that he had been, potentially, seriously hurt. We were all saying that he should just take his time, that the medics were on the spot and they would decide what was best no matter how long it took. Thankfully, after what seemed quite a long time, the feeling began to return to his limbs and Tim was able to go off for treatment. He was replaced by Dean Richards and although I don't think that Dean's appearance turned the game in England's favour, there's no doubt that his massive mauling presence more than suited the static type of game which England wanted to play at that juncture in the match.

So defeat at the hands of the Auld Enemy wasn't how I would have preferred to enter my final Five Nations' championship. We had played well in the first half and if we had managed to get over some of our penalty kicks then we would have been able to exert some psychological pressure on the English. At the end of the day, though, there's no doubt that Will Carling's men deserved their win.

Our season was very spread out. There was a lot of time between our matches. That makes it very difficult to maintain any kind of continuity. When we won the Grand Slam in 1990 there were just two weeks between each of our matches. When they follow on as closely as that then it is very much like being on tour.

Travelling to Dublin for a crack at the Irish, I found that I was under a great deal of pressure. We had lost three matches in succession (to England and New Zealand in the World Cup and England again in the Calcutta Cup). There was a suggestion that we were on a losing streak and that all the prophecies about this being a 'rebuilding season' were coming true.

The conditions at Lansdowne Road were lousy. There was what amounted to a gale blowing down the pitch. I won the toss and elected to play with the wind. Phil Matthews, the Irish skipper who was under even more pressure than I was, said: 'Thanks. That's one decision I won't have to make today.'

There was a nasty breeze blowing through Irish rugby too, with former Internationals queuing up in the Press to take pot shots at the players and coaching staff. Former coach Mick Doyle, in particular, had his knives out for the team and for coach Ciaran Fitzgerald. It was a particularly 'un-Irish' atmosphere which greeted us. The IRFU president Noel Henderson once said: 'While the state of British sport may be mostly serious but never hopeless, the state of Irish sport, though mostly hopeless, is never serious.' Someone should have passed these sentiments on to the Lansdowne Road crowd. I have played International rugby all over the world and have never heard a crowd barracking and slow-handclapping their team. That's what happened at Lansdowne Road and I couldn't believe my ears. Ralph Keyes, the Irish fly-half, had a nightmare of a game and the crowd gave him stick whenever he touched the ball. It was a shameful performance on the part of the crowd and so very unlike what had hitherto been my experience of Irish rugby. At International level, a player's commitment should never come into question. I don't think Ralph Keyes's commitment could be questioned but that is what the Lansdowne Road crowd were doing. I felt so strongly about what had happened that I made a point of mentioning it in my speech at the after-match dinner. We won 18-10 but rugby and not Ireland had been the real loser.

By the time we played the French my secret was out. Everyone knew it would be my last appearance at Murrayfield. Of course every player likes to perform in front of his home crowd but I like to think that the Murrayfield crowd means something even more special to me and to the Scottish team. Certainly, we have always felt that the crowd was involved. Whenever a back-row move had been called I never had to get my head out of the scrum to see whether it had been successful or not. The reaction of the crowd would let me know even while my head was buried in the deepest recesses of the scrum. Similarly, you never had to look to determine which way you had to run if you were buried in a ruck or maul. The rising crescendo of the crowd noise would tell you exactly where the action was.

I'll miss the Murrayfield experience greatly. But for my final appearance it was important that I didn't let my emotions run unchecked. The French came to us in some disarray, having been slaughtered by England at Parc des Princes and having had two men sent off in the process. Even allowing for that, the Tricolors are always difficult opponents. Next to the All Blacks they are the strongest and most physically abrasive of the world's top sides.

On the morning of the match, when the jerseys were handed out at the team hotel, Ian McGeechan said that he wanted to be absolutely selfish and to present personally the jerseys to myself and Derek White. Derek had intimated that he, too, was retiring and the game would therefore also be his last at Murrayfield.

Geech said that we had all come through a lot together and that he now looked upon us as friends rather than as players. It was a very emotional moment. I didn't want to get too emotionally involved as it would have dulled my performance as captain. I had toyed with the idea of giving a dressing-room talk to the boys which would have really tugged at the heart-strings but I rejected this as being too selfish. I didn't want to take anybody's mind off the game. Eventually, I said something along the lines of: 'It doesn't matter whether it's your first or your 41st Cap. We go out there to win. The priorities don't change. We play for each other and we play to win.'

By the time we were out on the pitch my emotions were, just, in check. Then, as we lined up for the anthems, I looked into the great West Stand and there was Jane with our three-year-old son Jamie. She had kitted him out in a Scotland shirt and it was his first time at the ground. This would be the first and last time that he would see his father playing for Scotland. That was a highly emotional moment and the thought of it brought a huge lump to my throat.

The game itself was a hard, physical slog. The French, as always, were tough men. I relished the hard physical contact but the match was marred by the incessant drizzle which made handling and running a nightmare. Neil Edwards scored his first International try from a lineout after only four minutes and Derek White brought off one of the tackles of his career with a superb, try-saving effort on Franck Mesnel. It wasn't a match for the casual observer. But there were some good things going on, especially the way we defended our line and, undoubtedly, it was a game we would have lost ten years ago. It wasn't the free-running, glitzy spectacle that I would have liked to have ended my Murrayfield career on but, with a final scoreline of 10-6, at least it was a win.

After the final whistle, on our way back to the changing-room, my direct opponent, tight-head Philippe Gallart, was fairly insistent that I swop jerseys with him. I explained that I preferred not to for the reasons that this was my last match at Murrayfield and that was the first time that we had worn our smart, new white 'change' strip with the blue pinstripes. I took his address and said I would send one on. So my International career had turned full circle. I had made my début at Murrayfield in 1986 with a win over the French and there I was ending my 'home' career with a similar result against the French. It had a tidiness about it which appealed to me.

Tidy is a description which could not be applied to my final championship outing two weeks later against Wales at Cardiff. The whole game was a mess. We played well below our capabilities and didn't really deserve to win. However, I feel obliged to make at least some mention of what became the day's main talking point and that was the standard of refereeing from championship débutant Marc Desclaux. At times the proceedings were reduced to the level of a rather third-rate French farce.

Before the kick-off Monsieur Desclaux had said that he did not speak very good English. I said that I spoke tolerably good French and that if he required to make any comments by way of law interpretation, or whatever, then I would be more than happy to converse in his native tongue. As the game got underway it soon became apparent to both sides that we hadn't been reading the same rule-book. Particularly as regards scrummage collapses we had no idea what the ref wanted and I don't think he did either. Eventually, after a string of collapsed scrums, he began penalising the front rows more or less on a tit-for-tat basis. If we had fallen foul of M. Desclaux in one scrummage then we could be almost certain that we would be in favour next time he blew his whistle. On one occasion he even penalised our hooker, Kenny Milne, for sup-posedly collapsing the scrummage on his own put-in. Unbelievable. I asked the referee what the specific problem was and he wouldn't tell me. We were operating in the dark.

Similarly, so far as the advantage law was concerned, it seemed that it had been repealed for the afternoon. Twice Scotland players broke free into potentially try-scoring situations only to be brought back for penalties in our favour. Then, when we were 12-6 down and fighting back in the last quarter, Iwan Tukalo scored what seemed to many neutral observers to have been a perfectly good try but M. Desclaux saw fit to disallow it. Our cause was not helped either by the appalling knee injury suffered by tighthead prop Paul Burnell. Paul, who has been referred to by the media so often as the 'unsung hero' of the Scotland side that he is referred to within the squad simply as 'unsung', was a real loss. We had to bring on Gloucester's Peter Jones who normally plays on the left of the front row. It just wasn't going to be our day. Coaches often say that to be successful you have to over-come not just one opponent but three: the opposition, the elements and the referee. Using these criteria our overall score at Cardiff Arms Park that afternoon wasn't particularly high. And lest the foregoing be mis-construed as a rather long-winded 'we wuz robbed' gripe then I would have to say that we didn't deserve to win. We never got our game out of first gear. I was disappointed mainly because we had played so far short of our true potential.

The Welsh won 15-12 but at the function after the match we were able to see just how much the win had meant to them. They could at last see some light at the end of the tunnel and be reasonably certain that it wasn't an express train coming in the opposite direction. I was able to meet up again with British Lions' chums Bob Norster, now the Welsh team manager, skipper Ieuan Evans, Robert Jones and Mike Griffiths. They were absolutely delighted. Perhaps at the end of the day, and despite the fact that it was to be my farewell championship appearance, the Welshmen just wanted to win more than we did. It would have been nice had I been able to bow out with a win and, maybe, even with a spectacular side-stepping try to my credit! However, life tends not to be like that.

On the Sunday after the match I was off to London to attend the BAFTA awards ceremony. I had been invited as the guest of United Distiller's PR manager Elaine Howie. It's always a treat to see how the other half live and it was a glittering affair with an absolute all-star line-up of the great and the good from the world of art and entertainment.

The SRU Patron, the Princess Royal, was the principal guest and during the meal she sent across a message asking if we would care to join her at a cocktail party later. She wanted to commiserate with me on account of the defeat the day before. HRH had been at Cardiff with son Peter and daughter Zara. All of them had been sporting the tartan and making no secret of which team it was they had come to support. She really has been a fine ambassador for Scottish rugby and we have been very lucky to have had her as Patron.

That, then, was how my Five Nations' career ended: in defeat at Cardiff and hobnobbing with the stars of stage and screen the following day. I would have gladly exchanged my place at the BAFTA ceremony for a victorious farewell at Cardiff. But there was to be no fairytale ending. I should have known. Fairies are an endangered species among the hills and valleys of rugby-playing Wales.

CHAPTER 6

LIFE WITH THE LIONS

Winning in Oz – 1989

SELECTION FOR A British Lions' Tour, even in these days of World Cups and overseas expeditions by national sides, has to be the pinnacle of any player's rugby career. As a schoolboy I had devoured newspaper reports trying to keep up with the progress of the victorious 1971 and 1974 Lions in New Zealand and South Africa. So far as I was concerned the Lions had about them a mystique which no other side came close to emulating and I can recall, as a 15-year-old, being bitterly disappointed when the 1977 Lions lost in New Zealand. That defeat turned into a losing run in South Africa and New Zealand in 1980 and 1983.

You are aware of the history and traditions which surround selection for the British Lions and after I was chosen for the 1989 tour I reminded myself time and again that it was the winning legacy of those '71 and '74 Lions that I should use as a personal bench-mark and that it was the example set by the likes of Barry John, JPR, Ian McLauchlan, Gordon Brown and by our two coaches Ian McGeechan and Roger Uttley that we should strive to emulate. That we did so against some pretty formidable odds, and after having made it almost impossibly difficult for ourselves by losing the first of the three Tests, speaks volumes for the character of the whole party and in particular that of our skipper Fin Calder.

Finlay was placed under almost intolerable pressure by uninformed media comment that he should drop himself after the first Test. Within the touring party there was never any suggestion that this would happen. Fin showed great strength of character and played a real captain's role by picking the entire tour up off the deck after that demoralising first Test defeat. It was due to his captaincy and to the fact that the entire party simply got on so well together that the wheels did not come completely off the wagon and that we were able to go on, as the history books show, to put that crushing first Test defeat behind us and achieve the first Lions' series win in 15 years.

But for me the tour began not in a rugby setting at all. I was in St Andrews, the home of golf, when word of my Lions' selection came through. At the time I was employed in the wholesale wine trade and with my boss, Susan Ramsay, I was visiting a customer at Rufflet's Hotel. I had been on tenterhooks all day. I knew the composition of the Lions' party was due to be announced and we listened for news on the radio as we motored from Edinburgh to the Fife golfing mecca.

Before we went into the hotel I called home on Susan's car-phone. 'Any news?' I asked Jane.

'No, sorry, nothing.'

I asked Jane to call up Ceefax on the television. Still nothing. I went back into the hotel and fidgeted all through our business lunch until I thought a decent enough interval had elapsed before I could excuse myself and sneak off to a phone again.

This time when I got through to Jane I didn't even have to ask. 'You're in. It's just been on the news,' she said.

I was absolutely delighted. I had reckoned that I had a fairly good chance of being selected but you can't take anything for granted. I had set my heart on going on the trip and it was such a relief to be told that I would indeed be travelling to Australia.

When I got word of the composition of the entire party I knew that we would have a pretty successful campaign. The selectors had chosen the in-form players and we had a large number of individuals of genuine world-class. The ultimate make-up of the touring party in national terms – nine Scots, eleven Englishmen, eight Welshmen and four Irishmen – I thought fairly reflected the playing standards of the Five Nations' Championship which had just ended. There were one or two guys who could consider themselves lucky to have been chosen and, equally, others unlucky to be passed by, but that's life. I was reasonably confident that with the chosen players allied to Clive Rowlands, who was to become a superb manager, plus Ian McGeechan and Roger Uttley as the two coaches, then the 1989 Lions would be as strong as any to have left these shores to do battle on the other side of the world.

We were a very happy band of brothers. The fact that no one nation dominated the others meant that nationalistic cliques didn't form and, in any case, Finlay went out of his way to ensure that every-one fitted in and was as committed to the party as a whole as he might have been beforehand to his mates in whichever national side he had came from. Of course, it helps when you're winning, as we did consistently with the exception of that blip in the opening Test match, but the generally good-natured and happy atmosphere of the Tour reflects tremendously on Fin's leadership qualities. He is a tremendously charismatic character, never lost for a word and endowed with a steely determination to get the job done. On the field, he also has that ruthless streak without which I don't think you can really survive at the top level.

I certainly didn't envy him his captain's role. There had been other contenders. Will Carling would, no doubt, have been considered had he not fallen victim to an untimely injury. Then there was Philip Mathews of Ireland. Phil was, perhaps, a bit of a surprise omission from the party although, by his own high standards, I don't think he'd had a particularly good Five Nations' Championship and the selectors do have to pick the guys on form. Paul Thorburn was the Welsh skipper and he didn't go on the Tour so I don't think there's much doubt that Finlay was just the man for the job.

Between the end of our season in Scotland and embarking on the Tour we had eight or nine weeks to kill. We put the time to good use by fulfilling a rigorous training schedule drawn up for us by the Lions' management team. The home-based Scots – Finlay, John Jeffrey, Craig Chalmers, Gary Armstrong, Peter Dods, Scott and Gavin Hastings and myself – trained regularly at Murrayfield, Earlston or Jedburgh under the watchful and unforgiving eyes of Scottish coaches Derrick Grant and Dougie Morgan. As a result, and despite the fact that we had played no rugby for a considerable period, by the time we gathered together as a party the Scots were fighting fit and raring to go.

One of the first things that we, as forwards, had to establish was whether we were going to ruck or maul. At that time, under the Jim Telfer influence, the Scottish game was based almost exclusively on fast, dynamic rucking. England on the other hand, although they were then in a period of transition, still utilised the traditional upper-body strength of their big forwards with much more of a mauling game.

At the time there was a lot of Press speculation as to what type of game we were going to play. The media weren't the only ones who were speculating. It was sorted out when we came together for a couple of weekend training sessions at the Oatlands Hotel in Weybridge. There was, as I recall, quite a bit of heated debate, but gradually a consensus began to form. When we were going forward we would ruck and when we were defending we would maul. It sounds so obvious that you wouldn't really have thought there was anything to discuss. But it did lead to a fair bit of good-natured but frank discussion within the camp. With this decided we were sure to get the best of both worlds. The reason why Scots have in the past decade become a fierce rucking side is not just because Jim Telfer, is thirled to anything remotely Kiwi in approach. Well, he is. But that's not the only reason! Scots ruck rather than maul because, generally speaking, we're smaller than the other top rugby nations. We traditionally don't have the big powerful men who can turn the rolling maul into an attacking platform. With the Lions, though, we had the likes of Dean Richards and Wade Dooley and Mike Teague. Big, strong men who would be able to hold their own in a maul with the best in the world.

With the kind of game we were intent on playing behind the scrum we were going to need fast second-phase possession and rucked ball is tailor-made for that. The debate didn't turn on nationality at all because the England hooker Brian Moore, for instance, was very keen on playing a fast, rucking game with the maul held in reserve for defence. At the end of the day Fin settled it by declaring: 'Look, if we're going forward stick the ball on the deck and ruck it. If we're on the back foot then keep it in the hands and we'll maul ourselves out of trouble.'

To win when you're so far from home takes a huge effort from everybody concerned. Every little thing has to be just right. Clive Rowlands was an outstanding manager. He was very much the spiritual leader of the tour. He was a great diplomat but, equally, when harsh words had to be spoken he didn't shirk the responsibility. He was superb.

Ian McGeechan, of course I knew well from his coaching duties with Scotland. He is as astute a rugby tactician as the world has seen and also a 'double' British Lion in his own right from 1974 and 1977. Roger Uttley I didn't know particularly well. A schoolmaster at Harrow, Roger, too, had 'been there' himself as a Lion in South Africa in 1974. So experienced were the forwards under his care that he was content to adopt an invaluable supervisory role. The medical team of Dr Ben Gilfeather and physio Kevin Murphy ministered to the lame and infirm. Kevin in particular really burnt the midnight oil as he eased aches and pains and laboured to get creaking joints and limbs back into action. It was much to his credit that we had only two seriously debilitating injuries throughout the tour – to Paul Dean and Chris Oti – and that players were invariably patched up and mended ready again to take their places in the front line.

The 12-match tour got underway against Western Australia at Perth where we won by the handsome margin of 44-0. At half-time we were only eight points ahead and perhaps this reflected the fact that having not played any rugby for nigh on ten weeks we weren't anywhere near optimum match-hardness. That, at any rate, was the verdict of the Welshman who coached Western Australia. After the game and after his guys had more or less been taken apart at the seams he sidled up to us and said: 'What's the stitch count?'

We hadn't a clue as to what he was talking about.

'The stitch count. You guys seem to have collected more than your fair share,' he said by way of explanation.

It was true that I'd had an ear stitched up and Donal Lenihan had also collected a few but we still weren't quite sure as to what our new-found Welsh-Australian friend was on about.

'You'll have to toughen up if you're going to make any sort of impact in this country. You guys have been cut to ribbons. If you don't tough up you're going to get whacked out here,' he said.

Point taken. We were soon to discover that Aussies set great store by the macho approach and some of the games we were involved in were intensely physical affairs. I was to discover even sooner, though, that it's not just your average Aussie male who tends to be ultra-macho. The Sheilas don't do too badly either!

The stitching in my ear had already been the cause of some grief. Before we left the UK Ben Gilfeather had been holding a tackle bag while we went through a training session. Unfortunately for Ben, when I hit a bag I do so as if I mean it, and despite having the bag for protection, Ben was caught under the ribs and winded. He limped off threatening vengeance. He got his chance during that Western Australia game. I got a boot on the ear and went into the changing room with blood running down my face to have some stitches inserted. The cut was right on the cartilage. Ben took a quick look and said: 'I told you I'd get my own back. No anaesthetic for you.' He then proceeded to stitch me up good and proper. It was absolute bloody agony.

However, the tale of the ear didn't end there. After the game we all adjourned to a nightclub in Perth. Suddenly two Aussie women started beating the hell out of each other. They went out on to a balcony, presumably for what in other circumstances might be termed a 'square go'. Scott Hastings and I were intrigued so we followed them out and peered around a corner to see what was happening. They were still at it. Unfortunately, Scott made some remark or other and the pair of them forgot about their not so private quarrel and bore down on Scott and me like a pair of avenging angels.

'Piss off and mind you own business, you Pommie bastards,' said one of them. She had a point and so we pissed off. We had just got back into the nightclub when, ten seconds later, one of the girls came up behind me and skelped me right across the cut ear. It was so painful I almost passed out. The stitches burst open and I started bleeding all over the shop. Bloody hell, I thought, if that's the Aussie women then what are the blokes going to be like!

The nightclub incident aside, though, Perth was a superb place in which to get the Tour underway. Our hotel was the last word in luxury and the weather was just like you see it in the Quantas adverts.

During one of our rest days we went cruising on the Indian Ocean. We were split up into various crews and I went with Brian Moore and Bobby Norster. Bobby wanted a picture taken as a souvenir of the trip and so when we got back to harbour he asked a passer-by on the quayside if he would do the honours. He handed the guy his camera and the three of us posed for the picture. Then, just like a slow-motion action replay, the poor bloke dropped Bobby's camera. It hit the ground and bounced. The guy was down on his knees making futile efforts to catch it. The camera bounced again and for a second time the guy grappled for it. Bobby, Brian and myself watched transfixed. After the second bounce the camera performed a perfect arc and dropped into the sea with a satisfying plop. Bobby stood there, disbelieving and mouth agape, as Brian and I creased up. We couldn't believe it. It was as if the whole episode had happened in slo-mo. Bobby didn't see the joke.

Next (minus Bobby's camera!) we moved on to Melbourne to play Australia 'B'. It was a hard, uncompromising game which we won 23-18. At this stage in a Tour you have to treat friends and colleagues who might be in with a shout for your position as rivals. You don't get bitter and twisted about it. That 'edge' is just one of the more interesting aspects of touring.

The management were keen, in the opening two games, to give everybody a run and to get the air-miles out of the system. By the time of the third game against Queensland, though, we would get an indication by means of the selection of how the team for the first Test might turn out.

Queensland had been having a superb season. They hadn't been beaten for something like 25 games and the last time they had lost had been to an equally strong Auckland side in New Zealand. Mike Griffiths of Wales and Gareth Chilcott of England were my rivals for the loose-head berth. Cooch came out with a damaged calf muscle and although he played throughout he was in some discomfort and tended to struggle a bit. I'm sure that had he been fully fit then he would have been challenging for a Test place. As it was I was picked for the

Queensland match in Brisbane and was glad to have got into what was being regarded as the embryo Test XV.

It was a hard, abrasive match which we really dominated up front. We won 19-15 and scored the only try of the game through Robert Jones. Queensland were restricted to five penalty goals from Michael Lynagh. From the very start of the Tour it had been our intention to play a rudely physical game, not dirty but extremely hard. The Australians set great store by the performances of their packs and we reckoned if we could get the psychological edge in the set piece and at the breakdown then we would be well on the way to winning the game.

Mike Teague played an absolute stormer that day. In fact, he really reached the peak of his powers on that Australian Tour. He is such a strong, abrasive character and he blossomed under the daily training regime that a Tour demands. He was undoubtedly the player of the Tour and it was against Queensland that he first showed the aggressive, driving form that would make him such a force to be reckoned with in the games to come.

We took the Queensland pack apart. Maybe we even won the stitch count! But it was never our intention to play dirty or nasty rugby. It was physical. It was tough. But dirty? No, definitely not. Afterwards, though, we had a taste of the Aussie whinge which would permeate so much of the Tour to come. It never ceases to amaze me how Australians have the nerve to refer to Whingeing Pommies. The Aussies are great when things are going well but when the going gets a bit tough or when events begin to unfold in a manner that isn't in their script then they don't half go on about it. As a nation they pride themselves on their macho image and they were very upset that we had taken them on and beaten them in the forward exchanges.

After the Queensland game their skipper, the Wallaby lock Bill Campbell, had a bit of a whinge. During the after-match function he indicated that he hadn't been too happy with the way that we had played and that we had been a pretty dirty outfit. He said that he was looking forward to meeting us again. The tone of his voice was more about throwing down the gauntlet than extending the hand of friendship. In truth, though, the game had been no harder and no more fiercely contested than your standard Five Nations' clash.

Wins followed against Queensland 'B' and New South Wales although in the NSW game we were at one point 20-12 up only to have the Australians come back into contention and snatch a 21-20 lead in injury time. Craig Chalmers notched up a hat-trick of drop goals with a particularly timely effort in the third minute of injury time and our unbeaten record was kept intact. I missed out on this match having injured my back against Queensland. Watching from the sidelines, what I remember most about the game was a spectacular stand-up fight in which Dai Young seemed to be centrally involved.

It was after that game that the British Isles 'Thugby' legend began to take root in the Aussie Press. From then on we were on the receiving end of some particularly sordid media coverage. Some of it was downright nasty. The way we looked at it, though, the more they squealed then the better we liked it. We weren't there to play pretty rugby. We were there to win. We were playing hard but fair. Adverse Press reaction merely underlined that thus far we had the measure of the best packs that they could throw at us. It meant that we held the psychological advantage.

By the time of the midweek game against New South Wales 'B' at Dubbo my back injury had cleared up and so I declared myself available for selection. With the first Test now just days away I didn't want there to be any doubt about my fitness. The day before the game Donal Lenihan, the dirt-trackers' skipper – the midweek side were christened Donal's Doughnuts – withdrew because of injury and I was asked if I would captain the side. I was delighted to do so. It's a great honour to captain the Lions and I treated the outing very much as that. We won 39-19 and went into the first Test with our record still in place.

We flew to Sydney for the Test quietly confident that we had seen the best that Australian rugby had to offer and that we were up to the challenge. As it turned out we were dangerously over-confident and our over-confidence would cost us dearly.

Four certain first-choice players were ruled out of the first Test because of injury. Mike Teague, Chris Oti, Scott Hastings and John Devereux had all been crocked and despite all the midnight oil burning sessions by Kevin Murphy they couldn't be restored to fitness in time.

No matter. We still felt that we had a strong enough side to do the business. The team was Gavin Hastings, Ieuan Evans, Mike Hall, Brendan Mullin, Rory Underwood, Craig Chalmers, Rob Jones, David Sole, Brian Moore, David Young, Paul Ackford, Robert Norster, Derek White, Dean Richards and Finlay Calder. Not a bad team in anybody's language. Unfortunately the vast majority of us chose this of all days to have a collective off-day.

I don't want to take anything away from the Australians because they played very well. We were quite simply hammered. On a beautifully sunny afternoon in front of a capacity 40,000 crowd at the Sydney Football Stadium we went down 30-12 and were, not to put too fine a point on it, pretty comprehensively done over. We were cleaned out in the lineouts where Steve Cutler in the middle of the line and Bill

Campbell at the front had a field day. Campbell and Cutler are very big men, each around six feet seven, and with Scott Gourley and Steve Tuynman not exactly dwarfs either, they had an imposing line-up along the touch line. They virtually threw the ball wherever they wanted with a cast-iron guarantee that they would retain possession.

We never really got into the game. Nick Farr-Jones and Michael Lynagh dictated play with some astute tactical kicking and we were unable to achieve the aggressive forward momentum which had been our hallmark up until that point.

When we got back into the dressing-room we were shell-shocked. The 30-12 scoreline almost represented a record whipping for the Lions and the try count of four to none fairly represented just how out of touch we had been. Collectively, we just couldn't believe how badly we had played. Also, though, and more positively, we couldn't wait until the following Saturday when we would have the opportunity to prove to ourselves and to everybody else that we weren't as bad as that display had just indicated.

The media had a field day. Suddenly it was open season on the Lions. To the Australian Press, which only days beforehand had been referring to us as 'Thugby' players, we were suddenly a bunch of pussy-cats. Certain sections of the British Press – and we had a large contingent of reporters travelling with us – were little better. They wanted blood and in particular they wanted Fin's head on a plate.

At the Press conference after the game Finlay was down-to-earth and characteristically straightforward. He spoke for all of us when he said that he was bitterly disappointed and desperately frustrated. We had committed far too many errors and hadn't come close to emulating the powerful forward displays we had shown up until that point. The Wallabies had struck peak form in their first International match of the season and they deserved full credit for that. However, said Fin, we had a week to sort things out and that was more than enough time. He ended on a defiant note. Many at the time must have written it off as empty bravado. However, he meant it and we knew that he meant it. 'These Lions,' he said, 'will never play so badly again.'

Fin then came under intense pressure from the media to make himself unavailable for selection for the second Test. Effectively he was being asked to drop himself just as Mike Campbell-Lamerton had done while skippering the 1966 British Isles side in New Zealand. The Press were blaming Fin for the Sydney defeat and they wanted him out and Andy Robinson in.

Finlay is a tough cookie and I know that the pressure he was under would have broken a lesser man. He discussed the situation with myself and JJ and Derek White. We spoke for all of the players when we said that he shouldn't even think about making himself unavailable. It was then that Finlay's immense strength of character came to the fore. It would have been all too easy in the aftermath of that Test defeat for the bitching and moaning to have started. Malevolent little cliques could have formed and the recriminations begun. The whole tour could have started to veer off course. Even while he was under so much pressure himself Finlay went out of his way to keep spirits up and to keep things on an even keel. We were all very low. But we couldn't wait to have a go at the Wallabies again, assuming, that is, that after the Sydney display we would be selected for a second chance.

The media are a fickle beast. While sections of the British Press were crying loudly for Finlay's head, the Australian papers had changed tack entirely. One minute we had been the British Isles rugby thugs and then after our defeat in the opening Test the reports were to the effect that these Lions were in reality just a bunch of pussycats. A headline in *The Australian* newspaper was representative. It read: 'Swift boot to the aura of the British Isles "Thugby" stars'.

The Sunday after the Test was a rest day and so we took the opportunity to unwind and get sorted out in our own minds just what had gone wrong at the Sydney Football Stadium. After lunch we boarded the plane for Canberra determined that we would make amends in the second Test just six days away. In many ways the fact that the Tests followed on consecutive weekends was a blessing in disguise. It meant that there wasn't that much time to brood on what had happened. We were straight into another midweek game and then into preparation for the make-or-break second Test.

We went through a rigorous training session on the Monday during which we concentrated on the areas where we had proved deficient. It was really a question of going back to the basics. So far as the forwards were concerned we re-examined our ball-winning and retention techniques.

The following day Donal's Doughnuts were playing Australian Capital Territories at the Sieffert Oval, Queanbeyan. ACT had a handy record against touring sides, having beaten Fiji, Japan, Wales, Italy and Argentina. In addition they had drawn with France and taken the All Blacks to the wire. If we were to get the Tour back on track then it was essential that we won against ACT and, in addition, won well. But it almost didn't happen. We were 18-4 down after 20 minutes and those of us who weren't playing were sinking deeper and deeper into our seats. Our worst fears were being realised – it looked as if a second humiliation was on the cards. An abiding memory is the jingle which was played over the public address system every time that ACT scored. As they did pretty well in the opening half it never seemed to be off the air. It went: 'Kookaburras, kookaburras 1-2-3, we are the boys from ACT'. Scintillating stuff. Gradually, though, the match turned in our favour and we ended with a convincing 41-25 scoreline.

That game also provided the basis for a trick sporting question. It was the only time on tour that the Lions fielded an all-Scottish back-row. Derek White, Fin and JJ? Wrong. White, Jeffrey and Sole. I was on the bench and when Andy Robinson had to retire hurt I got the call to go on and take his place at wing-forward. I must say, despite the fact that I hadn't much of a clue as to what I was supposed to be doing, I rather enjoyed the experience. But much more importantly, that victory over ACT was the turning point in the Tour. It had been supremely important that we won. To have come from 18-4 down and run out such convincing winners showed that we had deep reserves of character to dig into.

Psychologically, the Doughnuts' victory gave the entire party a terrific boost. I'm sure I hadn't been alone in thinking as ACT started piling on the points that the Tour was on the point of disintegration. But through sheer guts and determination imminent defeat and all that it stood for was turned into handsome victory.

The Wednesday saw us back on a plane and bound for Brisbane. We were training at the Brisbane Boys' College and we put in a couple of intensive sessions in preparation for the key second Test. By Thursday the Test side had been chosen but not yet announced. There were to be five changes. Wade Dooley and Mike Teague came into the pack in place of Bob Norster and Derek White, while in the backs Rob Andrew, Scott Hastings and Jerry Guscott replaced Craig Chalmers, Mike Hall and Brendan Mullin. The full team was Gavin Hastings, Ieuan Evans, Scott Hastings, Jerry Guscott, Rory Underwood, Rob Andrew, Rob Jones, David Sole, Brian Moore, David Young, Paul Ackford, Wade Dooley, Mike Teague, Dean Richards and Fin Calder.

The selection of Wade Dooley to partner his England colleague Paul Ackford in the second row really had a lot to do with our re-emergence in the second Test. Wade is a huge man, six feet eight and almost 18 stones. It meant that we had at least one guy who would be able to look Steve Cutler straight in the eye without getting a crick in the neck. It also has to be said that Wade and Paul really came of age in a sporting sense on that Tour. They were both fit, athletic men, particularly so Paul, who could more than hold their own in the lineout jungle with the best in the world.

The recovery of Mike Teague from a shoulder injury also gave us a tremendous boost. Mike, a Gloucester builder, is as hard as nails. He revels in the close-quarter stuff and his powerful driving runs around the fringes of ruck and maul provided us with an enhanced ability in this department.

Rob Andrew for Craig Chalmers at fly-half meant that we had more options. Rob, who had flown out to replace the injured Paul Dean, has faster hands than Craig and, at that time, was a lot more experienced. You have to remember that at that stage in his career Craig had been playing International rugby for only one season. He had done tremendously well to fill the breach when Paul got injured but obviously the management felt that Rob's experience would be what was required in the cauldron atmosphere of the second Test. Scott and Jerry had been shaping up well and Scott had overcome the injury which had kept him out of the first Test. We were more than happy with the selection. Every one of us was raring to go and to assuage the guilt that we all felt over the Sydney performance.

In the days before the game the English media were still harping on about Fin and how he should step down in favour of Andy Robinson while the Aussie papers were still chuntering on about toothless Lions. There was also a tale circulating within the Lions' camp that the England skipper Will Carling had been on BBC TV's *Rugby Special* programme giving his opinion on where these Lions were going wrong. That went down a bundle, I can tell you. I don't know whether it was true or not but that was the word which went around our Brisbane hotel. That, and all the criticism that was coming our way in general, really fired us up. I've rarely been in a side which showed more steely determination and utter commitment to win.

We arrived at the Ballymore ground about an hour before kick-off. There was a warm-up game on and because of the way the stadium is built we had to walk along the front of the stand in order to get to the dressing-rooms. We walked past the crowd, jaws set and determined to avenge the previous weekend's defeat. The Aussie crowd started barracking us. 'Look at them. Call themselves Lions? They're just a bunch of pussycats.' Then they started making miaowing noises. By the time we got to the dressing-rooms that graceless reception by the Ballymore crowd had as good as given us a three-point start. It had been rude, ungracious, very typically Australian but, so far as we were concerned, it was the very best welcome they could have given us.

By the time we had changed we were all very keyed up. Each one of us knew just how important this game was to the future of the Tour. The prospect of defeat and having to spend another fortnight in Australia with the series lost was just too awful to even contemplate. We were determined to take on the Aussies up front and to beat them. It wasn't going to be dirty so far as we were concerned but it was going to be hard, uncompromisingly so. It was never going to be a match for the faint-hearted. It's a cliché, I know, but there would be no quarter given and certainly none asked. If an alien were to stumble upon a Rugby International dressing-room in the minutes before kick-off then he would think that he had come upon a remarkably odd species. Most people get very het up. There's a lot of shouting, beating of chests, impassioned pleading, all of that kind of thing. There are, though, exceptions. The mighty Dean Richards felt that the tense, electric atmosphere in the dressing-room wasn't to his liking. He asked if he could just step outside and gather his thoughts in the corridor. Dean made his mental preparation in solitude on the other side of the door. Each to his own. Obviously that works for Dean. Different personalities react and respond to different stimuli in the emotion-charged quarter of an hour before International kick-off time.

By the time that René Hourquet, the French match referee, came around to say his final piece we were all clear what was required. We wanted a really physical match. We weren't going to intimidate the Wallabies by violence but we did want to intimidate them by the sheer physicality of our play, by the big hits, the driving rucks and the solid scrummaging. We wanted to keep them on the turn, with Robert Jones keeping the ball in front of our forwards and with punishing kicks into the box. We wanted to tease David Campese with kicks just short of him when he lay deep and kicks over his head when he chose to come up.

Both sides were very fired up. Punches were exchanged at a few lineouts early on but the first really major flare-up happened at a scrum in the most unusual of circumstances. The two scrum-halves, Nick Farr-Jones and our own Robert Jones, were crouched down ready for the ball to be put into the tunnel when Robert stamped on Nick's foot. Naturally enough Nick took grave exception to this and retaliated. Within seconds the pair of them were rolling around on the ground like a couple of rabid terriers knocking seven bells out of each other. Then the two packs got up and started slugging it out. Fists were flying everywhere. Poor René Hourquet didn't know what the hell was going on. Once the dust had settled the only casualty seemed to be Nick who had got a split lip. Unedifying though it had been, the punch-up did serve as a release valve for some of the mounting tension. It really was a pressure-cooker type of atmosphere.

There was a fair bit of niggle throughout the match but, truthfully, I don't consider that it was a dirty game. There were one or two unfortunate incidents, and none more so than Dai Young's stamping on

113

Steve Cutler's head, but taken as a whole the match was far from being the dirtiest or most brutal that I've played in. As a pack we were back to the form that we had shown in the matches leading up to the first Test. We were fiercely committed and ruthlessly aggressive in our efforts to secure and retain possession but it was, for the most part, completely above board and legal. That Dai Young incident was the exception which proves the rule. It was an aberration and Dai was lucky to stay on the field. He was given a severe dressing down by Clive Rowlands after the game.

With 20 minutes to go Australia were leading 12-6. They had a Greg Martin try converted by Michael Lynagh and two Lynagh penalty goals. For us, Gavin had put over a penalty goal and Rob Andrew had stroked home a drop-goal. Even six points adrift and with just a quarter of the match left I never felt that we were in danger. We had control and I was sure that we would prove victorious. Rob Andrew took us to within three points of the Wallabies with a penalty goal and then we had tries from Gavin and Jerry, and one conversion, to give us a 19-12 win. And what a win! We had confounded all of our critics and, more importantly, we had proved to ourselves that we hadn't become a bad team overnight just because of that first Test defeat.

Within hours of the final whistle, though, the legend of the Battle of Ballymore was born. Suddenly, it was the most brutal game of rugby that anybody had ever witnessed. The Aussie Press were almost frothing at the mouth. They can certainly teach the Poms a thing or three about whingeing. Nick Farr-Jones declared that so far as he was concerned the third Test could develop into open warfare. He said that the Lions had set the standards and if the officials weren't going to control the game then the Wallabies would have to do something themselves. He told an Aussie media revelling in mock outrage: 'We won't sit back and cop it again.'

Tom Lawton, the giant Wallaby hooker, was even more out-spoken. He had been particularly upset at the Dai Young incident and had waded in about us with his fists flailing. He said: 'I was incensed at some of the things the Lions did in the match. At times they behaved like hooligans and the best word to describe it is thuggery. If that's the price to be paid for winning then I want no part of it.'

At the after-match interviews Geech and Roger were pressed on the violent aspects of the game. Both rejected the assertion that we had needed to resort to rough-house tactics in order to win and both denied that the match had been dirtier than hundreds of other International games down through the years.

That was how I felt about it then and is still how I feel about it today. They are still whingeing about that game in Australia but it wasn't a dirty game. It was physically hard and some of the hits were as big as I've ever experienced in a career of International rugby but that is what the game is about at the highest level. The other point which must be made is that some of the treatment that had been meted out to us in the games leading up to the Tests had been uncompromisingly brisk and business-like. We didn't whinge, though, we just got on with the game.

In our dressing-room after the Test the primary emotion was one of relief rather than euphoria. We had squared the series in a manner which had never been done before. Finlay was particularly pleased. He was well chuffed. He had coped well with the sniping of the Press and now he had been exonerated. He had played particularly well and had proved his critics wrong.

At the after-match reception Nick Farr-Jones, in his skipper's speech, more or less threw down the gauntlet for the return bout in Sydney in a week's time. Like Bill Campbell after the Queensland game, Nick made a heavy point about how much the Wallabies were looking forward to meeting us again in Sydney. Even then, so soon after the Ballymore match, the third and deciding Test was being billed as the ultimate showdown.

The Sunday after the so-called Battle of Ballymore was spent reflecting on the scale of our achievement. It was a sense of quiet satisfaction rather than chest-beating or empty bravado. A few of us went for an early morning run just to get the stiffness out of weary limbs and then it was on to the bus for a couple of days' rest and recuperation at Surfers' Paradise on Australia's famous Gold Coast.

In this idyllic holiday setting we convened the first meeting of the Cocktail Club. It was a particularly exclusive set-up with, initially, only four members – myself, JJ, Craig Chalmers and Ieuan Evans. We found a quiet bar and began ordering up a string of cocktails. We began with Banana Daiquiris and Pina Coladas. They were going down a treat – perhaps too well – so we decided that we would have one nasty-tasting cocktail followed by a more palatable one. The 'nasties' had to be downed in a single gulp whereas you could take your time with the nice ones, meaning a couple of gulps. The evening flew past. By bedtime – around four in the morning – we were feeling no pain. A couple of hours later we were up and on the bus to take us to the airport for our flight to Sydney. The cocktails were still having a quite magnificent effect.

In Sydney it was decided that we should have a fairly hectic training session. I've never experienced anything quite like it. By now I should have been suffering a monumental hangover but I still felt absolutely on top of the world. Throughout the training session I couldn't stop giggling. I dashed around the training paddock like a buzz-bomb tackling anything that moved and really putting in an impressive amount of work. It couldn't last. Around three o'clock in the afternoon it was as if the engine had just run out of fuel. I ground to a halt and retired to my room. There was still no hangover – just terminal fatigue. From then on the Cocktail Club became an integral, if somewhat intermittent, part of the Tour itinerary as more and more of the players sought to join up.

In the days before the third Test the Australian media kept up their barrage of abuse. The *Sydney Morning Herald* plumbed new depths with the observation that the 'scum always rises'. Then, on a more civilised but nonetheless intimidatory note, the Australian Rugby Football Union chipped in with a Press statement obviously designed to unsettle the Lions. The ARFU declared: 'At a Council meeting held today at the Union headquarters at Kingsford, the Australian Rugby Football Union resolved the following:

To condemn violence in the game.

That the executive director prepare a video depicting certain incidents which occurred during the second Test at Ballymore, which were believed to be prejudicial to the best interests of the game. The video, when prepared, will be forwarded to the Committee of Home Unions for their information and for any action which may be deemed to be appropriate.

The ARFU delegates to the International Rugby Football Board have been requested to raise the matter of video evidence as part of the game's judicial system.'

The whole thing was getting way out of hand. The Ballymore Test was beginning to assume the guise of a full-blown diplomatic incident. Thankfully, the coaches of the two sides in their public utterances were playing down the likelihood of World War III breaking out at the Sydney Football Ground on Saturday.

René Hourquet, the referee, also found himself under a lot of pressure. He had taken a lot of stick for his handling of the second Test and, in particular, for not taking sterner action against Dai Young after the stamping incident. Like us – that incident apart, which he had not seen at the time – Hourquet was adamant that it had not been a dirty game. Nevertheless, he requested a breakfast meeting with Clive Rowlands, Ian McGeechan and Finlay. I went along as interpreter. He said that he had not seen anything particularly untoward during the Ballymore game but if anything happened on Saturday or if the game degenerated into a brawl then he would have no hesitation in sending off however many it took to restore order. René had made his position absolutely clear and we were all aware of exactly where we stood. He said he didn't want the Test match to become a boxing match and we told him that neither did we.

We fielded an unchanged side for the match. Despite the fact that the outcome of the series depended on the result, there wasn't the same tension as there had been before the Ballymore game. In Brisbane it had been all or nothing. If we had lost then we might as well have gone home.

Roger Uttley gave us our team-talk in the hotel before setting out for the ground. Roger's talks were totally unlike anything that the Scottish contingent had been used to. With Derrick Grant and Jim Telfer the psychology was that they would tell you how bad a player you were and then you had to go out and prove them wrong. Roger, though, concentrated on accentuating the positive. His little chat before the third Test was a classic. Roger has rather a nasal pronunciation, the result no doubt of being bopped on the nose too often. He began by recalling his days with the '74 Lions in South Africa. The atmosphere in the team room was very tense and we were hanging on his every word as Roger declared: 'In 1974 we were in a similar situation. I've never forgotten it. I remember it as clearly as if it were yesterday. We were playing in Durban' – thoughtful and absent-minded pause – 'or was it Port Elizabeth?'

Roger had a rather confused concept of 'remembering something as if it were yesterday'! The entire team burst out laughing. It was a spectacularly funny moment. Unwittingly, though, Roger had done the trick. The tension was broken and we were able to continue our preparations and get ready to leave for the ground with a smile on our faces. Even yet, whenever somebody says, 'I remember it as if it were yesterday', it brings an involuntary smile to my lips.

But, to the more serious business of the Test match. It was to the credit of all 30 players that the game was played in such a fine spirit. There was none of the nastiness which had been widely predicted. It was one of the most exciting games in which I have ever played. It was a real cliff-hanger. We ran out winners by a single point. The final scoreline of 19-18 in our favour probably flattered the Wallabies, well though they had played. Once again the Lions pack had the upper hand. We didn't quite get the supremacy we had enjoyed in the second Test but, with Fin, Mike Teague and Dean Richards immense, we kept the pressure on the Wallaby eight throughout.

Gavin was rock solid in defence and also turned our pressure into points by slotting home five penalty goals from seven attempts. The great talking point of the game, of course, was David Campese's momentary brainstorm which saw him absent-mindedly toss an in-goal area pass to Greg Martin only for the Aussie fullback to drop the ball and Ieuan Evans to pounce for our only try. After the game it was impossible not to feel sorry for Campo, such was the opprobrium to which he was subjected in the Australian Press. They really crucified the guy in a way that I have not seen before or since. It was shameful stuff. Basically, Campese copped all of the blame for the Wallabies losing the series. That's an awful lot of blame to heap on one man's shoulders. What the guys who write these things forget is all the good stuff that Campese had done in an Australian jersey. He is sheer class, a matchwinner par excellence. It's his unpredictability that makes him so dangerous. If Greg Martin had hung on to Campo's pass and the Aussies had scored from behind their own try line then Campo would have been hailed – as he had been in the past – as a real-life Wizard of Oz.

On this occasion it didn't come off but I don't think that the outcome of the match turned on that one incident. It was significant, sure, but it didn't cost the Aussies the match and by concentrating on that one incident I rather felt that the gloss had been taken off our victory. We won because we played well, not because of Campese's unfortunate lapse. As in the second Test I always felt that we were in control and OK, it went right down to the wire but at no time did I think it likely that we were going to lose.

Campo certainly left his mark on the game in those unfortunate circumstances and he also left his mark on me. I had tackled him, or he had come into a ruck, and I held on to his leg after the ball had gone. He lashed out with his free boot and a stud caught me in the left eye. I was quite worried because the vision was impaired for a while. The media picked up on the incident and Campese was quite apologetic about it afterwards but he needn't have concerned himself. I deserved it. I was, after all, hanging on to his leg.

After the game the feeling was one of quiet satisfaction; very much one of mission accomplished. But we didn't have long to indulge in bouts of self-congratulation. Another journey beckoned, this time to Newcastle where Donal's Doughnuts were to have their last game of the tour against a New South Wales Country XV.

I don't wish to offend the good people of Newcastle but Surfers' Paradise it isn't. Our hotel was being redeveloped. We had all the rooms facing out to sea while those facing landward were being reno-vated. From dawn until dusk workmen hammered and drilled and generally kept up a cacophony of irritating sound. We went down to the bar and one of the managers greeted us with a cheery smile. 'G'day.

Great hotel, don't you think? I guess this is probably the best hotel you've stayed in since you arrived in Australia,' he said.

He was so genuine and we didn't want to disillusion him by telling him that in the past six weeks we really had stayed in some of the best hotels in Australia, if not the world. We nodded politely in a noncommittal kind of way.

He continued unabashed: 'We've got everything you could ever want. Sailing, shooting, fishing. Whatever you want just name it. Shit, we've even got a brothel next door if it's Sheilas that you're after.' They had too. A few yards up the street stood a big red-brick building without windows and with a red light on the top. We didn't know whether to laugh or cry.

The NSW Country side were duly despatched and we had only the ANZAC game to win if we were to maintain our record of that solitary defeat in the first Test. We returned to Brisbane for the match with the combined Australia–New Zealand XV.

As a diversion, a 15-a-side cricket match was organised at the Boys' College where we trained. There were quite a number of handy cricketers in the party. Ian McGeechan had been on the Yorkshire books, Andy Robinson had been with Somerset and, of course, Rob Andrew was a Cambridge cricketing Blue. The rules were 25-and-out and everybody had to bowl. I was extremely bitter and twisted as I fell victim to a piece of Dean Richards subterfuge. I had played and missed a couple of times and on the third occasion, as the wicket-keeper caught the ball, Dean simultaneously threw a small twig at the stumps. It sounded for all the world as if I'd got a snick but my bat hadn't been near the ball.

Ian McGeechan was umpiring and he gave me out. An appalling decision, Geech, if you don't mind my saying so! We made 120-odd and then it was our turn to field. Fin put Stevie Smith on to bowl and he was clouted all around the wicket by Rob Andrew. We thought it was all over. But then wickets began to fall and the game started to drift our way. People began to take it seriously. Stevie Smith was bowling again and Scott Hastings, with typical bravado, rushed down the wicket thinking it would be an easy slog, a boundary and victory for his side. To our consternation and delight Stevie bowled him. In came JJ. He got an edge and was caught by the keeper. Peter Dods strode to the crease looking to win it in the last over. Unbelievably, Stevie was on a hat-trick. Everybody crowded around Peter and he popped up a catch which I held and they were all out. We had won. You would have thought we had won the third Test all over again!

For the ANZACs game Fin stepped down so that Andy Robinson, his understudy throughout, could get a prestige Saturday (Sunday actually) game. I was asked to captain the Lions for the second time and it was again an honour which I very much appreciated. Unfortunately, the game itself was a bit of an anti-climax. For reasons not unconnected with the fact that the Wallaby v All Blacks Bledisloe Cup series was about to get underway, the Kiwis were loath to take part in a combined effort against the Lions. At the end of the day only three All Blacks – Steve McDowell, Frano Botica and Keiran Crowley – took part. It was a shame really because McDowell told me afterwards that he had thoroughly enjoyed mixing socially with the Australian players. Their rivalry is a bit like that which exists between the Scots and the Auld Enemy.

However, in a keenly contested match we ran out winners 19-15. We did well to keep our 'one loss' record intact because the Aussies were keen to impress their selectors for the forthcoming Bledisloe Cup series while the Kiwis gave it their all so as not to let the side down while in the midst of their arch-rivals. Also, we were flying to the UK the very next day and the boys could have been excused if they had let their minds wander towards thoughts of last-minute presents and home.

I don't know if it's particularly well known even yet, but during the latter stages of the Tour the Lions were the subject of a bid – and I use the word advisedly – to bring us to South Africa as part of the South African Rugby Board's centenary celebrations.

After the third Test, Finlay took a call in his hotel room from a chap who introduced himself as Alec Kellerman, a SARB official. He wanted to know if we would be interested in being part of a World squad to take on the Springboks in a two-match series at Newlands and Ellis Park. A players' meeting was convened and Finlay outlined the approach that had been made. Various opinions were expressed but gradually a consensus emerged that yes, we would be prepared to go, but only if we were handsomely recompensed for doing so. We reckoned, I think rightly, that our acceptance of the invitation would have resulted in a most almighty row. There would be acres of bad Press publicity and many of the guys would probably have lost their jobs. We decided that if we were to accept then there would have to be substantial sums of money paid into individual off-shore accounts. We were talking about a six-figure sum per man – £100,000 apiece to be precise.

I think that to a certain extent we were purposely pricing ourselves out of the market. Anyhow, Finlay was delegated to call Kellerman back and to relay our terms. Fin said the chaps were quite keen on the idea but the cost would be a hundred grand a skull. There was a long silence. Mr Kellerman was horrified. He said he would get back to us. Subsequently, there was a lot of to-ing and fro-ing on the phone lines between

Pretoria and Brisbane but the whole thing just died a death. I thought no more about it until I was back home and heard on the grapevine that there were a couple of South Africans on a recruiting drive in the UK.

I got a phone call asking if I was still interested, but I had gone off the idea since my return from Australia and we never discussed cash. A World XV did go, though, and were beaten in both their matches. The word on the street was that the £100,000-a-head that we had asked for in Australia had been negotiated downwards to something in the region of £35,000 for two matches, to be paid secretly into an off-shore account. Only those who went and those who paid them will know the truth of that. So far as I was concerned once the Lions' party had split up the whole idea had lost its appeal and the matter was closed when I said 'no' in that phone call to my home.

One other 'extra-curricular' item intruded on the close-knit community of the Lions during the final days of the Tour. Unknown to the players, a midweek, floodlit game between the 'British Lions' and France had been arranged for Parc de Princes to form part of the Republic's bi-centennial celebrations. So far as I was aware the whole jamboree had been put together without so much as a 'by your leave' to those who would be centrally involved – the players. Again, we met to talk the thing through and the unanimous decision was that we would take part in the game only if the entire Lions' squad went and if our wives or girlfriends could be part of the official party. We had been away from home for eight weeks and we didn't think that it was asking for the moon. If cost was the problem then the financial burden was infinitesimal when set alongside the gate receipts from the Paris game. The authorities said no. Fin was adamant that he wouldn't go unless everybody went and I backed him wholeheartedly. I even wrote a number of letters to Five Nations' Secretary Bob Weighell explaining our position. He was perfectly polite but unyielding. We were then in a stand-off situation with the players on one side and officialdom on the other.

It had been a perfect opportunity for the players to have stood their ground but unfortunately quite a number who had been party to the decision in Australia backtracked and took part in the game. I felt that they had let the side, and in particular Finlay, down badly. Any ill-feeling that the incident caused has long since passed but at a time when rugby is at the crossroads and International players continue to be placed under quite unrealistic pressures it would have been a healthy sign if the players, for once, had showed some solidarity and had displayed the same kind of 'one for all, all for one' spirit which had paid off so handsomely against the Wallabies in Australia.

I don't want to end this Lions' chapter on a sour note. Touring with the British Isles was one of the highlights of my rugby life. It was a privilege and an honour to play alongside some of the best players in the world. Despite all the flak that flew after the Battle of Ballymore it was one of the happiest tours I have ever taken part in. We came from behind to win the series and in doing so were forced to dig deep into our reserves of resilience and commitment. In the end it was a victory for character as much as anything else. Friendships were struck and memories gathered which will last a lifetime. Such an experience is beyond price. The Welsh minstrel Max Boyce best sums it up. In the years to come I'll be proud to say that 'I was there'.

CHAPTER 7

THE FLOWERING OF
SCOTLAND

Grand Slam '90

THE GRAND SLAM. Even yet it has a nice ring to it. Only thrice in the history of Scottish rugby have we managed to perform consistently well enough throughout the championship season to defeat our Five Nations' rivals. In 1925 the side was captained by Phil Macpherson of Oxford University. Fifty-nine years later, in 1984, that honour went to Gala's Jim Aitken. Then, six years after that, it was my turn. That whole season, and in particular the emotion-charged memories of that wonderful afternoon at Murrayfield on Saturday, 17 March 1990, will remain with me until the day I die. For sheer tension, commitment, high drama and excitement I doubt if there has been a match like it. Certainly none of those who took part had ever played in a game even remotely resembling it. By the time David Bishop blew his whistle for the final time we were all drained – physically, mentally and emotionally.

It was a game in which the winners had taken all: the Calcutta Cup, Triple Crown, the Championship and the Grand Slam. It was unique. It had never happened like that before. Will Carling's England came to Murrayfield as the most incandescent of hot favourites. Those students of form, the turf accountants, had virtually closed the book on England, while the media, and in particular some of the Fleet Street papers, had, to all intents and purposes, written us off. And, in truth, could you really blame them? England had scored 83 points and we had managed only 47. They had scored 11 tries to our five. They had looked always to be in control while we had occasionally struggled. However, even taking all of that into account, the atmosphere south of the border was one of premature celebration. We had quiet self-belief. We knew that we could win even if few others did. We were perfectly happy to play the underdogs. It is a state of mind that, perhaps, we Scots assume only too readily and one which in years to come we should seek to redress. If you have aspirations to be the best then you have to win even when you are favourites. Few nations, save the New Zealanders, have managed that with any kind of consistency.

However, in Spring 1990, at that particular time and in that specific place, the role of underdog was one which suited us. We played up to it. It was a game of subtle psychological warfare. And we won. There is no doubt in my mind now that the England team were – from their point of view – adversely affected by all of the hype.

No matter how often they deny it, I am convinced that they had begun to believe their own publicity. Such was the blanket nature of the pre-match hype that it would have been difficult not to. In addition to the unique nature of the spoils on offer for the victors, the game was special, too, in the amount of media attention it attracted. A single game has never, in my experience, had so much written or spoken about it. During the week before the match there was unprecedented radio and TV coverage while the tons of newsprint devoted to it must have cut huge swathes through acres of best Scandinavian pine forest.

Our Grand Slam campaign ended amid scenes of great joy and jubilation around four o'clock on the afternoon of 17 March but it had begun 12,000 miles from Murrayfield during the previous year's British Lions' Tour to Australia. Nine Scots had been included in the Tour party which represented the cream of British Isles rugby. Peter Dods and Gavin Hastings were the fullbacks. Scott Hastings was one of the centres. Craig Chalmers and Gary Armstrong made up a half-back pairing while in the forwards Fin Calder, Derek White, John Jeffrey and myself were also members of that victorious Lions' party. As a nation I'm sure it's the case that Scots tend to have an inferiority complex. Probably it comes from co-habiting with a bigger and richer neighbour; someone once memorably described the unbalanced nature of the love-hate relationship which exists between Scotland and England as like being in bed with an elephant. That's a perfect and picturesque simile. But when we were out in Australia we realised that the guys from the other countries were no better than us and that in quite a number of ways we were, in actual fact, better than they were. We came back from Australia convinced that we could compete with them on more than equal terms.

Crucially, too, Ian McGeechan, chief coach to the Lions and Scotland's coach on the domestic scene, returned from Australia with first-hand experience of the players who would make up the hard-core of the Five Nations' opposition. Of course such an exercise works both ways. The English, Welsh and Irish players had seen us in operation when the going got tough and Roger Uttley, their coach, had been Geech's assistant in Australia. However, I like to think that we got the better of the deal. The powerful English contingent, in particular, had seen how the Scots hadn't been found wanting when push turned to shove. We all returned home with mutual respect for each other but for us Scots the shared experiences had been particularly fruitful. This is not a new phenomenon. In fact, the common denominator in each of Scotland's Grand Slam seasons is that on every occasion they have followed a Lions' Tour.

In 1924, the Scottish captain, Phil Macpherson, had been unable to take part in the British Lions outing to South Africa but eight other Scots were on the Tour including Dan Drysdale, Ian Smith, Doug Davies, Robert Howie and Herbert Waddell, who participated in the 1925 Grand Slam decider against England, in the game which heralded the opening of the new Murrayfield Stadium.

The 1984 Grand Slam Scots had also benefited from a British Isles Tour 'down under' in the summer preceding their domestic triumph. True, in terms of results, the New Zealand trip had not gone all that well. Nonetheless, the Scots boys – Roger Baird, Roy Laidlaw, John Rutherford, John Beattie, Jim Calder, Colin Deans, Iain Milne and Iain Paxton – returned home knowing that they were at least the equals of their colleagues and rivals from the other Five Nations' teams. And again, as in 1990, the British Lions and Scotland shared a coach. This time it was Jim Telfer, who compensated for the bitter taste that defeat in New Zealand had left with brilliant success in the Five Nations' Championship.

Jim was still around six years later and it is no coincidence and a massive tribute to the influence that he has brought to bear on the Scottish game that during his involvement with the national side Scottish rugby has gone through the most successful period in its history. The other survivor from the 1984 Grand Slam operation, and therefore the only player to have been involved with two Scottish Grand Slam sides, was Peter Dods, the Gala fullback who played such a crucial role in Jim Aitken's side and who acted as an able and willing deputy to Gavin Hastings during our 1990 campaign. Peter suffered a cheekbone injury in a league game against Heriot's FP on the Saturday before the Great Day and couldn't take his place on the bench for the final game. It was unanimously decided that he should be there at Murrayfield and afterwards with the boys as part of the official party. It was that kind of family atmosphere which made that 1990 team such a special one. Apart from the Telfer and Dods connection, the only other link between the two sides came via the brothers Calder. Jim, who scored that memorable 'turning point' try to set up the 1984 win over the French, and Fin are twins, yet strangely their International careers didn't overlap at all. And, stranger yet, Fin didn't make his breakthrough into the side until 1986, the year after Jim had won the last of his 27 Caps.

Finlay had captained Scotland in the season preceding the 1989 Lions' Tour and had captained the Lions throughout our victorious campaign in Australia. He had performed magnificently under great stress throughout that Tour and when we returned to this country he announced that he was taking a break from the game. Accordingly, for the first match of the new season, against Fiji at Murrayfield in October, the captaincy was offered to me and I accepted with alacrity.

We had no way of knowing that the season was to be anything out of the ordinary and we approached the game against the Fijians in our normal, business-like manner. Geech emphasised that what he wanted above all else was control. He was keen to ensure that we did not allow the Fijians a single inch of breathing space. They are past-masters at conjuring something out of nothing and so it was stressed that we should remain in tactical control and that we should dictate the pace, direction and development of the game. We won 38-17 and ran in six tries in the process, including two, in his first international, from Tony Stanger, the Hawick winger. We were content with our afternoon's work.

Six weeks later we faced Romania, again at Murrayfield. The Romanians posed a completely different set of problems from the Fijians. The strength of the Romanian game lies in their set-piece play. They are generally, like the French, strong men and they revel in scrummage and lineout situations. Temperamentally they are a bit like the French as well and not averse to delivering the odd skelp or three when the ref isn't looking. It was against the Romanians that we started to hone the offensive-defence which was to be crucial throughout the Five Nations' Championship and particularly so in the Grand Slam decider against England. We wanted to get the first tackles in and to arrive at the breakdown point in numbers, not in dribs and drabs. We defeated the Romanians by a pretty convincing 32-0. I got a try as did Derek White, who had an outstanding game, but Tony Stanger, making a huge impact in his first season, notched up a hat-trick.

The Romanian game was notable too because Fin was back in the side. This was bad luck on Graham Marshall who had played in the Fijian match but Finlay was refreshed after his brief sabbatical and was about to play some of the best rugby of his career. Iwan Tukalo and Craig

Chalmers both missed the game through injury, Lindsay Renwick and Doug Wyllie standing in as deputies.

There was a certain amount of conjecture at the time of Fin's return due to the fact that he had not resumed the captaincy. The reason, as I understood it, was simple. Finlay had indicated that he intended 1989-90 to be his last International season. In fact he went on to play in the 1991 World Cup but had to be enticed out of retirement to do so. However, in the winter of 1989, the coaches preferred the option of appointing a captain who would be around at least until the World Cup in 1991. In Scotland, unlike England, the captain is appointed on a match-by-match basis and so it was never said, in so many words, that I would be required to fulfil the role through to the World Cup and perhaps beyond but Geech has indicated subsequently that this was, indeed, the thinking behind the appointment. Fin and I are extremely good friends and although we have never talked about is specifically, the transfer of the captaincy never caused either of us any problems.

But the Romanian game grabbed the headlines for something even more mysterious than the identity of the new Scottish captain. After the match Cristian Raducanu, one of the Romanian lock-forwards, defected. There was a great hue and cry but Raducanu had just slipped away into the Edinburgh night. He wasn't heard of for weeks until he resurfaced playing for the Boroughmuir club in the city. He stayed on in Edinburgh for some time before going on to play rugby down south. More poignantly, within a month of our playing the Romanians, their country erupted in revolution and the Communist régime was toppled. Maybe Raducanu had seen the writing on the wall.

Although the basic shape of the team which would contest the forthcoming Five Nations' Championship was becoming clear there was still the annual ritual of the Trial to be gone through. This time, though, the selectors bowled a 'googly' by picking our Lions' flankers, Fin and John Jeffrey, to play in the junior Reds side. The senior side, the Blues, won well and Fin and JJ were forced on to the retreat for virtually the entire game. Obviously Geech and his fellow selectors wanted to see how they would perform under pressure and how well they had recovered from the arduous Australian tour. The pair of them were pretty dejected at the end, a situation not helped by the promising young Melrose back-row forward Carl Hogg who, with tongue stuck firmly in cheek, asked Fin what he was going to be doing with his boots.

'Why?' said Fin, who had just endured an afternoon of drudgery and torture.

'Because after a display like that you'll not be needing them for much longer,' said Carl with a huge grin on his face.

However, when the side was announced to take on the Irish in our opening championship game Fin and JJ were there. I had never been in any doubt. The team was: Gavin Hastings, Tony Stanger, Scott Hastings, Sean Lineen, Iwan Tukalo, Craig Chalmers, Gary Armstrong, David Sole, Kenny Milne, Paul Burnell, Chris Gray, Damian Cronin, John Jeffrey, Derek White and Fin Calder. One of the strengths of our game that season was that, with the solitary exception of Derek White's injury in the final game against England, we were able to go through the championship with the same personnel. That makes a tremendous difference to the general understanding within a team and to the all-so-important ésprit-de-corps. By the end of the season we had played and trained together so often that much that had been difficult at the outset had become almost second nature.

However, if the ability to name an unchanged side throughout the season had been a plus point then the way that the championship worked out, in terms of the fixture list, operated very much to our disadvantage. The championship season was two weeks old by the time we played the Irish at Lansdowne Road and, more importantly, we played every side on the rebound from a sound thrashing at the hands of the English. This meant that they each had something to prove. They all wanted to show that they weren't as bad as England had made them look.

During that first 'blank' championship weekend we were involved in a squad session at Gleneagles Hotel in Perthshire where the main attraction was a clinic held by the expatriate Scot Jim Blair, fitness adviser to Auckland and the All Blacks. This turned out to be an incredibly interesting session and once again we were pleasantly surprised at the great similarities between how we try to play the game in Scotland and how it is played *par excellence* in the land of the silver fern.

When eventually we got our championship campaign underway we didn't play well at all. In fact the entire weekend had a ring of doom about it. Ian McGeechan had been laid low with a virus and couldn't make the trip. Then our flight from Edinburgh was delayed because of gale-force winds in Dublin. When eventually we took off an hour or so late we had to return to base when it was discovered that one of the aircraft doors hadn't closed properly. By this time the less hardy travellers on board looked as though they would rather just have called it a day there and then.

We had gone to Lansdowne Road as favourites and although we sneaked a win we certainly hadn't performed like favourites. We were cleaned out in the lineout where the law of the jungle ruled and Noel Mannion and Willie Anderson profited as a result. We didn't adapt at

Graham Marshall comes up in support against the Fijians at Murrayfield in 1989

Murrayfield, 1990, and I'm on the charge against the Pumas

Murrayfield, 17 March 1990 – a day I'll never forget. We pose for the cameras before our Grand Slam encounter with England

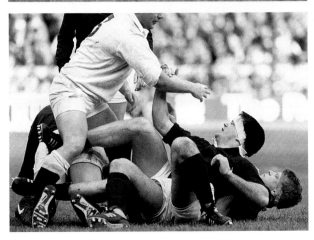

Just good friends. I seem to have upset my old adversary Jeff Probyn. An incident from the 1990 Murrayfield Grand Slam encounter. Damian Cronin is a horizontal eye-witness

THE HERALD

Sole possession? Not quite. John Jeffrey and I grapple for the ball against the Barbarians in their special centenary match at Murrayfield in 1991

THE HERALD

Back lads! I'm keen to get a tap penalty move underway against the Welsh at Murrayfield in 1991

Myself, Paul Burnell, Chris Gray and Derek Turnbull get a grandstand view of the art of passing, Robert Jones style. Gary Armstrong, on the right, has seen it all before

I'm led from the field by Scottish physio Dr James Robson after a clash of heads with John Jeffrey during our 1991 World Cup game against Japan. I came off second-best with a badly cut right ear

Arms and legs everywhere in a 1991 World Cup line-out against the Irish

A glower from me as we welcome the Western Samoans to Murrayfield during World Cup 1991. Doddie Weir, Gary Armstrong and John Jeffrey are equally unimpressed by the Samoan Manu

My 1992 Murrayfield farewell. Flanked by Scott Hastings, who has already swapped jerseys with Philippe Sella, I leave my favourite ground for the last time. Referee Freek Burger of South Africa brings up the rear

White-water rafting during a break in the 1990 New Zealand tour itinerary.
My 'shipmates' are Adam Buchanan-Smith, Sean Lineen, Doddie Weir, Tony Stanger, Finlay Calder
and Scott Hastings

Jubilation in Australia after Test match victory in 1989. In the dressing-room with Lions colleagues
Dai Young, Paul Ackford, Brian Moore and Wade Dooley

all well to the interpretations, or non-interpretations, of the referee Clive Norling, and we stuttered to an unconvincing 10-13 win. On the positive side, Derek White scored a couple of superb tries. Real beauties they were. Additionally, we showed that we were capable of changing horses in midstream by varying our tactics after half-time when we were 0-7 in arrears. I wanted the boys, and in particular the back-row, to drive much more at the Irish. It was that which eventually turned the tide in our favour.

In the dressing-room afterwards we were so despondent that you would have thought we had lost. We knew that we hadn't played to anything like our true potential. That fact alone served to underline how committed this team was. I had played in 22 internationals at the time and, having missed the 1986 Dublin victory through injury, that was my first 'away' win. No matter, we knew that we had sailed danger-ously close to the wind, both literally and metaphorically, and had come within a hairsbreadth of opening our campaign on a losing note.

In fact (whisper it) the SRU president, Jimmy McNeil, was firmly convinced that we had. He came into the dressing-room afterwards and, looking at the glum faces, started commiserating with us along the lines of 'better luck next time, boys' until some kind soul pointed out that, no matter how badly we had played, we had in fact been in front when it mattered most and that was at the final whistle. Once we had got over the initial disappointment at not performing as well as we, or our sup-porters, expected, we began to look on the bright side with the expecta-tion that things would, in all probability, get better once we had shed our ring-rustiness. Also, the lineout problems we experienced in Dublin were put to positive use because the coaches really turned their full attention on that area of play. The result was a dose of remedial action which transformed that aspect of our work.

There was precious little talk of Grand Slams after our Lansdowne Road championship début. We still had an awful lot of work to do before meeting our next opponents, the French, at Murrayfield a fortnight later.

Geech, along with fellow coaches Jim Telfer, Derrick Grant and Dougie Morgan, had done his homework on the French. The coaches homed in specifically on the threat the French posed by driving around the tail of the lineout. It was decided that on their throw-in I would be positioned in the scrum-half berth, Kenny Milne would join the lineout and Gary Armstrong would occupy the hooker's slot patrolling the danger area at the front of the line.

I would then target the number six slot in the lineout if they chose to come through that way. Finlay was charged with the same task at the rear. We planned to pressurise the French in the areas where they would expect to have the upper hand. We were going to deny them space and time, the two most sought-after commodities in international rugby. We also decided to target Serge Blanco. The French fullback was a mercurial character who could turn a game by a flash of brilliance. Equally, when things were going wrong, his performance had a tendency to fall to pieces. Our tactical kickers were instructed to torment the life out of him. We wanted to see the number on his back as he had to turn and retrieve our cruelly positioned kicks.

The French were a big, physical side as they always are. Again, they came to us having suffered a heavy defeat by the English and we were aware of the possibility of a backlash. It was a very windy day – the wind seemed to blow incessantly throughout the entire championship season – and we were only 3-0 up at half-time, having played with the gale at our backs in the opening period. The French captain Laurent Rodriguez, and what a powerful forward he is, had conceded weather advantage from the toss. I tend always to favour the discipline followed by toss-winning captains in Wellington, New Zealand, where the wind always blows and the decision, invariably, is to have the elements at your back in the opening period. Take the wind when it's presented; you never know what it's going to do in the second half.

However, with this in mind, I was more frustrated than concerned at the paucity of our half-time lead. We had created any number of chances in the first half but had failed to convert them into points. We should have been 15 points up and that would have been a reasonable cushion to have taken into the second half against the wind. But even with the meagre three points we had managed to put on the board I wasn't unduly concerned. I felt we were in the driving seat. We had control.

After the interval the wind dropped slightly in our favour and then French flanker Alain Carminati was sent off by Fred Howard for stamping on John Jeffrey's head. It was a blatant and dangerous foul and he deserved to go. Carminati's temperament was suspect and it was almost inevitable that when his path crossed that of Howard, a strict but fair referee, who had already sent off the Welshman Kevin Moseley in the Cardiff game against France the previous month, he would be taking an early bath.

However, I think it was French frustration at their inability to counter our hard, driving play which led to Carminati's moment of madness. In the second half we really got it together. Chris Gray had a superb game on the touchline and all of the tight forwards tackled as if their lives depended upon it. Quite simply we knocked the stuffing out of the French and their heads began to go down. The final scoreline of 21-0 was a true reflection of our superiority on the day.

Our confidence was rising. We felt we had done well against the French. But still there was no mention of the Grand Slam. We Scots are a canny race and it was very much a case, in the words of the old footballing cliché, of taking one game at a time.

Next we travelled to Cardiff to take on a Welsh side in disarray. Yet we were still fearful that we might experience the backlash of yet another side which had experienced a drubbing at the hands of England. Wales had lost heavily, 6-34, at Twickenham and in the fevered aftermath of that defeat the Principality's coach, John Ryan, had resigned. Into his shoes stepped Ron Waldron, coach of Neath, at that time the most successful club in Wales. Their game was based upon a fast, mobile pack which played the game at a frenetic pace. Seven Neath players were in the Arms Park side, including the entire front-row. The game was to be an object lesson in the old adage that what might work a charm at club level will go down like a lead balloon in the International arena.

Brian Williams, the Neath loose-head was just over six feet tall and weighed in at 13st 10lbs. This is ridiculously light for an International prop. Our tight-head, Paul Burnell, a genuine scrummager at six feet and 16st 3lbs, was given a couple of specific tasks for the afternoon. He was to scrummage Brian Williams out of the park and to make absolutely certain that whenever Williams's Neath clubmate Kevin Phillips took the ball on in one of those frantic tap penalty runs which he specialised in, he should be rapidly and unceremoniously decked. Paul performed both tasks to perfection.

We had absolute domination in the scrums. Rarely, if ever, at International level have I ever experienced one pack having such control over the other. Nevertheless, the Welshmen, playing for their country, their club and for Ron Waldron, put up stiff physical resistance and our domination in the tight wasn't reflected in points at the end of the day. It's never easy to beat Wales in front of the massed choirs at Cardiff. We had won there only eight times in 95 years. It was third time lucky for me as I had tasted Cardiff defeat in 1986 and 1988. Of the Scots on parade that afternoon only Derek White had known victory at the Arms Park. Even in the midst of Welsh troubles that was the nature of our triumph and we were well pleased. Now we allowed ourselves to think of the Grand Slam. We were three-quarters of the way there but the steepest hurdle was yet to come.

Until we had disposed of Wales nobody had dared utter the words Grand Slam. It just seemed too presumptuous, too much like taking things for granted. But, as soon as we got back from the Arms Park to the hotel, we started planning for the great showdown game. We were aware of the historical significance of the task ahead. For only the third time in history the championship was going to be decided on the final weekend; and for the first time ever France would not be involved. Very early on we took a conscious decision to play the whole thing in the lowest possible key. We knew that the players would come under intense media pressure and so it was agreed that all requests for interviews would have to be channelled through the SRU. It was decided, also, that only the side's senior pros – myself, Gavin, JJ and Fin – plus the coaches would be available for interview. In that way we ensured that the burden was lessened on the younger members of the team.

In that fortnight between Cardiff and the Murrayfield match the whole nation seemed to work itself up to fever pitch. All of the media coverage from south of the border concentrated almost exclusively on how many points England would win by. The fact that we were written off by many of the Sassenach pundits acted as a great spur to the team. We played up to it. We sang England's praises at every opportunity. We pondered publicly on how good a side they were and how impressively they had played all season. Secretly, though, we were thinking: 'We'll show them.' We were hard at work planning the strategies that would unravel England's game.

We knew that we had to match England in the set-pieces. In the time we had available we worked harder than ever on the scrummage. By match day we knew that we were technically proficient enough to more than hold our own in that quarter.

The other key area was the lineout. We knew from having played alongside them with the Lions that Dooley and Ackford posed a mighty threat. Ackford, in particular, had taken front-jumping on to a new level. The coaches devised fresh lineout drills which sought to mix the plays and the personnel to such an extent that England wouldn't know whether they were coming or going. I'll guarantee that the vast majority of the 54,000 people who cram into Murrayfield for every International match have scant idea as to just how technical the game has become and how the players nowadays have so much to remember. The lineout codes we used in the Grand Slam match are a perfect example.

Basically, the system was numerical. As we gathered for each lineout I would call out a series of four numbers. They would then be repeated by the hooker Kenny Milne to indicate that he had heard the call and for the benefit also of all the other forwards. Sometimes, amid the deafening roar at International grounds, the calls have to be repeated several times. Even then, there are times when the calls are misheard and the intended ploy falls to pieces.

On Grand Slam day the most important number for the guys to watch out for was that on the player's back. This was the key element of the four-number codes. 'Eight' would mean Kenny should throw to Derek White, 'seven' to Fin, 'six' to JJ, 'five' to Damian Cronin, 'four' to Chris Gray or, more unusually, 'three' to Paul and 'one' to me. Obviously, to hide our intentions from the England forwards these crucial numbers had to be disguised in some way. To achieve this end the field was split into four 'quarters' from try line to 22-metre line; 22-metre line to half-way; half-way to 22-metre line; 22-metre line to try line.

If the lineout was taking place within the 'first' try-line to 22-metre line segment then the 'key' number was the first one of the four called and Kenny knew to throw the ball to the player with that number on his back irrespective of where that player was standing in the lineout. For instance, if the call was 'four, eight, nine, one' then we would all know that the ball was to be thrown to Chris Gray. If the lineout was to take place within the second of our segments then the 'key' number would be the second one called; if it was in the third segment it would be the third number called and so on.

Those basic codes were just for starters. In the Grand Slam match we also called letter codes which indicated whether we were going to utilise a ball 'off the top', which meant that it would be disposed of swiftly to the scrum-half for immediate use by the backs, or whether we were going to catch the ball, bring it down and drive it on in a ruck.

Because we were convinced that the only way to counter the huge threat posed by the English at the lineout was to rush them out of their stride we also had a series of pre-ordained lineout plays which meant that there would be little or no time for the English pack to get their wits about them before Kenny had thrown the ball in and it was away.

The codes for these lineouts were centred around colours. If I called 'red' then that would be a seven-man lineout with, say, Derek White standing at number two with Chris Gray and Damian Cronin at the tail. If the call was 'white' this meant that I was looking for a five-man formation with the props out. 'Blue' would be a two-man line. If 'blue' was called then each of the forwards had a number associated with the two-man line and, for instance, the code 'Blue, one, three' would mean that Derek White and Damian Cronin were to be in the line and the ball was to go to Damian at the tail. If you consider that there are also variations in the type of ball thrown by the hooker – low and hard or in a more gentle arc and with the jumper taking it coming forward or going back – then you can see that the lineout is just a bit more complicated than it looks to the casual observer.

On the day, our never-ending stream of variations and constantly shifting targets had the Englishmen at sixes and sevens. I clearly remember that I took a ball at the front of the line as did Fin. By the end Wade and Paul just didn't know what was to going to happen next. We had achieved our aim of getting at least parity on the touchline and we had done so not only by outplaying the world-class England jumpers but, more specifically, by out-thinking them too.

We also intended to move the England pack around as much as we could. Craig and Gary at half-back would make them turn and chase. Some of the English forwards were getting on a bit while others weren't particularly mobile in the first place. We planned to make sure that they would know they had been in a game by the time 80 minutes was up. The key words were controlled intensity. Everything we did we would have to do with a ruthless ferocity designed to knock the English out of their stride. We were well aware that if they were allowed to establish control then they would be a real handful. We determined to get stuck in about them at the earliest opportunity.

By the time we gathered at the Braid Hills Hotel on the Wednesday before the game we all felt sharper than we had ever felt before. There was a feeling of intense expectation in the air. We knew that this was a now or never situation. We were determined that it would be now.

But even in the midst of preparing for the biggest game of our lives there was still time for fun. With Finlay Calder around how could it be otherwise! Fin was the architect and perpetrator of one of the most superb hoaxes that I have ever witnessed. And the victim of Fin's carefully laid plan was his old mate John Jeffrey.

On the Wednesday evening, a few of the forwards went for a pint in a pub just off The Meadows in the city-centre. Alex Brewster, Fin, JJ and myself took our drinks through to the quiet 'snug' at the rear of the bar. We were half way through our first pints when the door to the small room flew open in spectacular fashion and a young female burst in. She cornered Fin and, in straightforward terms, demanded that he make an honest woman of her. Fin is a happily married family man. This was a major problem. We all gaped in amazement, especially so JJ because what he didn't know and we did was that the 'spurned lover' was in fact Fin's hairdresser who had been primed to play the part. And she did, to perfection. She stormed out, followed by Fin and we sat looking at each other in 'stunned' silence. JJ, though, was genuinely stunned and he was the first to speak.

'Bloody hell. What on earth was all that about? Right, not a word to the others, OK. The last thing we want right now is a bloody scandal. I'll try and find out what's going on.'

At that, we finished our drinks and went back to the hotel. Fin, of course, had got there before us. He had primed Craig Chalmers to tell JJ that he had come in looking very upset and had gone straight to his room.

As we arrived back at the hotel JJ turned to us all and warned: 'Remember, not a word.' We all agreed that Fin's secret would be safe with us.

Craig was standing at the top of the hotel stairs. He zeroed in on JJ and said: 'What have you guys been doing to Fin? He came back here in a hell of a state. He looked really upset. He's just gone off to his room.'

'There's nothing at all wrong with Finlay,' said JJ. 'He's tired, that's all. He's going to have an early night.'

'He looked really upset if you ask me,' said Craig, by now really turning the screw.

'Look, there's nothing at all wrong with Finlay. He's tired. No need to mention anything to anybody,' replied JJ who was by now getting quite agitated.

We could barely keep our faces straight. The whole scam was working like a charm. JJ had bitten hook, line, sinker and then come back for a second helping.

He retired to his room that night deeply concerned that his pal was cheating on his wife and that a scandal was about to break. The next morning when we gathered for breakfast JJ was still solicitously reminding those of us who knew of Fin's 'secret'. 'Remember, not a word,' he said, and those of us who had been present at the scene in the pub nodded in earnest agreement.

When Fin came down for breakfast JJ asked him: 'OK?'

Finlay nodded sombrely and we finished eating so as to get on board the bus to take us to Murrayfield training. En route, it had become the practice for the cards and faxes from well-wishers to be read out to the company. Half a dozen genuine cards had been read out when Sean Lineen said that he had one marked 'Private and Confidential for the personal attention of Mr Finlay Calder'.

As Sean started to open the envelope JJ was almost beside himself and rose out of his seat to shout: 'No! Don't open it!'

We couldn't contain ourselves any longer and the entire bus erupted in hysterical laughter. JJ knew at once that he had been had.

'Bastards,' he swore, and shook his head. He had to admit, though, that it had been a spectacularly successful leg-pull. Everybody played their part to perfection. It had worked like a dream.

JJ imediately started planning his retaliatory strike. His chance came just a few weeks later when the Scottish team were invited down to London by the *Aspel* Show people to form part of the TV audience when our Patron, the Princess Royal, was to be the guest. Mindful of the fact that Michael Aspel also fronts the *This Is Your Life* TV show, JJ hit upon the idea that he would involve Michael in his revenge attack on Fin.

The plan was that as we gathered at the TV studio, ostensibly to see the Princess Royal, Michael would produce his famous red book and home in on Finlay.

'Finlay Calder. You thought you were here to record a TV show. Well, you're wrong . . .'

At this point in JJ's masterplan Finlay would step forward convinced that he was to become the latest *This Is Your Life* victim.

Michael Aspel would then add:' ... you are wrong indeed. And you're not going to be on *This Is Your Life* either. Because, Finlay Calder, all of this is by way of John Jeffrey's revenge.'

Unfortunately, Finlay couldn't make the trip and so JJ's great scheme never got off the drawing board. He never did get his own back. Better watch out, Fin!

The Friday training session at Boroughmuir RFC's Meggetland ground was just a half-hour affair, mainly for the benefit of the Press and TV cameras. All of the hard work had been done and we were ready. Now the waiting was to be the hardest part. There were still the final pre-match interviews to handle and then it was back to the hotel where the afternoon was spent trying to fill in the time and not allowing the mind to wander. In the evening some of the lads went to the cinema while others stayed behind to watch a stack of TV videos which Iwan Tukalo and Scott Hastings had organised.

Saturday dawned bright but windy. Geech's attention to detail is legendary and because it was felt that the weather conditions might have an adverse effect on the line and goal-kicking he took Gavin, Craig and Gary Armstrong down to Murrayfield in the morning just to acclimatise by kicking a few balls around. We picked up the first casualty of the day when a gust of wind caught one of Gavin's kicks and the ball struck Craig full in the face. He ended up with a bloody nose but, mercifully, no more serious damage. Back at the hotel we were running through lineout drills on the lawn and, generally, just getting the feel of the ball in the hand.

By this time on an International weekend you really do wish that you were a million miles away. The tension is incredible. I don't care how many Caps a player has won. If he tells me that he is not nervous on the morning of a match then I will tell him he's fibbing. By nervousness I'm not talking about a gentle nibbling away at the insides. It's a full-blooded gnawing at the pit of the stomach that renders some people physically sick. I found that the nerves and the tension got worse over the years. I often wished that I could have regained the nonchalance that I exhibited when winning my first Cap. However, after that début match I knew what to expect and the increased responsibility of senior-pro status and then that of the captaincy merely served to increase the state of nervous tension.

International day rolls on with an unstoppable certainty. You know that, inevitably, at 2.30 in the afternoon you are going to be out there performing in front of 54,000 people and the millions more watching on television. By then, though, you know that the nerves will have disappeared. Most International players, like me, relish playing in front of big crowds. It's our stage. That is the enjoyable part. It's a cliché, I know, but it's the hanging around beforehand that really gets to the players.

Before we left the hotel there was the usual team meeting addressed by Ian McGeechan. It was, quite simply, the most emotional team talk it has ever been my privilege to hear, and I've heard quite a number in my time. Ian isn't a tub-thumper. He speaks in a quiet, authoritative manner in that Yorkshire-Scot dialect of his. He reminded us all of why we were there, the work we had put in and what we had already achieved together. Then he spoke of how much a win would mean to the Scottish people. He said that the Scottish nation was dispersed all over the world. He had received letters from exiled Scots in every part of the globe and that to those people we were already special. No matter where these people were their thoughts would be on one small green patch of Scotland that afternoon. Ian said that because his father had been a regular serviceman he had spent almost all of his life outside Scotland. He had been told by his parents that irrespective of the fact that he didn't stay in Scotland he was never to forget that he was Scottish and to be proud of it. He knew, therefore, how these exiled Scots would be feeling. Our achievements, he said, had drawn together the Scottish nation and he wanted us to remember that and to carry those thoughts on to the field with us that afternoon.

Ian's address was heard in rapt silence. By the time he was finished there was barely a dry eye in the room. He had tugged the heartstrings with a vengeance but what he had said was true and we knew that it was true. We were playing not just for ourselves or for the shirts but for Scots everywhere. It was a huge responsibility but we considered that we were ready for it. Everything had been taken care of. There was nothing more the coaches could do. Now it was down to us.

On the way to the ground in the team bus we sang *Flower of Scotland*. We had almost always done so. The Corries' evocative call-to-arms, written by Roy Williamson, about proud Edward's army being sent homeward tae think again had virtually become our signature tune. But that day the anthem came of age. It played a formidable part in the emotional build-up to the game and, crucially and indisputably, it had an unnerving effect on the Englishmen.

The atmosphere in the dressing-room was one of grim determination. Geech had made all of the points he wanted to make before leaving the hotel and there wasn't any way that I could have topped his emotional charge to the team. I merely stressed again that we weren't there just to make up the numbers and that we could, and would, win. This was a unique day. We would never experience its like again. We had to make the most of it and make sure as we looked back that there was nothing more we could have done. Only our very best would be good enough. I was keen, though, still to retain a sense of perspective. Despite the high-voltage emotion and the saturation media coverage which the game had attracted it was still just another game of rugby.

'I spoke to Jane on the phone this morning,' I told the guys, 'and she said that whatever happens, win, lose or draw, she'll still love me. In the meantime, though, let's win for all of those Scots all over the world and let's do it for ourselves and our families. No matter what happens out there in the next 80 minutes, life will still go on but this afternoon we have a one-in-a-million chance to make history. Let's get out and grab it with both hands. Enjoy it, but let's go out and win.'

Then it was time for the talking to stop and the action to begin. We had already been out on to the Murrayfield turf for the team photographs and the presentations. Even at that stage, with the stands and the terracings still filling up, there was a unique buzz about the place. You could sense the tension in the air.

Among the 54,000-strong crowd was a very special contingent from Glenbuchat. Away back in January as we had seen in the New Year at the family home in Aberdeenshire, around 30 of our neighbours had decided that they rather fancied the prospect of a day out in Edinburgh to see the rugby. Of course, at the turn of the year we had no way of knowing that Scotland v England on 17 March would take on the significance that it did, and early in January I was able to buy 30 terracing tickets from the SRU. The Glenbuchat outing was arranged by Di and Alan Thomson, farmers on the estate, and a bus was duly hired for the occasion.

Some of those on the trip had never been to a rugby match before and they had the day out of a lifetime. Before the game I mentioned the presence of the Glenbuchat brigade to Bill McLaren and he gave them a plug during his Murrayfield scene-setter.

They thoroughly enjoyed their day out at Murrayfield but the celebrations didn't begin in earnest until they were back on the road to Glenbuchat. The bus broke down at Glenshee and one of the passengers, the local motor mechanic, repaired the damage with carpet tape. The bus limped on to the Inver Hotel, between Braemar and Balmoral, where my mum had told them that win, lose or draw there would be a drink waiting. I'm told that mum's round was just the first of many and that the celebrations went on in splendid fashion right into the wee sma' hours and beyond. The Glenbuchat celebrations were just a very small part of the general rejoicing which engulfed Scotland as news of the victory swept around the country. But first we had to win!

Much has been said and written about our slow walk from the dressing-room to the pitch. I had discussed it with some of the senior players during the week before the match. JJ was in favour but Fin reminded me what had happened the last time it had been tried. I didn't need reminding. The previous summer we had marched out for the British Lions' opening Test with Australia and had promptly lost.

I mulled it over further but decided to go ahead anyway. The walk was intended to be a public statement about why we were there. We wanted the 50,000 Scottish supporters in the 54,000 crowd to know that we thought we could win. I wanted to show that we were in control, disciplined, organised and throwing down the gauntlet to England for what would be the biggest challenge of our lives.

England ran out first to be greeted with the polite yet subdued cheer and half-hearted booing that is afforded all visiting teams at Murrayfield. We turned right from our dressing-room and then left and then right again to get into the tunnel leading to the pitch. It's a walk of, maybe, 40 yards. Normally when you emerge from an International match dressing-room you are so pleased to be able to vent the pent-up energy and emotion that you bound out like a greyhound from the slips. It was with the greatest difficulty that we maintained the walk down the corridor and along the tunnel. Behind me I could hear JJ shouting a reminder: 'Walk. Walk!' Then we came out into the daylight and the crowd caught its first glimpse of us. The usual ear-rending roar went up. But then, as they realised that something out of the ordinary was happening, the cheer ringing around the ground died fractionally and momentarily. Then, seemingly in a split second, it registered with the crowd that we were walking in single file and there was simultaneous recognition of why we were doing it. The cheers gathered in intensity until they reached a blood-curdling level which sent a shiver down the spine.

We could see England standing around watching all of this but for Will and his boys the emotional torture was only just beginning. We lined up in front of the huge West Stand for the anthems. First a few bars of *God Save the Queen*. Then, after a momentary pause, the pipes and drums of the Queen Victoria School, Dunblane, struck up the first chords of *Flower of Scotland*.

The effect was electrifying. For the first time, and at the team's request, we were to sing two verses instead of the normal one and, also for the first time, the words were printed in the programme. Fifty thousand Scottish voices joined the refrain in a wall of emotionally charged sound the likes of which I have never heard before or since. It made the hairs on the back of the neck stand on end. I managed to get the first verse out but I was so choked with emotion that I was unable to get through the second. I looked up into the stand. Ronnie Browne of The Corries was there. His partner Roy Williamson couldn't make it. He was gravely ill with cancer and was undergoing a course of radiotherapy. Sadly, Roy died a short while later. But before he did so he wrote to say that to hear his song being sung in such a manner and in such circumstances had been one of the proudest moments of his life.

My wife Jane was there with our families. A couple of hours beforehand she and the other Scottish wives and girlfriends had been in the foyer of the Carlton Highland Hotel in Edinburgh with their English counterparts. Jenny Ovens, Scott Hastings's then girlfriend, now wife, had said in a spirit of cameraderie to the English girls: 'Good luck. And may the best team win.'

'We will,' had come the reply from the English wives' party. They had obviously digested the pre-match hype in the same way as had done, I suspect, their 'better halves'.

The intensity of the emotional welcome that we received when first we came out of the tunnel was maintained for the full 80 minutes. The crowd obviously wanted to be involved and they were. The cheers that went up whenever Scotland were awarded a scrummage put-in was of a volume normally reserved for a try. The wall of sound rippled up and down the stands as play swung this way and that. I have never experienced anything like it. We played with a hunger and intensity that was unique. No Scottish team that I have been involved with or have watched has played with such ruthless commitment. I feel that we played better rugby on the Tour to New Zealand which followed in the summer but for sheer guts and determination the performance in the Grand Slam match will be hard to equal let alone beat.

We never let up, relaxed or allowed our concentration to be broken. It is quite a remarkable feat to sustain that level of concentration for 80 minutes but that afternoon we did just that. We just couldn't allow England any leeway at all. For the first ten minutes we drove at them as if there was no tomorrow. They rarely touched the ball. Craig Chalmers put us ahead with a penalty after Fin had charged on at real pace. Micky Skinner got in a big hit but Finlay stayed upright and we all thundered in behind him. England conceded a penalty and Craig popped the ball between the posts. We went six points up after Craig's second penalty goal when Jeff Probyn was penalised for stamping on me after a scrum had gone down. But then England showed what we knew they were capable of when, given just a little bit of space, Jerry Guscott ghosted in for a try after a drive by Mike Teague. Paul Ackford punched Chris Gray and the offence was signalled from the touchline by the Welshman Derek Bevan. Craig was well on target with the penalty kick and we reached half-time with a 9-4 lead.

England had been given a number of penalty chances but, with Brian Moore and Will Carling apparently in some disarray as to who was calling the shots, they opted to run or scrummage them rather than taking shots at goal. I go into detail on the series of scrummages on the Scottish line which caused the apparent dissent within English ranks in the 'Props, Propping and Improprieties' chapter and will just say here that I think the no-kick decision by Will and/or Brian was wrong. Had I been in their position I would have kicked for goal. The wind wasn't too bad and we now know that Simon Hodgkinson was more than willing to have a shot.

During that series of scrummages, around the half-hour mark, we lost Derek White with a knee injury. He was replaced by Derek Turnbull and JJ went to number eight with Derek taking over John's flank.

At half-time I was reasonably happy. We had achieved most of what we had set out to do. We had matched England in the scrummages, our lineout plays were working a treat, Gary Armstrong was giving my old Exeter University and Bath team-mate Richard Hill a rough old time at the base of the scrum, the defence was holding up and the running patterns we had worked on in practice were promising results.

Then, at the first scrum after the interval, came one of the turning points of the whole match. England won their put-in but instead of delivering the ball to Rob Andrew, who had been kicking really well,

Mike Teague attempted a pick up but knocked-on in the process. That meant the put-in went to us. We called a set move – it was codenamed Fiji – and it worked to perfection. Gary took the ball out wide, removing two defenders in the process. Gavin came up into the line and thundered up field. He got in his kick before being bundled into touch. Even in the difficult wind it was inch-perfect. Tony Stanger and Fin were in hot pursuit. Tony, at full-stretch, took the ball with his finger-tips. There's no doubt that if Tony had missed the ball then Fin, only a yard behind, would have snapped it up and we would still have scored. That, at least, is what Fin claims! The entire move from the scrummage put-in until Tony's touchdown had been planned. There was nothing *ad hoc* about it. It was a perfectly executed set-piece play.

England now had a bit of a mountain to climb. We had showed them that we, too, had a few tricks up our sleeves and if they gave us an inch of space then we wouldn't be slow in exploiting it. Neverthe-less, there was still a long way to go. England ran the ball back at us but then the offensive-defence that we had worked on came into its own. Time and again we drove the English backwards in the tackle. We got men to the breakdown point in numbers. You could have thrown a blue blanket over the Scottish defenders so together were we.

As the game wore on, Rob Andrew's kicking just got better and better. He really punished us with some raking kicks deep into our territory. But still our defence held out. Two incidents in particular still stand out. Scott Hastings pulled off a priceless, try-saving tackle on Rory Underwood. Then Will Carling was on the point of making a breakthrough when he was caught by what must have seemed to him like the entire Scottish team and he was driven backwards by a full 20 yards.

Simon Hodgkinson was successful from only one of three penalty kicks and Jerry Guscott had to go off with a hip injury. However, although we could never relax I always felt that our defence was going to hold. In the final ten minutes we were under siege but waves of white-shirted attacks foundered on rock-solid Scottish defence.

When David Bishop blew his whistle for the final time my immediate reaction was one of immense relief and of great pride. Chris Gray, Fin and myself just embraced each other. We were elated yet drained. Within seconds the pitch was engulfed by ecstatic supporters. The crowd were as relieved as we were. I tried to make my way back from the north-west corner of the pitch where we had been pinned down but my way to the tunnel was blocked by back-slapping sup-porters. Then I was hoisted on to somebody's shoulders and had a yellow and tartan Scottish "bunnet" stuck on top of my head. The whole pitch was by now just a sea of elated faces. Eventually we managed to find our way back to the tunnel. Fin was still outside consoling Brian Moore who was close to tears. Brian is a real competitor and defeat was hard for him to take. We knew most of the Englishmen. We had toured with them in Australia. In addition, I knew Richard Hill, Simon Halliday and Jerry Guscott from way back. They were still Damian's colleagues at Bath. Chris Gray, Simon Hodgkinson and Brian Moore were team-mates at Nottingham. We had a lot of respect for each other.

England accepted their defeat with impressive graciousness. It must have been very difficult for them considering all of the hype that had gone on beforehand. The way that they conducted themselves afterwards was something that earned them the respect of all the Scots.

In the dressing-room there was that deep-seated satisfaction from knowing that a job had been well done. The fatigue was forgotten as we drank in the atmosphere and considered the magnitude of our achievement. Nevertheless, we were all too tired to get involved in riotous scenes of celebration. The coaches arrived down from their seats in the stand and we broke into a spontaneous rendition of *Happy Birthday* for Jim Telfer who was celebrating his 50th birthday. Eight years before, to the very day, Jim had stood in the exact same spot celebrating the 1984 Grand Slam win over the French when he had been the side's principal coach. It was a great afternoon for Jim and Geech and Derrick Grant and Doug Morgan and everybody connected with the squad.

Then we had a surprise visitor. Peter Phillips came down from his seat in the Committee Box alongside the Princess Royal and sister Zara to offer us his personal congratulations. Peter was playing loose-head prop in his school side and so I thought it would be a nice gesture to give him my match jersey. I stripped if off and handed it over. He was as happy as a lark.

Will Carling and Roger Uttley popped their heads around the door to offer their congratulations and the place was mobbed by well-wishers, committeemen, pressmen, cameramen. It seemed that everybody wanted to get in on the act. But this was just a foretaste of what was to come. For the next month or so Scotland was swept by Grand Slam fever. We were fêted wherever we went. We were never off the TV or out of the newspapers. We made a record of *Flower of Scotland* with Ronnie Browne and the receptions just went on and on.

There was a humorous postscript and, of course, it involved one of the Hastings boys. We had a posh and private celebratory dinner with our Patron HRH The Princess Royal. All of the wives and girlfriends were there. It was a very informal and satisfying evening, towards the end of which Scott grabbed the microphone on the top table. Stone-cold sober he want on to say: 'There remains only one question still to be answered. Jenny Ovens, will you marry me?'

To say we were shocked would be an understatement. We weren't as shocked as Jenny, though. HRH took it all in her stride and Jenny recovered her composure to say, 'Yes.' A happy ending to a superbly happy season in the history of Scottish rugby.

CHAPTER 8

PROPS, PROPPING, AND IMPROPRIETIES

Tricks of the Front Row Trade

THE ALARM BELLS began sounding at the dance after the game. Luckily I hadn't been aware of it at the time but I subsequently learned that Jeff Probyn's wife had been, not to put too fine a point on it, rather upset at what had taken place between Jeff and myself at Twickenham earlier in the day.

It was February 1991, and Scotland had been beaten 21-12 as England trudged on in determined but stolid style to the Grand Slam which they maintained we had stolen from under their noses the previous season. In the course of the match I had become heartily peeved at Probyn's continuing use of illegal tactics in the scrum. It was nothing new. Jeff is known the world over for it. His singular scrummaging style has even given rise to a new fashion note for loose-head props. The Kiwi Steve McDowell first cut the left sleeve from his jersey for the opening game of the 1991 World Cup and I followed suit for our World Cup semi-final game against England and again for the 1992 Calcutta Cup match. Six months later that unique World Cup jersey raised £1,100 when it was auctioned in aid of the 1992 British Olympic Appeal.

Jeff is a strong, awkward customer and a useful enough tight-head prop but, in the sense that he habitually utilises illegal means with which to put pressure on his opposite number, he is effectively cheating. Probyn likes to get off the loose-head's right shoulder and come down into the middle of the scrummage so that he can pressurise the opposition hooker. He binds on the loose-head's left elbow and levers down on it. The laws state that props must bind on their opposite number by grasping the jersey of the upper shoulder or back. In my case this means that his right hand should rest on my left shoulder or back. Jeff, though, persists in employing the tactic of taking a fistful of jersey just at the left elbow and forcing down on it. This has the dual effect of de-stabilising his opposite number and of blocking the opposition hooker's view down the tunnel so that his sight of the ball being delivered by the scrum-half is restricted. It's a dreadful indictment on International referees that Probyn isn't pulled up short for it. It is blatantly illegal and everybody knows that he does it.

But if he can get away with it then good luck to him. I'm not going to whinge. It's a tough old trade in the front row at international level and we all use whatever means are available to us with which to put one over on the opposition. However, if what is being done is illegal and the referee seems unable or unwilling to administer the law then the player who is on the receiving end of the illegal treatment just has to administer his own brand of justice even if it means taking the law into his own hands. That's what I did. Literally!

When Jeff grabs hold of the loose-head prop's left elbow, he simultaneously bores in on the opposition hooker. He strives to lock out with his right leg now in a position from which it can be quite easily reached by the opposition loose-head. During that 1991 game at Twickenham he tried it on just once too often for my liking and I simply reached down and pulled his right leg out from under him. It wasn't something that was done on the spur of the moment. It was a ruse which had been imparted to me by a tough old Newbridge prop during my time with Bath.

As a young up and coming loose-head prop I was just learning my craft and becoming initiated into the freemasonry of front row play. I had found it pretty hard going against this gnarled Newbridge veteran. Try as I might I just couldn't get any change out of him. He would just lock-out with his right elbow on his right thigh and that was it. I couldn't budge him. It was a most frustrating experience. In the bar afterwards we were chatting about the mysteries and intricacies of front row play and I was telling him how difficult an opponent I had found him. He put his pint of beer down on the bar, moved a shade closer and in a deeply conspiratorial tone declared: 'You know how to play the likes of me? Just whip the right pin out from underneath me. I can't scrummage on one leg, can I?'

I must say I was rather taken aback by this gratuitous but nevertheless most welcome piece of advice. He had just shown me his Achilles' heel, so to speak, for the next time we would meet. But he wasn't daft. He was retiring. We never met again. However, in the week leading up to that 1991 Calcutta Cup game, as I pondered how I would play Jeff this time around, the leg-lifting tactic imparted by the sage of Newbridge came back to me. I determined that on the very first occasion that Jeff started his nonsense then in pretty smart order he would find himself minus a peg on terra firma.

Jeff never said a word to me during the game. Unlike his front-row colleague Brian Moore, whom I had played alongside during the 1989 Lions' tour to Australia, he is not one of the game's great 'sledgers', as they term it in cricket. However, within 24 hours the manure had well and truly hit the air-conditioning. The newspapers were full of stories whose general theme was 'He could have killed me – Probyn'. Jeff's apparent outburst wasn't particularly well received in rugby quarters where some felt that it smacked of squealing. Later that year, at the Hong Kong Sevens, he told me what had happened. He had been enjoying a quiet drink in the Twickenham Rose Room after the game. One or two journalists are allowed entry to the Rose Room so that they can gather quotes from the players as to how they felt the match had gone. Jeff had been asked what had been going on between himself and David Sole during the scrummages. He was quoted as saying that I had grabbed at his leg and that if the practice wasn't halted then somebody would suffer a broken neck. He said it was OK for seasoned internationals but if the tactic was copied by schoolboys then it could be dangerous.

On the Sunday after the game I received phone calls at home from journalists wanting my side of the story. I told them that Jeff habitually scrummaged in an illegal way and that if referees weren't prepared to penalise him then I would sort it out myself. The story ran for about a week. At the time I was writing a column for the Scottish *Daily Express* and under the heading 'You're out of order Jeff' I reiterated that Probyn was a habitual offender on the illegal binding front and I suggested that world-class tight-heads like Scotland's Iain Milne and Jean-Pierre Garuet of France possessed the strength and the technical ability to achieve the results they desired without resorting to Probyn's outlawed tactics.

I never considered that there was any bad blood between Jeff and myself but the row rumbled on in the background for a year and came to light again during the World Cup when the newspapers picked up on the feud that they now supposed existed between us. There were stories about how I never swopped jerseys with Probyn despite having played against him four times at International level before the World Cup competition. I had been quoted in the Press as saying that the new style England World Cup jerseys with their blue and red stripes would look good in a disco. I don't think that went down particularly well in the England camp.

Jeff and I have had some Herculean struggles in the matches that we have played against each other. He would be pleased with his performance against us in the World Cup semi-final but not so happy, despite England's win, with his showing in the 1992 Calcutta Cup game at Murrayfield.

On that occasion, with Fin Calder and John Jeffrey retired and Chris Gray unavailable because of injury, we introduced three new Caps in Ian Smith, Dave McIvor and Neil Edwards. England were without the retired Paul Ackford, Martin Bayfield came in at lock, and Tim Rodber was at number eight in place of Dean Richards. We scrummaged well that day and the England pack even conceded a pushover try. Something which, for sure, hadn't been included in their script.

Brian Moore was down injured in the corner to the left of the main West Stand just before the two packs came together. I had decided that we would go for the pushover try. I had felt that we had the measure of the England eight and that it was definitely on. It was a set move which we called McIntyre or Rodriguez after the Australian 1984 Grand Slam props. As soon as the call had been given all the guys knew what we were going to do. The key to the move was timing. Andy Nicol, the scrum-half who had taken over from the injured Gary Armstrong, was aware that we wouldn't be wasting any time and that the ball would have to be delivered simultaneously with the initial 'hit' as the two packs came together. The sequence, just as quickly as you could say it, would be Hit, Ball, Drive. It worked a treat. We drove them back over the line for the touchdown. That's a grand feeling for a front row forward.

I have lingered on the relationship between Jeff Probyn and myself because I hope that it gives at least an indication of the physical and psychological pressures which are brought to bear in the battle of wills which take place in the front row of the scrummage. From the terracings, and even from the close-up TV shots, it really isn't possible to gain any significant insight into what is going on. It's difficult for the outsider to capture the essence of what is a game within a game.

A rugby match represents 15 individual battles. In some positions the confrontational aspect is less evident than in others. But in each and every case, from full back to the front row, the team which comes out on top in most of these individual duels will be the team which wins the laurels at the end of the day.

Nowhere is this very basic one-on-one clash more graphically evident than in the front row of the scrummage and, specifically, in the

80-minute battle of brain and brawn between the opposing prop forwards. The front row is where ultimate success begins or ends. Very few
teams are able to paper over the cracks if the front five and, by implica-
tion, the props and hooker are not on song. Prop forwards may be the
unsung heroes of the game and undoubtedly they don't have the dash,
flair and flamboyance of a David Campese, an Andy Irvine or a Gavin
Hastings but while these guys might win a game for you, a below par
performance by your props will just as soon nullify the points that those
behind the scrum have put on the board.

I'm told that of the two propping positions – loose-head and tight-
head – loose-head is the more difficult to play. But as I've never played
tight-head I am really in no position to judge. Some particularly gifted
individuals, like the England and British Lions' prop Fran Cotton, are
equally at home on either side of the scrummage but they are the exception rather than the rule.

At loose-head, on the left of the scrummage and nearer the ball on
your side's put-in, all of the pushing is done on the right shoulder. You
ought to be bound tightly on your hooker and maintaining a position
which keeps him comfortable and which enables him to strike easily
with his right foot when the ball comes into the tunnel. On your put-in
the most important fellow in the pack is your hooker and his needs are
paramount.

I made a bit of a name for myself as a dynamic player in the loose
but really this was a bonus. Roger Spurrell, my captain at Bath as I was
breaking into the first XV along with Gareth Chilcott and Richard Lee,
drummed into me that the basic function of a prop forward was to
scrummage and to offer support at the lineout. Everything else was to
be viewed as an added extra.

The tight-head prop is generally, but not always, bigger and
heavier and performs more of a destructive role than the loose-head.
Because of the positioning in the front row, with the tight-head binding
on the outside shoulder or arm, it is much easier for him to be a disruptive force than it is for the loose-head. Sometimes, on your own ball, a
tight-head will just lock out and act as the bulwark of your scrummage
in an attempt to hold it steady. On the opposition ball he will attempt
to disrupt the opposing front row by unsettling his opposite number or
boring in on the hooker in an attempt to prise him apart from his
loose-head.

As I hope I have explained, the art of propping is as much a contest
of wills as it is of brute stregnth. You learn more about this art with
every game that you play. Even if you have played a particular opponent half a dozen times you find out something new about him on each

occasion. I tend to think a very great deal about whom I will be matched against on the coming Saturday. I will recall the last time we met and the various devices he employed in an attempt to get the better of me. I will then plan a strategy designed to counteract the measures he employed last time around and devise schemes of my own in an effort to get him into positions where his effectiveness is curbed. The day that you think you know it all is the day you will come unstuck.

As a loose-head prop your prime objective is to endeavour to get inside your man and to achieve pressure on his chest with your right shoulder and head. As a schoolboy, even at International level, I always found it relatively easy to achieve this optimum position. You work inside your man, get underneath on to his chest, straighten your back, thrust upwards with your legs and hey presto, your man would be left dangling clear off the ground. As I progressed up the propping ladder, though, and tested myself against more accomplished scrummagers it became more and more difficult to achieve this optimum position and this is where skill, rather than brute strength, starts to come in.

In order to exploit fully any ascendancy which a prop has achieved over his opposite number he has to have powerful support from behind. Good scrummagers who genuinely push their weight are worth that weight in gold. This includes not only the locks but the wing-forwards as well. During the 1992 Calcutta Cup match, when even our critics in the Press conceded that we had scrummaged particularly well against the England pack, we were scrummaging genuinely as an eight. We had two flankers winning their first Caps and they were told that their first priority at the scrummage was to push. We didn't want to complicate their International débuts with the myriad of back-row moves that we used when Finlay and JJ were still playing. When you have world-class flankers such as those two in the pack then it becomes very much a case of striking a balance that everyone can live with. Often, and they would be the first to admit it, Fin and JJ would be embroiled in an impending back-row move and the shove wouldn't be there for the initial hit. When you have five or six pushing against eight then it tends to put you on the back foot at the outset and it is very difficult to recover once you have started to go backwards.

This isn't a criticism of Finlay and John but is mentioned simply as another indication of the various factors which have to be taken into account in what, to the uninitiated, seems to be a simple matter of 16 guys getting down in a scrummage and pushing against each other.

So far as the actual physical experience of playing in the front row of an international scrummage is concerned it is supremely difficult to translate into words. Only those who have actually been there will have any real idea of just how physically demanding it is.

However, some indication of the pressures being exerted on the human frame can be gauged from the work that goes on during scrummage practice. Behind the main stand at Murrayfield we have a steel sleigh that we use for this purpose. On the sledge are 40 concrete blocks and each block weighs one hundredweight. That's two tons in total. Add on two or three spare bodies just to make it more difficult still and the Scottish pack is heaving around over two tons dead-weight. Virtually all of the massive pressure being exerted by the pack is concentrated on the two prop forwards who transmit the shove through the buttocks, along the spine and on to the shoulders. On a more high-tech piece of equipment which is kept under the Murrayfield stand we can simulate an opposed scrummage by squaring up to a hydraulic scrummaging machine. The machine 'pushes' back at you. We have held 4,000lbs of pressure on that piece of equipment. When you get up from a prolonged scrummaging bout you feel as if your entire body has been compressed like an accordion. In a live scrummage situation you have the added ingredients of a twisting and disruptive opposite number who might want to stick his fingers in your eyes, head-butt you as you wait to go down or stick his knee in your face as you break up from an improperly set scrummage. Interesting. Why do we do it? Well, strange as it may seem, we do it because we enjoy it.

In a game situation, at the first scrummage you will be determined to achieve an immediate psychological advantage over your opponent. As we wait to form the scrum I will be reminding myself about feet positioning and trying to achieve a good wide and stable stance. I will want to be in the optimum position to execute a good 'hit', the initial, jarring shock as the two packs crash together. Once the heads are down I will want to keep as stable as possible. Many props prefer to lock out with their legs straight but I tend to get a little bit of bend at the knees so that I can burst upwards into the chest of the opposing tight-head.

No matter what the pressures being exerted on you, the key to good scrummage work is to keep the back straight at all times. It is along the spine that the shove is transferred to the opposition and if the back is not kept ram-rod straight then the shove becomes misdirected and your scrummage will be in trouble.

On your own put-in you will be looking for a good solid 'hit' and will be seeking to get stable as quickly as you can and with a wide base with the feet so that the hooker can strike the ball through your legs. If you are unsettled and still moving around then you will be making it clear to your scrum-half that you don't want the ball into the tunnel until everyone is as comfortable as possible. On your own ball you are at an immediate disadvantage because with your hooker intent on securing possession, and not pushing, you start the scrummage with a numerical disadvantage. Very rarely, nowadays, does the hooker strike on the opposition put-in. He might do so occasionally, very much as a surprise package and as part of the battle of wits that goes on through-out the game, but generally speaking the pack without the ball will opt for the eight-man shove. With seven pushing against eight this means that you have to be rock solid if you are to protect and win your own ball, something which is more or less taken for granted at the higher level these days.

From my point of view I will be determined to stay as close to my hooker as possible. My opposite number will either be technically correct and pushing back at me – the really strong men like Iain Milne and Jean-Pierre Garuet come into this category – or the push will be of a twisting nature and directed at the link between me and the hooker. Essentially both varieties of shove have the same aim, which is to prise apart the hooker and his loose-head. It is just the execution of the shove which is different.

I must have taken part in hundreds, if not thousands, of scrum-mages over the years. Some stick in the memory. Pushover tries come into this category. But good defensive scrummages also bring with them a great deal of satisfaction.

During the Grand Slam game against England at Murrayfield in 1990 we were involved in a series of scrummages on our own line in the corner to the right of the West Stand. Derek White had been injured as Micky Skinner and Fin Calder had crashed into him after a tackle at the corner flag. He eventually had to leave the field with knee ligament damage and was replaced by Derek Turnbull.

There were five scrummages in quick succession, the first with Derek White hobbling with his knee injury and us with only seven men in the scrum. I was packing as low as I possibly could. The theory is that if I can get low enough then, OK, maybe I can't push but Jeff Probyn can't push me either. After the game I was accused of deliberately collapsing the scrum, and the English forwards were doing a fair bit of 'mouthing' to this effect, but that wasn't the case at all. The last thing I wanted was to concede a penalty try at such a crucial juncture of the game. During these scrummages the first cracks appeared in the English leadership set-up. Despite my contention that I wasn't intentionally taking the scrums down, the referee David Bishop thought differently and we were penalised time and again. Instead of taking the kick at goal, as I would have done, Brian Moore, the English pack-leader, obviously felt that England would eventually get the pushover try and they opted to scrummage again and again rather than take a pot at goal.

There were too many English 'captains' and they were arguing amongst themselves as to what they would do. I was delighted to hear it. That's always a good sign when the opposition starts yapping amongst themselves. Five scrummages later it finally dawned on Brian that they weren't going anywhere and, still just yards from our try line, they twice went for tap penalties with the English loose-head Paul Rendall taking the ball on rather gingerly only to be hit by a wall of Scottish defenders. At the sixth scrum, and remember all this had taken place within a pretty hectic and punishing five-minute spell, I finally got the nudge on Jeff, we drove the England eight backwards and Craig Chalmers got a boot to a ricocheting ball to clear the danger. England had missed a golden scoring opportunity but, more importantly, we had notched up a significant psychological victory.

On that occasion – I swear! – it was never part of my game-plan to take down the scrummage although, to be absolutely honest, I have been known to cause the odd scrummage to fall in. It's not a tactic that I employ regardlessly because there is no doubt that there are inherent dangers in a scrummage crashing to the deck. There are times, though, when you will try to con the referee into awarding your side a penalty by taking down a scrummage. In such circumstances I will get to my feet with a cherubic expression on my face such as to convey to the referee 'Me? Collapse a scrummage? Would I do such a thing?'

I have the greatest sympathy for referees. Honestly I do. Really most of them haven't a clue about what is going on in the front row and, in many cases when the scrum has gone down, they are simply guessing when they penalise one side or the other. In many instances, too, collapsed scrummages are simply a case of slippery conditions allied to missed footing and neither side has responsible for deliberately taking the thing down.

On the odd occasion that I do take a scrummage down then it will have been done in an attempt to 'steal' a penalty or simply to upset the opposing tight-head. There is, though, a specific ploy which we have used to good effect over the years with Scotland. Again, it is part of the 'all's fair in love, war and scrummaging' mentality which permeates the game at International level. It goes something like this. On the opposition put-in I will take the scrummage down in an attempt to entice the referee around to my side of the scrum. Normally the ref will stand at the side furthest away from me, behind the scrum-halves as the ball is being put into the scrummage tunnel.

Hopefully, the referee will come around to my side of the scrum in order to sort out the trouble which he by now thinks is taking place between me and my opposite number. Once the referee has been enticed around to my side of the scrummage then he can no longer see directly what is going on as the scrum-half feeds the ball into the scrum. At this point, as the opposition scrum-half bends down to put the ball into the tunnel, our man in the number nine jersey will kick or fist the ball into the scrum and we'll attempt to strike it 'against the head'. Cynical? It may well be. But at International level these days, for better or for worse, you have to be up with the lark (and up to all sorts of larks!) if you are to keep your head above water.

But, contrary to what many observers might think, there isn't all that much sheer physical skulduggery going on in the darker recesses of the scrum. Sure, there are the occasional flare-ups with punches being thrown right, left and centre but these incidents have more to do with ritual and momentary lapses of temper than premeditated violence. You do still get the odd haymaker being delivered from the second row. You can almost guarantee this against the French and one of the downright dirtiest games I've ever played in was the 'B' International against France at Albi in 1984. We won 13-10 but it was a battle from the first whistle to the last. Generally speaking, though, everyone is so intent on getting on with his job that there isn't all that much time left for gratuitous violence. That is not to say, however, that it doesn't happen.

There are some particularly cannibalistic citizens inhabiting the front row of the scrummage and ear-biting is still part of the repertoire of some props and hookers of my acquaintance. Because I always wore a tape headband I'm happy to report that my ears always ended a match relatively bite-free and intact. But I have to confess that on at least one occasion I have, myself, resorted to munching on the opposition. And once again the individual involved was that man Jeff Probyn. It was during a Calcutta Cup game at Twickenham and Jeff was attempting to inflict upon me a Bath Handshake. In other words his fingers had strayed with malicious intent towards my eyes. Unluckily for him one finger just happened to slip into my mouth and I bit it. Hard.

Verbal intimidation and good old-fashioned lip is much more prevalent than outright thuggery. In this regard Brian Moore is in a class of his own. I have known Brian for years. We first met when I played for Exeter University and he was gaining his law degree at Nottingham. Much later we both played in all three Tests during the Lions' tour to Australia in 1989. He is a very fine combative hooker and competitive to a fault. He sounds off constantly throughout the game. Some of his comments, heavily spiced with Anglo-Saxon expletives, are of a very personal nature. He seemed to have a 'thing' about our tight-head prop Paul Burnell and was forever telling him to 'Fook off back to London Scottish'. Or, whenever we had put in a really big shove, Brian's head would appear above the mass of bodies and he would bellow, 'Is that the best you can fookin' do?' I have the highest regard for Brian as a player but I sometimes think he is his own worst enemy when it comes to his publicly perceived image. His televised comment regarding England during the 1991 World Cup that 'Nobody likes us but we don't care' was straight out of the Milwall FC supporters' phrase book and I don't think he did anybody, least of all himself, any favours by adopting such an attitude.

The Kiwis are also great talkers. The All Black hooker Sean Fitzpatrick keeps up a fairly constant flow of 'advice' and all the rest. He's not so vindictive as Brian, though. Brian's intention is to rattle people, to get them upset. Once you know what he's about then you just get on with the game and it becomes just so much water off a duck's back.

Of course, I wouldn't want to convey the impression that we're all plaster saints and I have been known to offer the odd word of 'advice' myself. But the greatest talker in the Scotland side in my experience was Finlay Calder. He was in the Louisville Lip class and could have taught old Cassius Clay himself a thing or two about unsettling the enemy. He was never vindictive but at lineouts in particular Fin would keep up a constant commentary on the merits and de-merits of the opposition jumpers. During the 1989 Calcutta match when Finlay was paired against Bath's Andy Robinson at the tail of the lineout he had one of those days when almost everything goes right. Fine player though Andy is, he was on the short side for International duty and Fin ran rings around him in that crucial area at the tail of the lineout. At every lineout you could hear Finlay asking Andy, 'Where's this one going to? To the front? Middle? D'you think it'll come to us?' Fin kept this up throughout the entire match and by the end poor Andy didn't know whether he was coming or going.

In my six years with Scotland, the British Lions, the Barbarians and the French Barbarians I have locked horns with all of the world's leading tight-head props. Yet, as I've already suggested, I have to look no further than my own backyard for at least one of the two that I admire the most. Iain Gordon Milne, known to the rugby fraternity the world over simply as The Bear, is such a strong man and so technically sound that he has never, ever had to resort to underhand or illegal methods with which to get the better of his man. Similarly, because he is so proficient, he has come in for more than his fair share of stick from opposition forwards who have so run out of ideas as how to cope with him that in sheer desperation they have opted for the tactic of last resort and have given him a good skelp.

Iain was no shrinking violet and was well able to look after himself but it was simply his way to soak up all the punishment that was meted out and then to get on with his job which was to destroy the opposition scrummage. This was never more evident than in the 1984 Grand Slam game against France when The Bear was immense. He soaked up all sorts of cynical punishment from Jean-Pierre Rives's rattled Frenchmen and just got on with his game. I had just broken through into the Scotland 'B' side that year so was just an immensely interested spectator but I was hugely impressed with Iain that day and it came as no surprise when the Scotland coach Jim Telfer singled him out for special mention after the game. And for Creamie to do that you really do have to have turned in something a wee bit special!

I've played against Iain many times in matches between our Edinburgh Academicals and Heriot's FP sides but the very first time that I found myself up against him was in the Anglo-Scots versus Edinburgh District championship game at Richmond in 1983. Iain was then at the top of his form – he went on the British Lions' tour to New Zealand that summer – and I was very much a wet-behind-the-ears newcomer to the representative scene. I was playing a pretty high standard of rugby with Exeter University and had come up against some impressive scrummagers on the English club scene but at the first scrummage in that District championship game I was stunned by the amount of pressure that Iain was able to exert. He did so absolutely legally and was binding correctly and properly up on my left shoulder and back.

The reason why many, lesser, tight-heads don't like to do so is that it exposes their chest area to attack by the loose-head. In such a situation any loose-head prop worthy of the name should be able to get underneath and 'explode' upwards, wreaking havoc on the opposition scrummage. No such chance with The Bear. He exerted so much pressure that as I got up from that first scrum I felt, quite literally, dizzy. My head was spinning, my legs had turned to jelly and it was a real effort to put one foot in front of the other. That was my introduction to Iain and it was one that I never forgot. He was a much handier guy to have on your side than to have ranged against you!

It was a real blow when he finally lost his battle against injury and had to pull out of our World Cup squad in 1991. He is a real character off the field as well. He is not averse to the odd glass of ale and has a devastating repertoire of one-liners. He was once asked for his thoughts on the strains of captaincy and replied, 'Well, it doesn't affect my running!'

On another occasion a rugby writer asked him for his opinion on the state of the pitch only to be told that the conditions were 'bloody awful'. Translated this meant that the sward was in perfect nick and just right for fast, open rugby. But my favourite Milne-ism which sounds apocryphal, but I like to believe that it's true, occurred when a table collapsed under him at a post-match banquet in Paris. Quick as a flash The Bear raised his hand and declared, 'Waiter, bring me another table.' Nice one, Iain.

Jean-Pierre Garuet was the tight-head who has probably given me the hardest game I've ever experienced. He has immense upper-body strength and brings all of that strength to bear, absolutely legally, in the scrummage. Like Milne, he binds on the back or shoulder and pushes as straight as a die. The game was at Parc de Princes in 1989. France beat us 19-3 and the French pack had us on the rack. If Garuet hadn't been playing then we could have given the French a game. As it was he was in spectacular form and we never got a look in.

The All Black Richard Loe is another very strong scrummager. Like his fellow countryman John Drake he is technically very correct and somebody that nobody has managed to get much change out of over the years.

It is a very small and close community in the front row of the scrummage. Once you have been around for a while you get to know your fellow props and, where appropriate, to build up a bit of respect (hopefully mutual) for them. Despite everything that I've said up to now about Jeff Probyn I must stress that there hasn't really been any bad blood between us, at least not on my part! In January 1992, after what I knew (but few others did) would be my last Calcutta Cup match before retirement, Jeff and I met for the usual pint or two, and we even exchanged addresses.

Similarly, I first played against the Frenchman Pascal Ondarts at Murrayfield in 1990. Pascal is a tough old bird. He's not one to walk away from a scrap and he had the nose to prove it. He had played in the infamous Nantes Test against the All Blacks in 1986 when the French ran out 16-3 winners after one of the most brutal games that most people can remember seeing. As we squared up to each other at Murrayfield I was expecting the odd skelp and was getting quite excited about when it might come and, more to the point, what I was going to do when it did. There are times when you just have to stand toe-to-toe and slug it out. If you allow yourself to be intimidated then you're finished.

I waited and waited and waited in vain. Pascal never laid a finger on me throughout the whole match. In the bar afterwards I told him in my best French that I had been expecting a skelp or three. He seemed miffed that I should even suggest such a thing. 'I would never hit you, David. I respect you too much,' he said.

Well, maybe. It could equally have been the case that he had known only too well what he would have got in return if he had laid a finger on me. But I prefer to believe that Pascal's attitude really did sum up the cameraderie that genuinely exists among those of us who have toiled away in that harshest of rugby schools – the front row of the scrum.

CHAPTER 9

THE ULTIMATE CHALLENGE

New Zealand, 1990

IT WAS the morning of the first Test in Dunedin. The countdown to the kick-off had begun and I was in my hotel bedroom taking care of a few last-minute bits and pieces when the telephone rang.

'Hello, is that David Sole? It's Widnes Rugby League Club here,' said the heavily accented north of England voice on the other end of the line.

'Like hell it is,' was my initial reaction. The dialect was so theatrically 'flat caps, mufflers and whippets' that I was certain one of the boys or a Kiwi joker was winding me up. I said: 'Yeah, yeah. What can I do for you?'

The voice, ever so polite, said: 'We were wondering if you'd consider coming to play rugby league for us at Widnes when you get back.'

Still convinced that the boys were having me on, I said: 'Well, strange as it may seem to you, we're playing the All Blacks in a couple of hours' time and really, playing rugby league for Widnes, or anybody else for that matter, is the last thing on my mind at the moment. If you would care to call me when I get back to Scotland, I'd be quite happy to talk to you then.'

The voice, cheered by this reaction, said: 'Oh, that would be fine. Could you give me your telephone number.'

I could just imagine some of the jokers in the team sitting huddled around a telephone in a neighbouring room as they carried on with the wind-up. I said: 'Well, the best thing to do is to call the Scottish Rugby Union at Murrayfield and they'll give it to you.'

The voice sounded genuinely aghast at the suggestion: 'We couldn't do that. That wouldn't be proper. We couldn't phone the Scottish Rugby Union.'

'OK then,' I said, 'call me at work.' And I gave the telephone number of my Edinburgh office.

Right up until we hung up I had been convinced that it was a wind-up but it had been, after all, a genuine approach. On my return to the UK I was contacted by Doug Laughton, the Widnes coach who later went on to Leeds. He was very pleasant and basically asked if I was interested in principle in playing rugby league. I think from the tenor of the conversation he quickly realised that my heart wasn't really in it and our discussion never progressed much beyond niceties. We certainly never got as far as talking about financial terms and so on. The ball was always in Laughton's court. We agreed that I should think about it and that he would call me back. I think, though, that he realised I was going to be a difficult convert because he never called back and there my flirtation with rugby league ended.

It seems that Widnes had become interested in me on the very first day of our arrival in New Zealand. At the time, All Black rugby had been stunned by the decision of fullback John Gallagher to sign professional forms. At our first news conference in New Zealand I had been asked what my reaction was. I replied that every man had his price. Obviously, in retrospect, I can see that in some rugby league circles this observation has been viewed almost as a job application. Actually, I never had any intention of going to rugby league although I stand by my 'every man has his price' comment. It is just that in my case, to have given up my lifestyle in Edinburgh and the captaincy of Scotland would have taken a spectacular amount of money, so much in fact that there was no way any rugby league club could have looked at it. If I had been serious about switching codes I suppose I could have taken the initiative and got back in touch with Widnes for some serious discussions. But I never did. In addition to the upheaval that would have been involved in uprooting the family for the move to Widnes, I was also extremely wary of the pitfalls and pressures involved in playing sport for a living.

I hope I am not being unduly immodest when I say that with my natural style of play I think I could have made quite a mark in rugby league. However, there is a world of difference between playing for fun, which is what rugby union players do, and being obliged to perform as a paid participant. I don't think that rugby league players enjoy their sport nearly as much as we do. That, certainly, has been my impression of those who have changed codes. Fun, even when things were deadly serious at International level, was always what the game was about for me and, undoubtedly, the fun factor would have been drastically reduced had I signed for Widnes or any other rugby league club.

Although I had no wish to sign professional forms, I do have to admit that I am a fan of the game itself. I think that we in rugby union can learn a fair bit from it. The ball-handling skills, tackling and angles of running in rugby league are absolutely first-rate. I've seen a lot of the game in Australia over the years and it impresses me more and more. It is tremendously exciting and the athletic abilities of the top players really have to be seen to be appreciated. There's no doubt that rugby union can adopt and adapt the best bits from the league game. In fact many of the more progressive union coaches have done just that in terms of contact drills, the taking and giving of a pass, running angles and so on.

We arrived in New Zealand as holders of the Grand Slam and were therefore European champions. The All Blacks were the reigning world champions and the two-Test series was being billed in New Zealand almost in the manner of a world title boxing bout. Rugby is, of course, the number one sport in New Zealand but they certainly don't rest on their laurels. Our arrival and the build-up to the Test match was given big licks on the TV and this is an area in which, I feel, we still have a great deal to learn in Scotland and in the UK as a whole.

Although we didn't do as well as we thought we could have done in the Tests (but came desperately close to winning the second) there is no doubt in my mind that the team played the best rugby of any Scottish side that I have ever been involved with. We had made huge strides since the Championship decider against England in March and there is no doubt at all that the Grand Slam side reached its peak during those weeks Down Under when we came close, but not close enough, to pulling off a superb win over the then invincible All Blacks.

We did, though, go through the Tour undefeated in the Provincial matches – only the fourth side ever to do so – and that in itself is quite an astonishing feat. This was, as much as anything, a tribute to the work put in by the dirt-trackers' skipper Alex Brewster who really got the midweek side firing on all cylinders. We had a fine blend of experience and youth. The young 'up and comers' being blooded on that Tour included Doddie Weir, Adam Buchanan-Smith, Graham Shiel, Craig Redpath, Stuart Porter and Alex Moore. The fact that every single member of the Tour party performed outstandingly was one of the things that made it for me such an enjoyable and rewarding experience. Ultimately we lost both Tests but, in the second especially, we really took the Kiwis on and gave them a hell of a game. We lost 21-18 in Auckland but even in defeat that was one of the finest Scottish performances that it has ever been my privilege to be associated with.

Before we set out, Ian McGeechan had told us that the one thing above all else that we would have to do was to earn the respect of the New Zealanders by the style of our play and the manner in which we conducted ourselves off the park as well. As the Tour progressed, we made it clear that we were not going to intimidated and that we would give as good as we got. The Kiwis began to show us a great deal of respect and after the second Test there is no doubt at all that the standing of Scottish rugby in New Zealand was as high as it has ever been.

At the airport in Auckland on the opening day of the Tour we met up with our bus driver, 'Beatle', who was to become one of the trip's characters. Beatle – on account of a more than passing resemblance to one of the Fab Four – was much given to hyperbole and overly prone to exaggeration. He told us that he owned a fleet of buses. As the Tour progressed the fleet grew and grew until he claimed to have 24 gleaming omnibuses in his garage. By the end, the story had grown to such an extent that Beatle practically owned and operated Air New Zealand! We had plenty of time to make Beatle's acquaintance as the SRU had decided upon a seven-hour bus trip to Gisborne as the best way of introducing us to the delights that New Zealand has to offer. We broke in mid-journey for a training session and that, I think, was the first indication to those who were in New Zealand for the first time of just how seriously the Kiwis take their rugby.

It was a tiny town in the middle of nowhere but within minutes of our arrival the word had spread and soon there must have been 1,000 people lining the pitch and watching us go through our paces.

Gisborne, which boasts that it is the first place in the world to see the sun every morning, was a delight. It was a wonderful spot in which to begin the Tour proper. We attended barbecues and generally had a good time. Then, in the opening game itself, against Poverty Bay-East Coast, we had a fairly easy 45-0 win and the campaign was off to a first-class start.

Next on the agenda were Wellington who have a much coveted reputation against touring sides and who would obviously be a much tougher proposition. We wanted to give everybody a game in the opening two matches and the team was picked accordingly. We didn't play particularly well and ended up with a fairly lucky 16-16 draw. That was just the experience we needed, though, after our relatively simple opening match. Those who were new to the country began to appreciate at first hand just how physical the game is in New Zealand. If I had to choose one factor from the Kiwi game which more than any other characterises the way the game is played Down Under then I would have to say that it is its sheer physicality. They really relish the body contact situations. The Maori influence has a lot to do with this but every New Zealand rugby player that I've ever encountered – from fully-fledged All Black to the most junior of junior club players – really gets stuck in. They have superb body position. It seems to be something that is drummed into them at school and colt level. The All Blacks are very hard men. I don't mean that they are 'hard' in the sense of being street brawlers and so on. I mean the word in its truest, literal sense. Whether by breeding or exercise or a mixture of both they are tough hombres and when they run into you, or you run into them, you know that you've been in a collision.

There is a knack in the physical contact side of rugby. It is some-thing which, I think, I became quite proficient at over the years. You learned to make contact with the opposition on your own terms and to tense-up your body so that you could, quite literally, 'bounce' the guy who was your target. Even at International level not everyone can do this. Sometimes, when you had run at an individual – no names, no pack drill but a number of England players come into this category – you felt that you had run into a soft mattress. This was never the case with the All Blacks. From full-back to loose-head prop, they were invariably all raw-boned, muscular men and running into them was often like colliding with a brick wall.

The game also provided John Jeffrey with a day he'll never forget, or, more accurately, a day he'll never remember! JJ was minding his own business at a lineout when he was belted by the Wellington lock, Chris Tregaskis. Tregaskis, who had played a season with Boroughmuir in Scotland and later went on an All Black Tour to Argentina, caught John when he wasn't looking and he went down like a sack of potatoes. John got to his feet and was quite obviously in some difficulty. The ref was going through the normal routine of holding up a number of fingers in front of the player's eyes and asking how many were on display. All that JJ would say, though, was that he wanted to speak to me. 'I want to talk to Davie,' I could hear him telling the referee.

I walked across and it was quite obvious that John was totally out of it.

'Where are we?' JJ asked.

'We're in Wellington, New Zealand,' I said.

'Wellington. Why the hell are we in Wellington?' said JJ incredulously.

As gently as I could I told him that he had been playing rugby and that he had hurt his, ahem, shoulder, and that maybe the best thing would be for him to go off and have it seen to. Whereupon JJ toddled off to the dressing-room, no doubt to become even further bemused when the medics made no effort to look at his injured 'shoulder'.

Our visit to Wellington coincided with a *Star Trek* convention. Fans of the TV space series from all over New Zealand converged on our hotel. The 'Trekkies', as they called themselves, had virtually taken over the hotel and it was often an unnerving experience to come out of an elevator to be confronted by a brace of Klingons or a couple of Mr Spocks. They had part of a room decorated as an exact replica of the Starship Enterprise flight-deck – bizarre.

Next stop was Nelson for the game against Nelson Bays–Marlborough. But before we could even think about playing we had some rather delicate business to attend to. It has become the tradition on rugby Tours to have special T-shirts printed up, usually with a suitable motif on the front and the players' autographs on the back. The garments are then sold to augment the players' Tour fund which is used to buy beer and so on. For this trip the T-shirt operation had been entrusted to Scott Hastings. He had a New Zealander and a Highlander design for the front. So far so good. On the back we had the Tour itinerary and all the team signatures. Unfortunately, Scott had thought that it would be a bit of a wheeze to include the signature of an additional Tour member – one AS Hole. It was doubly unfortunate that the aforementioned AS Hole appeared just after the name of the Tour manager, Dunc Paterson. The manager didn't see the joke and we were told in no uncertain terms that not one of the T-shirts could be sold until something had been done about AS Hole.

We decided that we would use our laundry markers to transform 'Hole' into 'Haley'. One thousand T-shirts were deposited in the team room at our Nelson hotel and we set to work. It was like an old-fashioned sweat-shop. There we were, Scotland's finest rugby players, sitting for hours bent over piles of T-shirts. We took it in shifts. Scott, we decided, had to suffer for his 'joke' and he was told that he would have to sit through the entire session until every single T-shirt had been amended. Typically, though, Scott came into the room, did a dozen, and then disappeared claiming to have an unbreakable appointment with someone. The rest of us were left sitting there working our way through pile after pile of cellophane packaged T-shirts. It was a nightmare. It took us the better part of five hours to work through them all. Scott Hastings, as you might appreciate, was not the most popular guy around Nelson that Sunday afternoon!

Throughout the tour we were serenaded with *Flower of Scotland* almost everywhere we went. Before the Nelson Bays-Marlborough game it was sung as usual as our anthem. Or rather it was sung but not as usual! An elderly gent had been nominated to sing the song but the musical accompaniment was obviously in the wrong key for him. Poor bloke, he was all over the place. Pavarotti he wasn't. Those of us not playing were in hysterics.

Alex Brewster's men turned in a convincing performance to win 23-6 and we adjourned to the after-match function in a good frame of mind. The same bloke who had sung *Flower of Scotland* was there, too, giving the Address to the Haggis. Unfortunately, he chose to give a running Scots/English translation of the entire address which rather detracted from its impact. When he had finished his simultaneous translation he went through the whole thing again without stopping. It was a bit of a marathon.

Afterwards, he approached Alex and asked him how he thought the Address to the Haggis had gone. Alex, who had been too engrossed in the forthcoming game to have paid too much attention to the indentity of the *Flower of Scotland* singer, replied: 'That was fine. Which was more than I can say for that bugger who sang *Flower of Scotland* this afternoon.'

The old chap cleared his throat and said: 'Well actually, that was me.'

Alex, absolutely mortified, made his excuses and slipped away into the body of the kirk!

After Nelson we upped sticks and made for Canterbury. We regarded the Canterbury game as a crucial pointer to how we were going to do on this Tour. Canterbury is one of the big New Zealand provinces and, on their day, New Zealand provincial sides can represent maybe not quite the challenge of a Five Nations' game but not all that far short of it. There is the added incentive from their point of view in that they really relish the prospect of lowering the colours of a touring side. With this in mind and knowing full well that Lancaster Park is traditionally a hostile venue when you are playing the Cantabrians, we picked what we reckoned at that stage would be more or less our Test XV.

Canterbury listed half a dozen or so well-known players. Steve and Graeme Bachop were in the line-up as were Andy Earl, Warwick Taylor, Dallas Seymour and Arthur Anderson who actually retired with rib damage, having come off decidedly second best in a Finlay Calder shoulder charge. We won 21-12 but it was a very physical match and never easy. They tried to intimidate us out of the game but we weren't having any of it. We gave as good as we got. We had always considered ourselves to be a fair old rucking side – in fact based largely on the New Zealand model – but after the Wellington game a few of the Wellingtonians had told us in the bar that we would have to be even more brutal in our approach to opposition players on the deck.

Generally, in New Zealand if a player is on the ground then he is out of the game and the onus is upon him to get out of the way. The opposition can ruck him out of the way and referees will usually penalise him for impeding play rather than the pack which rucks over the top of him. We kept in mind the Wellington players' advice and put it to good use in the game against Canterbury.

Canterbury was the scene, too, of some of the most graphic reporting of a rugby match that I have ever encountered. We had been awarded a penalty try when the Canterbury forwards had taken down the scrummage after we had twice gone for pushover tries from five yards out. This incensed the spectacularly partisan Canterbury crowd who had taken up with gusto the refrain: 'The referee's a wanker.' Soon the chant was reverberating around the entire ground and there was no mistaking what it was the crowd were chanting. It was quite extraordinary. Even more extraordinary was the fact that in the local paper the following day the crowd's displeasure with the referee had been reported in precise detail.

Next, we had a midweek outing against Southland at Invercargill. We felt that a number of potential Test players were still not firing on all cylinders and it was decided to give them a run with the dirt-trackers – or Brewsters' Beezers as they became known – in order to see whether that would help their confidence. Included among them were Grand Slam regulars Scott Hastings and Iwan Tukalo. There was also a bit of a debate going on over the respective merits of Kenny Milne and John Allan for the hooker's berth. Kenny, it was felt, wasn't quite as sharp as he had been during the previous season. There was a long and hard discussion over who should get the number two shirt for the first Test. Eventually we opted for John, although he gave way to Kenny for the second encounter with the All Blacks a week later.

The other big selection debate concerned Iwan Tukalo and Alex Moore. Iwan played in the opening Test at Carisbrook Park, Dunedin, and didn't have a good game. He was replaced by Alex for the second Test but made it known that he considered Alex only to have taken out a lease on the left-wing berth. Iwan said he would be back and it is to his credit that he stuck to his guns and eventually won his way back into the side.

You can never underestimate the All Blacks but I at least went into the first Test thinking that we had a pretty good chance of getting a win. Grant Fox kicked the All Blacks into an early lead and then we scored a superb try from a loop move when Sean Lineen went in under the posts. Sean, our naturalised Kiwi, was absolutely thrilled. He is a New Zealander by birth, and his father Terry played for the All Blacks, but Sean qualified for Scotland on account of a Hebridean grandfather. To have returned to New Zealand as a member of the Scottish side and to have scored a try against the All Blacks at Dunedin was a big moment for him. Chris Gray, who had a superb Tour, also had a try and for a while it looked as if we were going to pull it off.

As the game developed, it struck me that the guys were giving the All Blacks too much respect. They are a pretty formidable bunch and their reputation goes before them. Jane, my wife, remarked on the telephone after the game that she had watched the match on television and that on the TV close-up shots before the kick-off, as the New Zealanders performed their haka, we had looked overawed; afraid almost. It wasn't something that I was conscious of at the time but in retrospect she was right. We had put the All Blacks on a pedestal and it was almost as if we were frightened to knock that pedestal over and bring them crashing to earth. We made a number of basic errors and eventually the New Zealanders romped home 31-16. We felt we hadn't done ourselves justice and were tremendously disappointed.

It was essential that we pick ourselves up after such a deflating experience and so immediately on our return to the hotel we decided to hold a Happy Hour. Well, it turned into more like a happy two and half hours at the end of which the players were feeling no pain. We had also decided to have an after-match party and Brewster's Beezers had been performing the traditional rugby Tour ritual of going around handing out tickets for the bash. Doddie Weir, not long out of school, showed his inexperience when it transpired that he had been the only one handing out invitations to blokes! Nevertheless, what could have been a post-Test wake turned into a good night and the air was cleared for a positive approach to the two remaining games.

The midweek game between the two Tests was against Manawatu at Palmerston North and it was especially significant because, if we won, our unbeaten record in the provincial games would be maintained. Accordingly, the game took on even more significance than it might otherwise have done.

It wasn't a particularly good game and we didn't play particularly well. The Beezers had really peaked the previous week against Southland when they had produced some superb driving play to achieve a convincing win. Against Manawatu the play was more fractured, not helped by the fact that the Kiwis had a big second-row man sent off for, literally, slapping Damian Cronin. There had been a bit of a set-to and Damian was holding the guy at arm's length and got slapped across the face for his trouble. The poor Kiwi – harshly in my opinion – received his marching orders and I've no doubt on the basis of being hung for a sheep rather than a lamb wished in retrospect that he had sent Damian to the deck with a full-blooded skelp.

When the composition of the original Tour party had been announced there had been criticism in some quarters over Alex Brewster's selection. He was considered by some to have been well past his prime and to have been a waste of space on the plane. How wrong the critics were. Alex was worth his weight in gold throughout that Tour. He shaped the midweek side in his own uncompromising image and because they were winning, and winning well, that took an awful lot of pressure off the rest of us.

In Auckland for the second Test we determined that we had nothing to lose and that if we were going to go down then we would do so with all guns blazing. Jane had been right. We had given the All Blacks far too much respect in Dunedin and this time we were going to get stuck in amongst them.

We had a team meeting before the game and talked it through. I said that the All Blacks didn't have some God-given right to expect victory and that there was no reason at all why we should fear them. We had come up against the best that New Zealand had to offer in the provincial games and we had beaten them. I said that we should all put the previous Saturday's defeat out of our minds and that there was absolutely no reason why we couldn't win this time around. We hadn't played to our full potential in Dunedin and yet for long periods we had been more than a match for our opponents. At the conclusion of the meeting I felt the mood was right. There was a much more positive 'feel' about the team than there had been the previous weekend and we entered the second Test with our confidence and spirits high.

We now know, of course, that after a superb performance by all concerned we were beaten 18-21, and that defeat remains one of the biggest disappointments of my rugby career. We outscored the All Blacks by two tries to one and, without doubt, it was a game which we deserved to win. However, Grant Fox was in spectacular kicking form and he was 100 per cent successful from six shots at goal. There were a couple of curious incidents which went against us. Gary Armstrong was off injured just before a scrum at a corner flag. We were a man down and Finlay Calder got caught offside as the scrum wheeled. Fox put over the penalty goal and that was a lucky three points for them.

Then, the referee was undoubtedly wrong when he penalised Gavin Hastings for not releasing the ball after a Grant Fox garryowen. Gavin had fielded the ball and Mike Brewer appeared from a blatantly offside position to tackle him. There was no way on God's earth that Brewer could have reached Gavin from an on-side position. That was a real kick in the nuts for us. You get over these things, of course you do, but I shall go to my grave convinced that this was a Test match we could and should have won and I am sure that the 'Brewer on-side' call was a major turning point in the game.

The All Blacks had been unbeaten since 1986 but behind the scenes there appeared to be some serious politicking going on. The skipper, Wayne Shelford, was dropped after the game and never won back his place. He was a world-class player who, I feel, was the victim of the various backstage rivalries which sometimes seem to afflict New Zealand rugby. I have played with and against Shelford. He is great with the ball, great in contact situations and invariably takes all the right options. Most recently, in 1992, I played against him in a Barbarians game and he still has all the touches. I suppose in a way I should take some sustenance from the fact that the New Zealand selectors felt obliged to discard their captain even after beating us. Obviously, many felt that it had not been a game that they deserved to win. However, there's little doubt in my mind that Buck Shelford was made a scapegoat and that he was discarded far too soon.

After the game I was, as they say, absolutely gutted. I don't think I have ever felt so deflated. I felt we had been robbed. We had given our all and had failed to get the win which I felt we had deserved.

We were then given the opportunity to delay our departure by three days. The original plan had been for us all to begin our homeward journey on the Sunday morning immediately after the Auckland Test. This had been a bad idea because, with the 1001 things that have to be done in preparation for the journey home, it would have detracted from the total concentration that would be required from the Test players. Accordingly, we delayed our departure until Wednesday of the following week and we had an extra three days to wind down after the Test match.

We bade farewell to our departing colleagues with an impromptu haka on the hotel steps and then those of us who were staying on were driven by 'Beatle', the bus driver, to a nearby winery. We had a great day. They laid on wine and beer and a barbecue. Kenny Milne uttered one of the all-time great Milne-isms when during our conducted tour he asked: 'What are those oak casks made of?'

Big brother Iain was also a star that day. He had recovered from injury during our domestic season to play fantastically well throughout the Tour. He really unwound at the winery. He found his way to a raised platform and started performing his party-piece 'head, shoulders, knees and toes'. For anyone who has not seen the Bear performing this ritual I can only say that it is one of the funniest routines around.

Picture the scene, this huge front-row forward performing the delicate manoeuvres that the thing demands. It's outrageous. They could sell tickets for it.

The following day 'Beatle' drove us to Rotorua where we wanted to go white-water rafting. That was certainly different. You rush down-river and over serious rapids in these inflatable boats. It is quite danger-ous and almost proved to be the undoing of one young woman who was swept overboard and was going down for the obligatory third time only to be plucked from the water by one of the rafting guides. We would meet up with her again just a few days later. It turned out that she was a Cathay Pacific air hostess and she was on duty on our flight home. Talk about it being a small world.

We hadn't realised at the time that the NZRFU had agreed to pick up the accommodation costs for those remaining behind. Accordingly, we decided that we would stay at a 15-bucks a night dive in Rotorua. We had a couple of beers in the bar before going out for a Chinese meal. When we returned the local pipe band had turned out in our honour. It was as if the word had just gone out – 'Come as you are, bring your pipes' – and the bandsmen had just turned up in their working clothes. It was another good evening.

We were really making the most of our remaining time in New Zealand, which is the most wonderful country for outdoor pursuits, and the following day was spent at a luge run in the mountains. On the way back to Auckland in the bus we stopped off at a pub run by a mate of Sean's and, no doubt fuelled by the hospitality provided, we decided that it would be a splendid idea to bring the curtain down on our New Zealand safari with a 100-metre bungee jump from a crane into Auckland harbour.

Basically, bungee jumping entails the attachment of an oversize elastic band around the ankles and a headlong jump off a raised plat-form. I said that as captain I would go first and the others drew lots to decide the order thereafter. Finlay was making the draw and, of course, John Jeffrey drew number 13! There was a lot of high-spirited comment about how much we were all looking forward to the jump but as we drew nearer and nearer to the harbour the bus became quieter and quieter. By the time we had actually arrived at the harbour-side you could have heard a pin drop. We drew up outside the bungee jumping office and Fin got out to make the arrangements.

A couple of moments later he came back on board to announce: 'Sorry, but it's closed on Tuesdays.'

He had no need to feel sorry and he knew it. The look of relief which came over the faces of the 16 hitherto brave souls told its own tale. We had all been terrified but hadn't wanted to admit it.

That brought the curtain down on the best Tour that I have ever taken part in. The rugby was great, the company was better and the country itself was out of this world. If only we had won that second Test in Auckland.

CHAPTER 10

THE OVAL GLOBE

Two World Cups

THERE CAN BE no doubt that whatever the profit and loss account may show at the end of the day, as a festival of rugby and as a showcase for the game, Rugby World Cup '91 was a roaring success. It was a rare delight to be involved when rugby was grabbing the headlines, monopolising the airwaves and, for once, rivalling the round-ball code as a topic for universal discussion.

I had played in the inaugural RWC 1987 and so the uniquely intense, knock-out nature of the competition – and from which it derives its special drama – hadn't come as a complete surprise to me. In New Zealand and Australia in 1987 it had been very much a 'toe in the water' kind of exercise. Nobody knew exactly what to expect and the rather *ad hoc* nature of the event, with for instance the final TV contract not being signed until literally minutes before the opening ceremony, added to its appeal. We all felt like pioneers. As the competition progressed I became convinced that we were in at the start of something big and there was never any doubt in my mind that the Rugby World Cup would prosper and act as a superb companion to Five Nations' and Antipodean domestic competitions.

Four years later, RWC '91 was more professional and, of course, for the UK teams it was significantly different in that we were, effectively, on tour at home. For us Scots that rather unreal state of affairs was magnified by virtue of the fact that all of our matches up to and including our semi-final with England were played at Murrayfield. We stayed predominantly in a hotel on the outskirts of Edinburgh. For those of us who lived in the capital this meant that we were 'on tour' for nearly a month just half an hour from our homes. This took some getting used to.

I felt under intense pressure throughout the 1991 competition. The draw had been extremely kind to us. Playing virtually all of our games at Murrayfield represented an enormous psychological boost. However, it was a double-edged weapon. Throughout the Eighties and into the Nineties the expectations of the rugby-watching Scottish public have been raised enormously. The Murrayfield crowds have come to expect success. This meant that the pressure was on us to deliver the goods. In a World Cup context it also meant that when we won at Murrayfield then there would be those who would put it down to unfair ground advantage while if we had lost a succession of games on our own patch then defeat would have been doubly difficult to endure.

RWC '91 got underway at Twickenham during the first week in October with the opening game between England and New Zealand. However, for me – and I've no doubt for most of the other players involved – the competition had actually begun four months earlier when I embarked on a summer fitness routine. In June I had returned from a family holiday in Majorca (the first non-rugby summer break since 1986) and immediately started my personal fitness and weights programme. We were due to start working as a squad the following month and I wanted to ensure that when the group sessions began I would already have achieved a satisfactory level of personal fitness. So far, so good. Then, in the second of our Murrayfield squad sessions, I pulled a calf muscle. The damage was done just at the insert to the Achilles' tendon. I didn't know it at the time but that pulled muscle was to be the first of a whole series of injuries which dogged me throughout the summer and throughout the competition itself.

Donald Macleod, the SRU medic, sent me for treatment to Tom McNiven, the Hibernian FC physioptherapist. I received virtually daily therapy at the Murrayfield Hospital, nearby the rugby stadium and, luckily, near to my office as well. After an intensive programme of ultra-sound, deep-heat and electro-magnetic treatment, the damaged tissue began to repair itself but the injury had already set my preparations back by about a fortnight, which doesn't sound a lot but, in the context of an on-going fitness programme, was a real blow.

As a team, too, our campaign did not get off to a promising start. Mindful of the fact that the nature and timing of the competition meant that we would be undertaking a series of full-blooded Test matches at the 'wrong' end of our domestic season, we were keen to get up to speed and to achieve match hardness with games against genuine opposition.

With this in mind, and a month before the tournament was due to get underway, we travelled to Bucharest in order to take on Romania. There's no point in mollycoddling yourselves. Quite simply, the best preparation for International rugby has always been International rugby. We were experimenting in a number of areas and took a relatively inexperienced side to Romania. Chris Gray was injured and therefore couldn't play. That turned out to be a piece of fortuitious planning on his part. We lost 18-12 and what had been intended as a tolerably tough but most definitely winnable warm-up game became something of a morale crusher.

The next weekend we were on duty at Murrayfield against a powerful Barbarians side. The Baa-Baas had spread their net wide to put together a star-studded XV. They had a very big pack. Their front row, comprising such solid citizens as the former Argentinian and Australian prop Topo Rodriguez, his fellow Wallaby Tom Lawton and the South African Guy Kebble, probably weighed as much as our entire front five. The Baa-Baas took the game very seriously and, played on a warm and humid September afternoon, we were tolerably happy with a 16-16 draw.

Our preparations continued with a change of identity. We became the SRU President's XV for a game against the Anglo-Scots which we won 32-4 and then came the Murrayfield encounter with Edinburgh Borderers (who would later claim to be the unofficial third-placed team in the world!).

The game was played on a Friday afternoon. That very evening we were due to board the bus which would take us, now as a properly constituted squad, to St Andrews for the official start of our World Cup campaign. After St Andrews it would be a case of travelling down to London for the grand opening dinner and the competition would be underway. Accordingly, although a lot of the boys might have been at Murrayfield in person, in spirit they were already on board that bus to St Andrews. We played very badly and lost 13-9 to a very psyched up Edinburgh Borderers outfit who were led by Jeremy Richardson. Afterwards we were pretty gloomy. It wasn't, for sure, the kind of result we had most wanted on the eve of the competition but we held to our belief that it would all come right 'on the night'.

The following day we were off to the Royal Lancaster Hotel in London for the official opening dinner. It was a glittering occasion but, in retrospect, it did seem rather a waste of time, not to mention money, to have all the players interrupt their preparation just to attend a dinner. We returned to our training camp at St Andrews the following day. It was an intrusion we could have done without. The French had the right idea. They flew into London from Paris, instructed the pilot to carry out the aeronautical equivalent of keeping the engine running and flew out again as soon as the meal was over.

Our Sunday training session at the Madras College pitch in St Andrews almost had dire consequences for me. I suffered a potentially serious training injury and for a worrying 24 hours my World Cup participation hung in the balance.

We were involved in a pretty hectic contact session and my old mate Finlay Calder stormed in to a maul and caught me under the ribs with a shoulder. Now, as many a player will testify and sadly I must now include myself among their number, Fin has the boniest shoulders in world rugby. When he hits you, you tend to stay hit. I knew right away that it hadn't been just a run-of-the-mill collision. The pain, of a searingly sharp variety, had been unusually severe. I went down for an 'eight count' but, after a while, managed to get my breath back and continued with the session.

Back at the team hotel overlooking the 17th fairway of the famous Old Course I was still feeling pretty groggy and so went for a jacuzzi and a swim in an attempt to ease the pain. That didn't do much good and I was still feeling under the weather when I paid a visit to the loo. I looked down and my urine was bright red in colour. Hello, I thought, that's not too clever. I sought out Donald Macleod, the SRU medical officer. He was working-out on a rowing machine in the hotel gym and so I waited until he had finished his session and then, as undramatically as I could, informed him that I thought I had a bit of a problem because I was passing blood in my urine.

'Yes,' said Donald, who is one of the most imperturbable blokes I know, 'that would be a bit of a problem.'

He asked what, when, where, how and why and explained that I was probably right and that as there was very little that could be done immediately I should keep taking lots of fluids. He then went off to fix up an appointment at his hospital in Livingston for first thing the next morning.

At that stage we didn't know how seriously the kidney had been damaged and therefore didn't want a lot of scare stories circulating. We decided to keep the problem to ourselves for the time being. That evening we had a management meeting involving myself, the medics, the coaches and the team manager, Dunc Paterson. We got around to injuries and Dunc asked if there were any problems on that front. Donald and I looked at each other but simultaneously decided that we would have to come clean.

I mentioned what had happened to Fin and he was suitably

apologetic. The rest of the squad were informed the following morning after Donald and I had left to drive the 50-odd miles to St John's Hospital at Livingston where we had an eight o'clock appointment with a specialist. Everybody was sworn to secrecy. We were desperately keen that news of the injury didn't leak out and that, in particular, the Press didn't find out.

Before they had run the tests at the hospital there was no way of knowing just how bad the injury was. Nevertheless, with only four days to go until the opening game, I was pretty dejected. The St John's people, who were absolutely marvellous, ran a whole series of tests. They wanted to make sure that the kidney was still functioning properly and so I had a number of x-rays and scans with dye injected into the bloodstream by which means they were able to monitor the performance of the damaged kidney. It was all done very clandestinely and, like the squad, the medical staff were asked not to say anything to the media about my visit. When the results came through, the diagnosis was severe bruising but with no lasting damage. They reckoned that after a couple of days' rest the bleeding would stop and I would be as right as rain. I was mightily relieved, I can tell you.

The return trip to St Andrews was completed with me in a much easier frame of mind. I was forbidden to train with the squad the following day. The attendant press people were told that I was suffering from a heavy cold and this was what appeared in the papers. Meanwhile, I couldn't force myself to sit idly by and, stupidly, did some light running on my own. The blood duly made a re-appearance in my urine. When I told Donald he was not best pleased.

The trouble cleared up, just as the medics had said it would, within a couple of days. But with only three days remaining until our opening game against Japan that was just too close for comfort for my liking. Our schedule, and what makes the competition so demanding, was three Test matches within the space of a week. On the Saturday we were due to play Japan, followed by Zimbabwe on the Wednesday and Ireland the following Saturday.

We spread our time between the Dalmahoy Golf and Country Club on the outskirts of Edinburgh and our Old Course hotel at St Andrews. We were keen to prevent the onset of boredom and it certainly helped to have the two centres working in tandem throughout the competition. As I've already related, one of the strangest things about the entire campaign was the fact that we were 'touring' at home. I live only ten miles from Dalmahoy and it was quite bizarre to be so close to your family and yet, to all intents and purposes, they might as well have been on another planet. The SRU had sanctioned family-day visits but

I'm sure some of the lads managed illicit assignations with wives and girlfriends as well. Jane was none too pleased that my only contact with her other than at an SRU-sanctioned family-day was in the form of a request to bring my guitar out to Dalmahoy!

We watched the opening ceremony and the England v All Blacks game at our Dalmahoy HQ. We weren't particularly impressed by either side. England looked rather ponderous and both sides seemed to have been badly affected by nerves. What did impress us, however, was the way that the defending champions had changed tactics and taken control in the second period to win 18-12.

With the opening ceremonial and the first game now out of the way it really did feel as though the whole thing was for real. We had a couple of days to wait until our Murrayfield debut against the Japanese and it certainly wasn't a game that we were taking for granted. We knew from past experience that the Japanese prepare meticulously. They really do their homework. We knew that they would have put our playing style under the microscope and that they would be attempting to capitalise on any perceived weaknesses. We knew, too, that the Japanese would have appreciated that if they were to defeat one of the competition's top sides – which we were – then they would be most likely to do so in the first game when they would be hoping to catch the opposition cold.

The other point that has to be borne in mind about the Japanese is that despite their lack of inches they are an amazingly physical outfit. They really do put themselves about and they are never defeated until the final whistle has blown.

As I had expected, the Japanese threw everything at us and we led by only 17-9 at the interval. The physicality of their approach was underlined in spectacular fashion when Scott Hastings found himself on the receiving end of an amazing tackle by the Japanese centre, Katsuki. Scott was making for the line when the little Japanese player shot into view like an Exocet rocket. He slammed straight into Scott, who had seen him coming but reckoned that he would just give him 'the bump' and proceed on his merry way. As it was the sound of the impact was like a couple of cars colliding and Scott almost finished up in the fourth row of the stand.

Then, by the same token, I suffered a painful gash on my right ear as John Jeffrey took the full brunt of a Japanese charge from a kick-off and our heads collided. I was waiting to secure the ball as JJ came back to earth but this guy hit him like an express train and in the ensuing collision my ear came a very poor second. I was a bit woozy and had to go off for some stitches. 'Thanks for breaking my fall,' said JJ rather wickedly as I was led away.

The doc put three stitches in the ear and because I was still a bit groggy it was decided that David Milne should go on for the final five minutes. David is the least well-known of the three Milne brothers and had waited a long time for his Cap. He is an absolute tryer and had put in so much work to make the squad that everybody was delighted for him. Unfortunately, in his eagerness to get on the pitch, and to complete the family hat-trick in the list of Scottish Internationalists, David missed his footing on the concrete steps which lead down to the pitch from the replacement players' seats in the stand. He sustained a very bad groin stain and, truth to tell, so bad was the injury that he should never have gone on the pitch at all. He should have gone straight to the treatment room. Looking back the incident does, of course, have its funny side (although David certainly wasn't laughing) but at the time it represented a major blow. Again, to underline just how physical the Japanese were, we had to replace Craig Chalmers ten minutes before the end when he took a knock on the throat. We eventually disposed of our Oriental opponents by the margin of 47-9 and despite our rather alarming casualty list we were delighted to have got the first game under our belts. We were pleased, too, that we had improved greatly on the form that we had displayed during our warm-up games. The Edinburgh Borderers' ghost had, for the time being, been exorcised.

David's injury, allied to mine, meant that we went into our next game, against Zimbabwe, somewhat short on the propping front. I wasn't fit to play against the big Zimbabweans and we decided to switch Paul Burnell to the loose-head side of the scrum and to play big Alan Watt on the tighthead. Despite his groin injury David was listed for a place on the bench. By rights he shouldn't have been there but, I guess somewhat ruthlessly, the selectors had decided that he was more expendable than I was if he had to go on while 'carrying' the injury.

One of the most important lessons we had learned in 1987 was that in a prolonged competition such as this, you really do have to spread your playing resources. Without giving away Caps just for the sake of it, if your second string players are up to it – and if they are not then they shouldn't be in the squad – then they have to be played at some point in the tournament. With this in mind, we made a total of eight changes to the side which had proved victorious against the Japanese. Against Zimbabwe it was important above all else that we won. There would be no points awarded for style and so it was simply a case of registering a victory in whatever manner came most easily. After a sticky start, when we were only 15-12 ahead at one point, we went on to win by a convincing 51-12, Iwan Tukalo scoring a hat-trick of tries in the process.

Throughout the entire competition we were absolutely aware of the fact that we had to keep capitalising on the luck of the draw. With victory over the Zimbabweans we had confirmed our qualification for the quarter-final. All that had to be decided then was where we would play it. Obviously, we much preferred to continue playing in front of 'oor ain folk' at Murrayfield. To do that we had to keep on winning.

Next it was Ireland. Over the years the Scots and the Irish have been involved in some rare old tussles. Despite the fact that there was perhaps more in it for the Irish if they had lost at Murrayfield, in as much as that would have meant they would play their quarter-final at Lansdowne Road, we knew perfectly well that the Irish would have no intention of throwing the game. It just isn't in their nature. They play at 300 miles an hour and they play to win. For us, on the other hand, it was crucial that we won. We had no wish to go to Dublin for our quarter-final tie. The odds would have been stacked very much against us if that had been the case. Accordingly, the pressure upon us was intense.

Things weren't going tremendously well against the Irish. Ralph Keyes had on his kicking boots and just after the interval he slotted home his fifth successful penalty goal to give his side a 15-9 lead. Craig Chalmers had been in the wars again and had to be replaced when he damaged a hip in a tackle by Gordon Hamilton. His young Melrose club-mate Graham Shiel came on to win his first Cap in a real pressure situation and in such an atmosphere it was as well that our scrum-half Gary Armstrong was playing a game right out of the top drawer. Gary protected Graham at first but once the young Melrose player had found the pace he came on to a really fine game. He put in some first-class tactical kicks and his distribution was as if to the manner born.

Eventually, we triumphed 24-15 over Ireland and the feeling of relief was tremendous. The major talking point of the game, however, revolved around an incident involving Finlay Calder and the Irish full-back Jim Staples. The sequence of events, as I recall them, was as follows. From a scrummage just inside the Irish half at the 'clock' end of the ground, Gary Armstrong hoisted a wicked high ball which Staples came forward to mark. Tony Stanger got to him first and then Finlay, following up milli-seconds later, caught the Irishman with his left shoulder. He was caught on the side of the head and went down like a sack of potatoes. After the match there were allegations in the Press that Finlay had executed a forearm jab or a stiff-arm tackle on Staples. Well, I didn't think that was the case at the time and subsequent viewing of the match video confirms my initial impression.

Finlay is a great man for the shoulder charge (as I had already discovered to my personal cost!) and it was a tremendously potent and effective weapon. Some of the Press coverage was hysterical in the extreme and Finlay found himself on the receiving end of hate mail from outraged Irishmen. I know that he was considerably upset by this.

What happened next on the field of play was that, with Staples still groggy, we won a lineout inside the Irish 22 and Gary sent up another perfectly placed garryowen which poor Jim Staples misjudged. The ball bounced off his right shoulder and a delighted Graham Shiel snapped up the loose ball to crash over for his first International try. Gavin slotted home the conversion to level terms on 15-15.

After a penalty goal by Gavin, Staples was tested yet again when Graham, this time, put up the high ball and the waiting Staples was engulfed by Sean Lineen and Scott Hastings. This time it was Gary who was on hand to pounce on the ricochet and scramble over for a try. We were criticised in some quarters for capitalising on Staples's discomfort but I make no apologies. This was Test rugby and at that level there are no prizes for coming second. It was entirely legitimate for us to target the weak link in the Irish side. It was clear to all that Jim hadn't recovered from his earlier injury and he should have gone off. Sad though it was for Staples on a personal level, it would have been naïve in the extreme had we not sought to capitalise on his misfortune.

I was grilled about the 'Calder Affair' at the news conference immediately after the game. I was amazed that the subject had been raised at all. It had seemed totally unremarkable in the context of the game itself. We followed the Irish coaching and managerial hierarchy into the Murrayfield interview room and it became clear that they had either raised it themselves or had responded to questions from the media. It left rather a sour taste and to some degree took the edge off what we considered to have been a good win.

That evening we were able to unwind with a party attended by wives and girlfriends and held at the Royal High Club's new premises in Edinburgh. The following day, at our Dalmahoy base, we were again joined by our families and that was the perfect way to ease into the second week of the competition. On the Sunday, too, we learned who our quarter-final opponents would be. At that stage it could still, theoretically at least, have been Wales, Argentina or Western Samoa but it came as little surprise to anybody when it was the South Sea islanders who eventually turned out to be our next Murrayfield 'guests'.

Western Samoa had been, in the memorable words of Aussie coach Bob Dwyer, the 'dark horses' of the tournament. They had seen off Wales and Argentina and given the Wallabies a run for their money in the driving rain at Pontypool. We had watched on the telly as they had smashed their way to a quarter-final berth with some of the hardest tackling that the rugby world had ever seen. Additionally, to those of us who knew something about New Zealand provincial rugby it was clear that as most of the Western Samoans actually lived in New Zealand and played on the Kiwi provincial scene they weren't going to be anybody's mugs. Their skipper, the prop Peter Fatialofa, who was to become the most famous piano shifter in the world, was an Auckland provincial regular. Throughout the squad the Kiwi influence was evident and underlined by the fact that the Western Samoan coach Peter Schuster was aided throughout the tournament by Bryan Williams, the much respected, former All Black wing-threequarter. Not for nothing did the Polynesians become known as New Zealand 'B'.

A number of Western Samoa's World Cup stars have reverted to the rugby colours of New Zealand, their country of adoption. I'm not entirely sure that this should be allowed. The Northern Hemisphere equivalent would be for someone to play for England and then, only six months later, transfer allegiance to Scotland. In the Spring of 1992 I was a member of a World squad in New Zealand for the NZRFC centenary celebrations. I skippered the opening Test and one of the questions I was asked at the after-match news conference was what I had thought about the new-look All Blacks. I replied that they weren't all that 'new look' to me as I had met quite a number of them playing for Western Samoa during the World Cup. I'm 12,000 miles from the issue and so can't afford to be too judgemental. However, one cannot help thinking that if the Polynesian nations were to have first choice of their expatriate stars then the power centre of world rugby would switch with tidal-wave rapidity to the Pacific Ocean.

We prepared thoroughly for our quarter-final tussle with the Western Samoans. We had watched as they had put in the big hits which had reduced some of their opponents to the ranks of the walking wounded. However, we reckoned that we had detected a flaw in the Samoan technique. They had become so intent on getting in the crunching tackle that they became victims of tunnel vision. Like sharp-shooters, they liked to be able to draw a bead on their target and line him up for the kill. Like sharpshooters, too, their concentration on the task in hand was total. If they were allowed to get in the big hit then the results were pretty devastating. We planned, though, to turn their great strength into a weakness.

The Western Samoans liked nothing better than to have an opponent running straight at them. Invariably, because they were physically strong and mentally tough, the opponent would come off second best. We decided that by constantly moving the target we could negate much of the advantage which their heavy tackling prowess had given them. The plan was perfectly simple. It was really just a development of the old coaching principle of drawing your man. The ball carrier would head for his would-be tackler and once the tackler had been committed then the ball would be transferred out of the contact area to a supporting colleague. We had deduced, rightly as it turned out, that the Samoans weren't particularly flexible. Once they had committed themselves to the tackle they would go through with it whether or not the tackle victim still had the ball. That this was the case was evident in the relatively high number of late tackles which the Samoans had been guilty of in their earlier matches. It wasn't, I think, a case of deliberate transgression but simply evidence of the 'tunnel vision' which we hoped to exploit. We hoped, then, by judicious use of running angles, by laying off the ball late and by aggressive support play, to take the edge off what had been up until then the Western Samoans' most productive gambit.

Additionally, we considered that a touch of their own medicine might be no bad thing either. Gavin Hastings, at six feet two inches and nearly 15 stones, is one of the most powerful runners in world rugby. We reckoned that even the Western Samoans wouldn't much relish the prospect of bringing him to earth once he had got up a head of steam. We intended, therefore, to take them on physically, with Gavin coming in on short balls off Gary. The strategy worked a treat, something which was borne out by Peter Fatialofa when we were team-mates during that centenary Test series in New Zealand. Fats said that it had been his side's intention to intimidate the Scots. His guys really relish the physical stuff and it had been the plan to knock the stuffing out of us by getting in a few really big hits early on. On the day the strategy had worked in reverse with the Scots getting in the big ones and the Samoans being given much food for thought.

For both sides victory meant a place in the semi-finals of the World Cup. It was a huge incentive. We really wanted it. We had finished the game against Ireland with two players crocked. In addition to Craig, Sean Lineen had taken a bang on a knee which had dislodged the knee-cap. Both players spent time in a hyperbaric-oxygen chamber in an effort to speed recovery. The device, which utilises high-pressure oxygen, is used in deep-sea diving and, more controversially, in the treatment of multiple sclerosis. Exposure to oxygen under pressure is known to speed recovery from injury and both Craig and Sean undoubtedly benefited from its use. Craig was fit in time for the Western Samoan game while Sean was back in harness for the semi-final which followed.

The performance against the Western Samoans was, in my opinion, our best of the entire tournament. We led 13-3 at the interval and went on to win 28-6. I had chosen to play against the stiff breeze in the opening period. This, I had hoped, would spur us into a more urgent and constructive start than had been the case in our earlier games. We took on the Samoans at their own game and beat them but the Polynesians had indeed been one of the big hits of the tournament. They were given a standing ovation at the conclusion of the game when they returned to the Murrayfield turf to bid a final farewell to the competition. In 1987, the Western Samoans had been justifiably upset when they had not been invited to take part in the inaugural competition despite the fact that they had just beaten Fiji and Tonga who were invited. Their performance in the 1991 competition signalled their arrival on the world scene. If they can entice their best players, including second generation expatriates in New Zealand, to turn out for them then they will continue to be a force to be reckoned with. Scotland have recognised their enhanced status with a Tour in 1993 so their 1991 World Cup campaign has already brought positive rewards.

However, back in 1991, they were out of the competition and we now had a semi-final to look forward to. While we had been engaged with the Samoans, England had been winning their torrid quarter-final tie against the French at Parc des Princes and it was the Auld Enemy who would be coming to Murrayfield for a semi-final joust with ourselves.

But before we could lock horns with them again my World Cup injury jinx struck for the third time. After the Western Samoan game we had six days in which to prepare for the England game and we returned to our 'country home' at St Andrews. On the Tuesday before the game we paid a visit to the Cameron Brig whisky distillery where we enjoyed the hospitality of the manager, Donald Stewart. On returning to the hotel we went through a few late afternoon lineout drills in the process of which I damaged my back. I didn't do anything about it immediately but by early evening I was in excruciating pain. Nothing that I did helped to ease the discomfort. I couldn't sit, stand or lie down. The team physio, Dr James Robson, who is also a Dundee GP in his own right, was summoned and he advised me, initially, to go and have a hot bath. That eased the pain slightly but I was still in a great deal of discomfort.

James gave my back the once over and discovered that a vertebra had slipped out of alignment. He manipulated it back into shape and immediately I felt better. Nevertheless, the last thing a prop forward wants is a 'dicky' back. With the huge stresses and strains that are exerted on a front-row player the one part of the anatomy above all others that you want to have complete faith in is your back. The realisation that a disc had slipped out of alignment didn't do much for my confidence. However, James had put it back in and I felt much happier. Then, on the day before the game, the same thing happened again. Luckily, James was on hand and he popped the vertebra straight back in again. However, with yet another confrontation with my old sparring partner Jeff Probyn only 24 hours away, spinal problems were absolutely the last thing that I needed!

As it turned out, I took a fair bit of stick for the quality of my scrummaging against Jeff in this game. At the time I never mentioned the disc problems. It would have sounded too much like a, literally, lame excuse. However, I'm convinced that the vertebra problems and the other annoying injuries before and during the campaign didn't help my cause at all. I satisfied myself, at any rate, that this was the case five months later when, I think, I redressed the balance in my personal duel with Jeff during the 1992 Calcutta Cup game.

John Jeffrey, winning his 39th Cap, led us out on to the pitch and what an ovation he got. It was to be JJ's final appearance in front of the Murrayfield crowd and we reckoned it would be a nice moment. Fin, whose last home appearance it also was, had led the team out before the second Test against the All Blacks in 1990 on what was to have been his farewell appearance. He was persuaded to return to the International arena for one final fling during the World Cup. Finlay and JJ constituted one of the most devastating breakaway units in the history of Scottish rugby and they will be sorely missed.

England played exactly as we had expected them to. They set out to grind us down up front and the hugely exasperating thing from our point of view was that although we knew that was what they would try to do we couldn't do anything to counteract it. God, it was a dull game. England won 9-6 but I felt sorry for the poor spectators. England under Geoff Cooke and Roger Uttley have had some superb players at their disposal – the kind of players, like Guscott, Carling and Underwood who could have crowds on their feet yelling for more. I feel, though, that England sacrificed a lot of the talent they had to offer in the unremitting search for success and the overwhelming need to grind out another victory. I feel, too, that this ultra-cautious approach was the psychological legacy of defeat by us in the 1990 Grand Slam match.

They would argue that what the 1990 game taught them was how to win; how to beat teams like ourselves. There is no doubt that the strategy they adopted was effective. It has brought Will Carling and his men two Grand Slams and second place in the World Cup. I remain convinced, though, that with the pots of playing talent at their disposal they could have continued to win but, with a more expansive approach, they could have done so with some style. Ultimate defeat at the hands of the Australians in the World Cup final when they did try to throw the ball about does not adversely affect my argument. In the final England tried to adopt a style of play which by then had become alien to them. They had been conned by the media who were crying out for a more adventurous and entertaining style of play and by Aussies like the worldly-wise David Campese who embarked upon a one-man psychological warfare campaign with regular, damning indictments on England's lack of style. Had I been Will Carling, Geoff Cooke or Roger Uttley then I would have said, 'Sod the lot of them, we'll play exactly the same brand of rugby which got us to the final.' By then it was far too late for them to change.

Anyway, two penalty goals by Jon Webb and a drop goal from Rob Andrew in reply to two penalty goals from Gavin Hastings were, sadly for us, sufficient to gain England their place in the World Cup final.

And what can I say about Gavin and that penalty miss of his in front of the posts? The first thing that has to be said is that it didn't cost us the game. The scores were tied at 6-6 and we were awarded a penalty when England killed the ball at a ruck just inside their 22 at the 'clock' end. It looked like a formality as Gavin stepped forward to take the kick. When he pushed the ball a yard outside the right upright I think the entire Scottish nation stared in shocked disbelief. What made it especially hard was that Gavin had kicked beautifully throughout the competition. He was really striking the ball well and had kicked so sweetly against Ireland that you could argue the case that if it hadn't been for him then we wouldn't have made it to the semi-final in the first place. It was an horrendous miss but I feel certain that even if it had flown straight and true then England would have persevered with their 'grind 'em down, slow it down' strategy and they would still have proved victorious. We really needed the kind of cushion that a converted try would have provided to have forced them out of their game-plan and into the kind of fast and furious tactics which would have suited us.

So we exited at the hands of our oldest International foe. We were very very down. We felt that we really hadn't been able to get our game up and running. It was a very empty feeling; a feeling that after three weeks of furious competition it was all over. We still had the third-place play-off to look forward to but before that there was one last thing that remained to be done. We wanted to thank the Murrayfield crowd for the amazing support that they had provided throughout the competition.

It was a spontaneous thing. We had gone to the tunnel in traditional fashion to see England off the pitch and then we went back to offer our own thanks to the crowd which even in defeat was quite marvellous. That defeat had ended a superb run of 13 consecutive Murrayfield victories and the crowd had played its part in each and every one of those wins. I've said it before elsewhere in this book and I make no apologies for saying it again: Murrayfield and the Murrayfield crowd are two of the things that I shall miss most about my departure from the game.

Afterwards in the dressing-room it was very anti-climactic. We were out and yet we still had to go to Cardiff for the third-place play-off. The prospect didn't exactly fill one with glee. We had a day to wait before finding out who our opponents would be. We watched the New Zealand v Australia encounter on the television from Lansdowne Road and, strangely, I perked up a bit when the New Zealanders lost to become our Arms Park opponents. I always enjoy playing against the All Blacks and, optimist that I am, I always reckoned that the more often you played against them then the greater chance you had of actually winning!

Before the game in Cardiff there was a rather desultory atmosphere. Both teams, I think, would rather have been somewhere else. However, once combat had commenced, that feeling was soon put aside and both sides entered the fray with gusto. I had picked up a 'dead leg' in the game against England and within 20 minutes at Cardiff I got another knock in almost exactly the same place. I was never happy with my fitness level throughout the competition. That early summer calf muscle problem had set me back at the outset and I'm afraid the situation is that if you are not 'there' at the beginning then you are always going to struggle; it's going to be a constant battle to catch up. I don't think I ever really did. Mentally, too, I found the whole experience quite gruelling. It took a great deal out of me.

And I wasn't, either, to get my long-cherished win over the All Blacks in a Scotland shirt. There was a distinct lack of commitment in the first half. First-time tackles were missed by the barrow-load. The cover defence – usually in the shape of Gary Armstrong – invariably snuffed out the threat before it got too serious. But if it hadn't been for Gary I shouldn't have been surprised if we had been 30 points adrift at the interval. Then, noteworthy to the last, Fin found himself in the headlines again. He head-butted the All Black hooker Sean Fitzpatrick. It looked absolutely dreadful afterwards on telly but the TV pictures didn't tell the whole story. What they didn't show was that Fitzpatrick was dancing a fandango on John Jeffrey's head at the time. It was this to which Fin had taken grave exception and which had led to delivery of the old Glasgow Kiss.

The other talking point of the game was Gavin's cavalier treatment of Richard Loe. Gav had just missed a relatively simple kick at goal and wasn't in the best of fettle when he fielded a high ball and ran it straight back upfield. He had obviously made up his mind that nobody, but nobody, was going to stand in his way. Loe, at 17 stones not exactly a shrinking violet, was shoulder-charged out of the way as if he were a seven-stone weakling. The affrontery of it! The aggrieved and indignant look on Loe's face as he picked himself off the deck was a real treat.

I was happier with our performance in the second half and we were still in with a shout right up until the final moments when Walter Little went over for the only try of the game. I was very frustrated by the circumstances of the All Black score. We had been awarded a penalty inside our own 22 and, without asking me what I wanted done with it, Craig chose to run it rather than putting the ball safely downfield. It was never really on, the ball went loose and, in a trice, Little was in for the try. They won 13-6 and we had still to notch up our first win over the Kiwis in 16 encounters. End of competition. But not quite.

We had thoroughly enjoyed it. Despite the injuries and the pressures that I felt I had been under it had been something which was good to be involved in. We had done what, I think, had been expected of us and to come fourth in the world has to be gratifying. It wasn't our doing that we played most of our games at Murrayfield. However, we made the most of the good hand that we had been dealt. To appreciate that this need not necessarily have been the case one need look no further than Wales where the Welsh side played all of their games on the Arms Park, and look what happened to them!

We had been staying as a team at Bristol for the Cardiff game and afterwards we were east-bound for London. All four of the semi-finalists were invited to the final at Twickenham and we decided to make the most of what remained of our World Cup. We arrived in London on the Thursday before the final and arrangements had been made for us to attend a West End Show. Unfortunately it turned out to be quite the worst show that it has ever been my misfortune to see and so a few of us left early and went to a nearby pub. The evening had begun badly but rapidly transformed itself into one of those good nights out that you couldn't plan.

We moved on to a pub in Cambridge Circus. It was a lovely evening and we sat outside – Paris style – at pavement tables. Soon, a sing-song started. A gorgeous-looking Swedish girl gave a rendition of an unintelligible Swedish song and we responded in kind. The singing seemed to attract more customers and the manager astutely decided that this was good for business and so he kept on supplying us with free ale.

Then the cabaret began. Our revelry was interrupted by what seemed to be a running gang-fight. Groups of youths, each knocking seven bells out of each other, were running up and down the street. Soon, the police arrived and the youths ran off. One was just running past our table when a female police officer brought him to the deck with a copy-book tackle around the ankles. The WPC, with her eyes shut tight, was hanging on to the struggling yob's legs as if her life depended on it; whereupon I jumped on top of him, closely followed by Fin. To paraphase Humphrey Bogart the guy must have wondered why, of all the 'gin joints' in London, he had chosen to become involved in an affray when the Scottish rugby team were in residence. By now the villain had decided that further resistance was useless and agreed to go quietly with the WPC.

Having discharged our duties as model citizens we then decamped for Chinatown where the evening was brought to a close with a superb Chinese meal. It was one of those spontaneous and hugely enjoyable evenings that will linger in the memory for years. The following day we had a touch-rugby tournament at Richmond where we were the guests of London Scottish before meeting up with wives and girlfriends for a dinner on the Friday evening. We used the occasion to honour two of Scottish rugby's most influential and faithful servants. Coaches Jim Telfer and Derrick Grant were retiring after a decade of service at the 'sharp end' where, with limited resources, they fashioned teams which could hold their own with the best in the world.

We were keen to mark their departure in fitting manner. Normally, on Tour, the players' kitty – basically beer money – is augmented by the sale of unofficial Tour T-shirts and so on. Because this had been an internal 'Tour' there hadn't been the opportunity to become involved in this kind of fund-raising. Nevertheless, we did have some cash in the kitty and it was decided to spend it on watches for Derrick and Jim. That was the least we could have done for the sterling service which the pair of them had provided over the years.

The following day we were off to Twickenham for the grand finale. When we arrived at the ground we nailed our colours firmly to the mast by buying Aussie hats and scarves and were amazed to see the huge number of 'Jocks' wearing kilts and gold Wallaby jerseys.

It was a superb occasion with a real cosmopolitan atmosphere but not a great game. As I've already written, England were more or less conned into altering their style of play for the final. The Wallabies were a very impressive side. That was obviously the first time in the entire competition that I had seen them in the flesh. They were a side devoted to total rugby who managed to cover up their lack of a genuine number eight forward. I don't think there's much doubt that if a fully fit Tim Gavin had been around then the Aussies would have been truly invincible. However, they were very worthy winners and there's no doubt that the Wallaby world championship will have given a huge boost to the game in Australia where, traditionally, it has come a poor third after Aussie Rules and Rugby League. And that can only be good for the future worldwide development of the game.

The 1987 World Cup was my first experience of touring with a Scotland side and, to this day, I remain very much of the opinion that New Zealand is still the number one destination for a rugby tour. I was very much a new boy on the Scotland scene, having broken through into the national side just the previous season. The whole concept of a World Cup competition was new too. Nobody really knew what to expect, but at the outset, at least, we treated the adventure very much like any other Tour.

The trip began badly when our scheduled 28-hour flight to Auckland via Los Angeles and Honolulu was diverted, because of bad weather, to Christchurch. There we refuelled and charged back to Auckland. By the time we checked in at our Auckland hotel we had been on the move for 40 hours. We barely had time to get our bearings in Auckland when coach Derrick Grant decreed that the best way of getting the air-miles out of the system was a light run around and within a couple of hours of arriving in New Zealand we were out on the training paddock. That was an early indication of just how seriously we were taking this trip into the rugby unknown.

The country itself was a rugby players' paradise. Reared as we had been on the Scottish game where rugby plays a poor second fiddle to association football, it came as a pleasant surprise to find that in New Zealand rugby is, often quite literally, the only game in town. All Black rugby stars are revered in the same way that soccer stars are back home. In pubs and clubs and even in taxis, rugby was invariably the sole topic of conversation. To those of us who hadn't been in New Zealand before it was a real eye-opener.

The attention which the game attracts in New Zealand, though, does have its down-side. We were keen to get in some good training sessions well away from the prying eyes of the media, which was why the entire Scottish party ended up in jail. Through the good offices of an expatriate Scot who worked with the NZ prison service the squad were introduced to the delights of Christchurch's Paparua Prison. Sometimes Derrick Grant's training sessions felt like rugby's equivalent of 'doing time'. Now we were behind bars almost for real. The jail's playing-field facilities were excellent, though, and it was a worthwhile venture. We returned a couple of times and at the end of each session the inmates would serve us with rejuvenating mugs of tea. They seemed pleasant enough chaps and we asked what they were in for. We were told that they were murderers and rapists. It was quite an eye-opener. That brief experience of life on the inside was certainly a reminder to us all that we would have to get our income-tax returns in on time!

The party was captained by Colin Deans, the exceptional Hawick hooker. He would retire at the conclusion of the campaign with 52 Caps to his name, equalling the record set by his fellow Hawick player, Jim Renwick. Colin was a prop forward's delight in that he had the knack of still being able to strike at the ball even when the front row as a whole was in some difficulty. He also, of course, was one of the best throwers-in of lineout ball that the game has ever seen.

We were coached by Derrick and Ian McGeechan and managed by Bob Munro. It was a well balanced party of young up-and-comers and old heads. We were confident that we would be able to give a good account of ourselves.

From a Scottish point of view one of the major talking points of the World Cup build-up had been the knee injury sustained by our stand-off John Rutherford. Rud had injured his left knee during an unsanctioned trip to the Bermuda Rugby Festival along with fellow World Cup party members Iain Paxton, Iwan Tukalo and Matt Duncan. The SRU had imposed a cut-off date after which players going on the NZ trip were to abstain from further rugby. The four of them would probably have got away with it had not John arrived back in the UK on crutches.

Ironically, the injury, which was ultimately diagnosed as a ruptured anterior cruciate ligament, had occurred as John was attempting to side-step Iwan who was playing for the opposition. There had been no physical contact and the knee just went as John came off his left foot. In the period between the injury and our setting off for the World Cup, John had undergone intensive physiotherapy and we were all keeping our fingers crossed that the knee would hold out. John was a world-class fly-half and it was a tragedy, as we now know, that the injury should have cut short his career.

Our injury worries were further compounded when, in a rather bizarre training session with the Irish squad who were also in Auckland, Scott Hastings pulled up with a leg injury and, privately, there were doubts about his fitness for the impending fray.

We were drawn in the same pool as Romania, Zimbabwe and France. We weren't done any favours when the draw dictated that our opening game was to be against the French in Christchurch. We were going straight in at the deep end but we were confident that we could give Daniel Dubroca's Frenchmen a good game. The feeling was that a win against the French would open up all kinds of possibilities and that thereafter the sky really would be the limit.

Very early on, Derek White put us four points up with a try. We were just settling in to our stride when John rushed in to collect a high-ball after a lineout. He was tackled by Philippe Sella and ended in a heap clutching his left knee and grimacing in pain. He was stretchered off and out of the World Cup. He had lasted just six minutes. There were no recriminations, just sadness that such a talented player had been denied the opportunity to display his gifts on a world stage. John was utterly distraught and one of the saddest sights I have ever seen in rugby was that of John sitting huddled against a pitch-side advertising hoarding as he waited for an ambulance to take him to hospital.

Doug Wyllie moved from centre to stand-off and Kelso's Alan Tait – a powerful player who would later sign professional forms with Widnes and go on to play International Rugby League – came on to win his first Scottish Cap.

Despite the disruption caused by Rud's injury we stuck to the task and really got in amongst the French. At half-time we led 13-6 through Derek's try and three Gavin Hastings' penalty goals. The French had managed just a couple of penalties and that was a fair reflection of how the opening period had gone.

We were still confident as the game kicked off for the second half and even tries by Pierre Berbizier and Sella didn't particularly knock us out of our stride. Gavin had another penalty goal and with just ten minutes to go we were 16-14 in front.

Then, disaster. You would have thought that we would have learned our lesson from our Five Nations' tussle with the French at Murrayfield the previous year. It had been my first International match and Berbizier had scored virtually from the kick-off. Gavin's starting kick had gone out on the full and we had all trooped back for the scrummage, not noticing that the French had taken a quick throw-in and scampered away for a soft try. The lesson should have been 'never trust the French'.

In Christchurch they sneaked in again. Matt Duncan had been penalised for not releasing the ball. He was bleeding from a nasty head cut. We were distracted as he sought medical attention. Simultaneously, Berbizier was on the sideline being attended to by the French physio. While all of this was going on Serge Blanco took a surreptitious tap penalty and ran in to score unopposed. We were not amused.

We were trailing by four points and mounted one final effort to claw back into contention. With just moments to go Matt bulldozed in

Scotland representative début: Scotland 'B' v Ireland 'B' at The Greenyards in 1983. My Press 'reviews' were not entirely flattering

The 1985 Scotland 'B' squad.
Back row: *Me, Jerry Macklin, Billy Murray, Gavin Hastings, Derek Turnbull, Ian McKie, Jeremy Campbell-Lamerton, Hugh Parker, Ronnie Nichol, Andrew Ker, Matt Duncan, Brian Hislop*
Front row: *Brian Edwards, Iwan Tukalo, Alan Tait, Bob Hogarth, Rob Cunningham, Stuart Johnston, Keith Murray, Colin Gass, Paul Hogarth*

Scotland's international trial match in January, 1986. The underdog Reds won by the spectacular margin of 41-15 and six new Caps was the result.

Colin Deans with his six new Caps for the 1986 game against France: Fin Calder and me, Scott Hastings, Colin, Matt Duncan, Jeremy Campbell-Lamerton and Gavin Hastings

John Jeffrey in the thick of things against the Irish in 1987. Help, though, is at hand

The Scotland squad for the 1987 World Cup.
Back row: *Gary Callander, Scott Hastings, Finlay Calder, John Jeffrey, Jeremy Richardson, Jeremy Campbell-Lamerton, Derek White, Derek Turnbull, Gavin Hastings, Alex Brewster, Doug Wyllie*
Middle row: *SRU secretary Bill Hogg, Dr Clark Sharpe, Norrie Rowan, Peter Dods, Roger Baird, Alan Tait, Matt Duncan, Greig Oliver, Iwan Tukalo, David Sole, SRU technical administrator John Roxburgh, physiotherapist David McLean*
Front row: *Coach Derrick Grant, Iain Paxton, Roy Laidlaw, Alan Tomes, manager Bob Munro, Colin Deans (capt.), SRU president Dr Doug Smith, John Rutherford, Iain Milne, Keith Robertson, coach Ian McGeechan*

Bloodied but never bowed: the Bear, aka Iain Milne

The Scotland front row against Ireland in 1988. Norrie Rowan, Gary Callander and me

We got our Grand Slam season underway with a convincing win over the Fijians at Murrayfield in 1989

Jim Telfer and Ian McGeechan, coaching architects of two Scottish Grand Slams

Damian Cronin towers above this lineout from our Grand Slam season game against France, 1990

*Finlay Calder, typically direct in his running, against Western Samoa during the
1991 World Cup*

Sailing during the 1989 British Lions tour to Australia. With Robert Norster, Gareth Chilcott, Brian Moore and Kevin Murphy

The other team: with Jane, Gemma and Jamie

for the equalising try and it was down to Gavin, with a difficult conversion, to try to win the game for us. The ball flew just wide of the posts and we had tied 20-20. It had been a great game of rugby and, as it turned out, one of the best matches of the entire tournament.

The concept of a World Cup competition had been born in the Antipodes. From the early Eighties, New Zealand and Australia had been pushing the International Board along the path which led to a truly global competition. In view of the impetus that the concept gained from Anzac determination it was only right and proper that the inaugural competition should have been held in the two Antipodean countries. I can't speak for Australia because all of our matches took place in New Zealand but it was clear to us that the competition had really captured the imagination of the New Zealand public.

I've been back to New Zealand twice on rugby business since that first trip in 1987 and never cease to be amazed at the similarities which exist between Scotland and the land of the long white cloud. There seems to be an affinity between the two nations which, I suppose, isn't really surprising when one considers the very large number of New Zealand families who are proud to claim a Scottish heritage. On the 1987 trip my mum and Jane decided to come along, not just because I was making my touring debut with Scotland, but because we have a number of relatives out there that Mum was determined to visit. Jane was in the early stages of pregnancy and, sadly, started to miscarry. She eventually lost the baby on our return home but at the time we were very appreciative of the assistance given by Dr Clark Sharpe, the SRU medic on the trip. I'm willing to wager that Clark's emergency visit to Jane's hotel was the first time that a rugby tour doctor has ever been called out to deal with a threatened miscarriage!

Our next outing was against the Zimbabweans in Wellington. The game represented Colin Deans' 50th Cap, a real milestone. As a contest it was a bit one-sided, as many of the matches in that first World Cup were. We led 40-6 at half-time and eased off a bit in the second period when Zimbabwe got more into the game, yet we still won 60-21.

Afterwards in the dressing-room, Colin missed one of the greatest speeches of all time. To mark his 50th Cap we had bought him a salver and four goblets. The Jed scrum-half Roy Laidlaw was to make the presentation and to preface it with a few well-chosen remarks. Roy really turned it on. He reminded us all how superb a player Colin was and how, both on and off the field, he had been a great ambassador for Scottish rugby. Sadly, in the confusion, Colin never heard a word of it. He had been outside doing after-match press interviews. Roy then had to do a 'take-two'. As was bound to be the case, his second effort hadn't been a patch on the first. Nevertheless, Colin appreciated the gesture.

Romania was the next hurdle that had to be negotiated. Because of the knock-out nature of the competition it was still imperative that we kept on winning. We moved to Dunedin – the Edinburgh of the Southern Hemisphere – where the match took place at Carisbrook. Again, we played hard to win and were leading 33-7 at the interval before eventually winning 55-28.

For the Hastings brothers the game offered mixed fortunes. Scott, who had never really recovered from that leg injury sustained in the training session against the Irish, was making his competition debut. He pulled up with a hamstring gone after just 20 seconds and was out of the campaign. At the other extreme, Gavin had a field day with a world-record haul of 27 points from two tries, eight conversions and a penalty goal. However, it was one of the shortest-lived records on record, when, within a couple of hours, Didier Cambarabero supplanted Gavin with 30 points in France's 70-12 win over the Zimbabweans.

We were now into the quarter-finals and our 'reward' was a match against the All Blacks on their own patch back in Christchurch. That was always going to be difficult. We aimed to keep it simple; to play the Kiwis at their own game. This was my first confrontation with the mighty All Blacks. They have a mystique and an aura which is unique in world rugby. They are, almost always, genuinely hard men. They are invariably rangy, raw-boned and made to look even bigger by the intimidating nature of their 'all black' strip. The addition of the Polynesian element acts as the catalyst to draw the whole thing together.

We immediately found ourselves under pressure and only some superb defensive play kept the score down to a respectable 9-3 at the interval. But it was hard going. The All Blacks, as they very often are, were quite 'lippy' into the bargain. The Auckland wing John Kirwan was particularly heavily into 'sledging', as the cricketers call it. He was making sarcastic comments about our early trip home. The following year we had revenge of sorts when Finlay Calder was playing for an invitation outfit at a seven-a-side tournament in Australia. He put in a crunching tackle on Kirwan who complained: 'Hey. That was a bit late.'

'Aye, about a year too bloody late!' replied Fin.

We struggled for possession and inevitably our defensive wall cracked. Alan Whetton and John Gallagher got tries, both converted by Grant Fox who also had three more penalty goals. I felt that 30-3 flattered the New Zealanders but they had given a powerful display of pressure rugby. So that was it. We were out and on our way home which was via Los Angeles and a visit to Disneyland, courtesy of the SRU. It was a gesture much appreciated by us all. On the rugby front, we had played both of the ultimate finalists and given a tolerably good account of ourselves. On a personal level, the trip had whetted my appetite for touring with the national side. I had thoroughly enjoyed the 24 hours a day immersion in rugby that touring provides and I was hungry for more.

CHAPTER 11

THE MONEY GAME

I Almost Quit

JUST BEFORE the start of the 1992 Five Nations' Championship I was on the brink of quitting. After more than 20 years in the game I felt so disillusioned that I just wanted to get out. A number of circumstances had combined to drive me to this lowest of low ebbs in my rugby career. I had taken stick in some quarters for recharging my batteries on a family ski-ing holiday rather than taking part in the annual Murrayfield Trial. Then, as one of the players' representatives, I was in the midst of ongoing and vexatious professionalism negotiations with the Scottish Rugby Union. Finally, word began to filter through that I was the subject of a rather nasty whispering campaign by at least one senior Murrayfield committee man.

I was doing a TV interview when, at the close of the session, a journalist whom I have known for years and whom I trust implicitly, said that just the other day my name had come up during a casual discussion with a senior SRU man. I was, according to this SRU chap, 'a cancer at the heart of Scottish rugby'. I was considerably upset. What angered me wasn't just the sentiment but the terminology used to express it. My initial reaction was one of 'Why the hell do I bother?'

By the time I got home I was seething with anger and indignation. The Five Nations' Championship was almost upon us but I was so hurt and upset that someone apparently in a position of real power and responsibility at Murrayfield should be saying such things behind my back, that I had more or less decided to chuck it all in.

I discovered the identity of the SRU man involved some months later. I'm not going to name him. There's no point. His comments were made against an unpleasant backdrop of ongoing negotiations with the SRU on the question of what the players could or couldn't earn as a result of their off-the-pitch activities. The negotiating role hadn't been one which I had particularly wanted but as captain I had felt it to be one of my duties. Similarly, at a time when the whole question of rugby professionalism was exciting the media my views as captain were quite often sought.

The upshot was that I often appeared in the papers as an advocate for easing the financial restictions placed upon players. This, obviously, had not gone down well at Murrayfield with some officials and committee men.

Then another acquaintance told me that he had been speaking to a selector who, during their conversation, had been voicing serious doubts about my ability to hold my place in the side. There was obviously a school of thought within Murrayfield which considered that Sole was over the hill. It was presumably no coincidence that a story appeared in the Edinburgh evening newspaper which suggested that my days were numbered and that I was about to be sacked as captain. People are, of course, entitled to their views but perhaps, too, they should make these views personally known to the target of their attack. If somebody in a position of power at Murrayfield felt that my game wasn't what it had been or that I wasn't performing well as captain then he should have come to me and told me face to face rather than gossip about me behind my back. We had, after all, just a couple of months beforehand reached the semi-finals of the World Cup. That wasn't a bad achievement and it wasn't easy by any means.

I was on the point of writing out my resignation note but before doing so I decided that I would discuss the situation with the Scottish coaches, Ian McGeechan and Dougie Morgan. I informed them both what I had been told from two separate sources. Both coaches are men that I respect and admire. If they had told me that I was over the top or that I had become an embarrassment due to the professionalism issue then I would have gone there and then. They both told me to forget it. They said that I had their confidence and that they wanted me to carry on.

I followed their advice and played throughout the 1992 Five Nations' campaign. However, the back-biting had left its mark. I had already been in two minds as to whether I would retire after Scotland's summer tour to Australia or whether I should play on for another season and try to make the 1993 British Lions' Tour to New Zealand. I knew that career and family commitments indicated that I should call it a day but up until the 'cancer' jibe there had still been an outside chance that I would have stuck around for the 1993 Tour.

The whole professionalism issue is one which has caused a great deal of upset within the game these past ten years and more. But until my involvement at the sharp end through the negotiations with the SRU I had no real idea just how strongly many people felt about it.

During the time that I have been involved in the game it has changed out of all recognition. It may still look much the same to the casual observer but behind the scenes, and especially at international level, the intensity of approach and preparation has reached quite staggering proportions.

To survive at international level the players and coaches have to be utterly professional in their outlook and approach. We are professionals but for the small matter of money. We train as hard as professional sportsmen. We play as hard as professional sportsmen. And we are expected to make the same all-encompassing commitment and sacrifice to the game as professional sportsmen. International rugby players are the poor relations of sport as it is played at the highest echelons.

We are involved in a multi-million pound industry. I am talking here about the international game and not the grassroots. I am talking about the tours, the world cups, the international seven-a-side tournaments, the Five Nations' Championship. This is big business. Tour itineraries are arranged so that the rugby authorities can fill stadia and make more money from the game. Just as the former Australian coach Alan Jones predicted several years ago, the players have indeed become mobile money-makers.

The whole rugby union professionalism debate is riddled with hypocrisy. At a very elementary level the definition of the true amateur must be someone who plays but pays his own expenses. We are, therefore, all professionalised to a degree. However, the situation is worse than that. Much worse.

By that simplistic definition you are either an amateur or you are not. As things stand at the moment, though, international rugby players are neither one thing or another. We are neither fish nor fowl.

We hear so much about how rugby union is the last bastion of the true Corinthian ethic, or that it is the only international sport where the ethos of the gentleman amateur holds sway. It is this purity, it is argued, which makes the game what it still is today. We are told that it is this lack of professional cynicism which makes rugby union such an attractive vehicle for commercial sponsors.

Well, I am sorry to disillusion anyone who genuinely believes this to be the case, but all of the foregoing is just so much hot air. The real hypocrisy and the real cynicism is displayed not by the players who are being paid but by those who know perfectly well what is going on but choose to turn a Nelsonian eye to it.

Rugby union is most definitely not the last true bastion of the Corinthian ethic. For instance, when players spend their close-season turning out for Italian clubs they do so not because of a passion for pasta but because it is a highly lucrative exercise and because in whatever guise it might appear, they are in receipt of copious supplies of lira.

This is not just rugby folklore. In a court of law it might be dismissed as hearsay evidence but I have spoken with players who are involved in the Italian game and I have no reason to doubt what they tell me. Even in rugby, market forces prevail. A prop forward might get, say, £10,000 plus board and lodgings for a season's work. For a match-winning fly-half or a crowd-pulling threequarter the sky would be the limit. Italian rugby, despite its lowly status on the world stage, is well sponsored. The clubs are thus able to import the big money stars from abroad. I can't prove it. It's not my job to prove it. It is, though – however much the authorities would like to believe that it isn't the case – a fact.

Many of the players involved in the Italian game are household names. They are professionals but I am not condemning them. If they can get away with it then good luck to them. The double standards come in when the game's legislators choose to ignore abuses like these and pretend that everything is rosy when in fact it isn't.

It's fairly well known that the French, too, pay their players. Again, I have no documentary proof. It's not my job to go around collecting proof that players have professionalised themselves. However, the fact that French clubs pay their players is so commonly known within the game that it hardly needs remarking on. French clubs not only pay their players a weekly wage, they also pay them bonuses for a win. The wage-scale is borrowed almost in its entirety from rugby league. Again, I am sure that the authorities know this but, once again, they choose to turn a blind eye.

Of course, the French are not going to admit that they pay their players any more than will the Welsh, but professionalism is rife within the rugby union game in Wales as well. An international colleague of mine received a very handsome offer from a top Welsh club to go and play for them. When I played for Bath we had long-standing fixture relationships with Welsh clubs. In many instances Welsh club players from the colts to the first XV were being paid and it was well known that the international stars were being paid very handsomely indeed. A Welsh international player of relatively recent vintage reputedly switched clubs because he was being paid £200 a match at one and £300 a match at the other.

The hypocrisy of those supposedly in charge of the game is appalling. Rugby at the top level is now a shamateur sport. The game is in the same situation as athletics was before the athletes went legitimate and established trust funds and as tennis was before it went open.

I think that the International Board chooses to turn a blind eye rather than conduct a thorough-going investigation because there is too much at stake. If they were to carry out a proper confidential inquiry then a real can of worms would be opened up.

If the International Rugby Football Board and the individual unions accepted that in almost every rugby-playing nation players are currently being paid then the situation would in all likelihood have to be legitimised.

And lest it be thought that the underhand payments are confined to our colonial cousins or to Five Nations' clubs where we might all have expected it to be going on in any case, the practice comes right home to us here in Scotland. I know of a handful of players in the Scottish game who are paid for playing. Again, no names, no pack drill. I will not break their trust by naming them or their clubs but they are being paid and that is a fact.

The problem is this. I know that it is going on and I presume that the authorities know that it is going on (and if they don't then they should), but I don't know what we should be doing about it. I have no ready-made solutions. I think the concept of a player's trust fund, along the lines of that set up for international squad members at Murrayfield, is something that should be looked at. Players who were considered to be crowd-pullers or match-winners could perhaps command a match fee which would be paid into their trust and they wouldn't be able to touch the cash until they were of pensionable age, say 35.

Of course, in Scotland if every club paid their players then the game would soon be bankrupt. The Scottish game just doesn't have the commercial infrastructure to support such a scheme. Maybe the players who turned out in District games could benefit from a trust fund scenario but it would be unrealistic to think that it could go much further than that. I feel that there is still a lot that could be done by aggressive marketing of the game in Scotland to increase the amount of revenue which the game attracts but even then it is unlikely that across-the-board payments could be made to, say, every player in the first division.

To those who still say that rugby union has something special – which it has – and that this something special can only be attributed to its amateur status, I say that the amateur status is a myth and that it no longer exists. It hasn't existed for years and years. The abuses which I have referred to have been going on for a very long time. The game has passed on from being an amateur game and it passed that point many, many years ago.

I think we all had our eyes opened during the inaugural World Cup competition in 1987. There on the TV screen, quite blatantly and for all to see, was Andy Dalton, the All Black captain, endorsing the off-road capabilities of a little four-wheel-drive tractor-cum-buggy. This was at a time when the commercial and sponsorship situation in the northern hemisphere was screwed down tight. The Kiwis were driving a coach and horses, not to mention Andy Dalton's little tractor, through the amateurism regulations. The letter of the law might not have been breached because the advert didn't actually mention that Dalton was the All Black skipper, but the spirit of the law had been rent asunder.

This was really the first time that we had seen just what was going on elsewhere. The cry went up that we all wanted to be treated equally and in the three or four years which followed, the northern hemisphere players have been campaigning in order to enjoy the same endorsement type deals that have abounded in New Zealand throughout the mid to late Eighties.

The time is now right for the authorities to grasp the nettle and to bring everything out into the open. Either the match fee payments should be legitimised so that we can all play on a level playing field or they should be banned and rigorously policed. Either way everybody would be aware of what was going on and the blatant shamateurism which exists just now could be averted. It often seems to me that critics are more upset by the efforts of those who try to nudge the unions along the way towards a fair recompense for the huge efforts that inter-national players are now expected to put in, than by the blatant profes-sionalism of those who accept cash for playing.

I have always believed that the game is about players and those involved at the sharp end. We are only there for a short space of time. We are passing through, if you like. But what is given to the game in that period, in terms of time, commitment, and self-sacrifice, is immense.

I love the game, I have devoted almost all of my adult life to it. It has been a great privilege to play for Scotland and to have captained Scotland and the very last thing that I have ever wanted was to be paid for playing. Playing for Scotland has brought with it many perks and spin-off activities but it has also been very costly in terms of the reduced amount of time that I have been able to devote to my family and to my career. Most people have two important facets to their lives: their families and their careers. An international sportsman has a third factor to contend with – his sport. An international rugby player is in all but name a professional sportsman. I trained four nights a week. I also had club training sessions, district training sessions and international training sessions – more often than not over a weekend. There are only 24 hours in a day and it is simply not possible to pay proper attention to all of these three facets and give each the attention which it deserves. It was my choice to pursue a career in international rugby. But it was not my choice that the game should develop in such a way that to compete on equal terms with other countries the players have to devote such a huge slice of their lives to it. Even in the seven years I have been involved with the Scottish team there has been a massive increase in the demands being made of the players.

The increasing 'professionalism' on the field and the massively upgraded levels of fitness required to play the game at international level have just developed over the years. It has been a never-ending process of evolution which has swept the coaches and the players along in its wake. We have, in a sense, all become prisoners of the incessant quest for higher standards.

The trend has percolated down to the lower levels of the game. It is with some horror that I learn that the 1991–92 Scottish league champions, Melrose, coached by one of the world's most respected coaches, Jim Telfer, have felt it necessary to introduce a Sunday coaching session to their schedule in addition to the regular Tuesday and Thursday night get-togethers which are the norm in Scotland. No doubt other clubs will feel that if they are to wrest the title from Melrose then they will have to follow suit. For younger players with no family ties this will not be a particular hardship but for those with wives and young families it represents another encroachment into one of the other two facets of a rugby players' life. And so it goes on. The demands on time and commitment are increased season by season and year by year.

Of course, by making these comments I lay myself wide open to the charge that if I didn't like it then I shouldn't have become involved. Or that there were others standing by more than ready to fill my boots if I didn't like what was on offer. In fact this was the exact tactic employed by a senior RFU official at Twickenham when faced with outspoken comments by members of the England team. But surely that misses the point. The game has changed out of all recognition. It is now more commercially orientated than it has ever been. For better or for worse, the world has changed.

In the business world people are making their mark at a younger and younger age. Sure, firms still enjoy employing international rugby players and the benefits are obvious to both the player and the employer. But the downside is that it is not possible to devote the time necessary for genuine career advancement while simultaneously coping with the wants and needs of a young family and a virtually 'full-time' rugby career. The equation just doesn't balance.

The sport's governing body – the International Rugby Football Board – recognised that the professionalism issue had to be addressed when it met in Edinburgh towards the end of 1990. It was a timely meeting because with the second World Cup coming up the following year the sport was going to find itself under more commercial pressure than it had ever experienced before.

The main impetus for change came from the southern hemisphere unions. Despite the more relaxed attitude towards professionalism, they had seen their game suffer at the hands of rugby league which was attracting big name players to the legitimately paid ranks. It was reported that, just in case any of the home unions proved difficult, the New Zealand representatives had come armed with a dossier containing the names of New Zealand players who had been paid to turn out for clubs in the UK.

Whether or not the Kiwis had to use their allegedly damning dossier I have no way of knowing, but the result of the IRFB's deliberations was the 'communication for reward' dictat which meant that players could legitimately be paid for various off-pitch activities and for the endorsement of a variety of products just so long as they weren't rugby-orientated.

In essence, what happened next was that it was left up to individual unions to interpret the IRFB ruling. The problem with this was that the 'level playing field' which had been the Board's intention was denied from the outset. Effectively, this ensured that the southern hemisphere unions, plus France and Wales (which had also traditionally operated under the threat of rugby league cash luring away international stars) could go one way, while the more conservative unions such as the RFU, the Irish union and our own SRU could go another.

Towards the end of 1990 and during the run-up to the World Cup competition, the commercial side of the game was exercising many minds. I wouldn't like to give the impression that it was continuously at the forefront of the Scotland squad's mind because that wasn't the case at all. Nevertheless, we appreciated that we were operating in the market place and that, in the buzz phrase of the times, market forces would prevail. We discussed the possibilities with our counterparts in England who were further down the road than we were north of the border.

Brian Moore, the England hooker, told us that the English lads were setting up their own company and that any commercial monies which accrued from off-pitch activities during their 1991 Five Nations' Championship campaign and the World Cup competition would be channelled into that.

We talked the issue through amongst ourselves and decided that we, too, should go down this route. So, with the full cognisance and backing of the SRU, we set about appointing an agent to tend the commercial activities of the squad.

Myself as captain plus Iain Milne, John Jeffrey and Gavin Hastings as the team's 'senior pros', along with SRU secretary Bill Hogg and team manager Dunc Paterson, held a number of meetings when we talked to the various contenders. Basically, it was our choice and we decided to appoint the Glasgow firm Proscot. The choice was announced at a Murrayfield press conference with senior committee members alongside us and they fully endorsed our choice. So far as we were concerned Proscot were now looking after our commercial interests and it would be up to them to liaise with the SRU on interpretation of the IRFB regulations and hopefully to bring in some revenue. Having done that we felt we could then concentrate one hundred per cent on preparation for the World Cup.

At that stage it was very much an untested market. We were sailing in uncharted commercial waters and we had no idea how much, if any, money there was to be made. Two of the major deals that Proscot tried to secure for us involved an association with Famous Grouse whisky who were already one of the tournament sponsors, and with Tennent's, the brewers. The deals were worth substantial sums of money, perhaps totalling £90,000. I had made it plain, in my capacity as captain and as the player responsible for liaison with Proscot, that because the competition itself was now very close, I would not allow commercial interests to interfere once the squad was 'in camp' and when preparation was underway in earnest. Whatever the Famous Grouse and Tennent's people had in mind specifically vis-à-vis the squad's involvement with the product, they appeared to be quite happy to go along with that. Therefore, the next stage was to put the arrangements to the SRU for sanction.

Much to the dismay of Proscot and subsequently the players, both deals were vetoed by the SRU. The reasons given were that they were likely to conflict with existing sponsorship arrangements and impinge upon player preparation time.

It was, to put it mildly, very frustrating to see these opportunities fly out of the window. Personally, I never got bitter and twisted about it but my impression at the time was that the SRU never really had their hearts in it. Nothing that has happened since has led me to modify that view. I'm sure that had they really wanted to then they could have moved with more speed and determination, but the lingering impression was that they were involved only as the most unwilling of participants and that there were few tears shed at Murrayfield when the players' commercial hopes began to unravel.

I think the problem was that the SRU were quite happy to see the boys earn a few quid here and a few quid there from personal appearances and such like but when it came down to the players attracting some serious money in the form of five-figure sums from internationally known companies then it began to upset the established order and, not least, existing sponsorship arrangements. If Tennent's had come in with a package to sponsor the Scotland World Cup squad then, understandably, their rivals, Scottish Brewers, who are already handsome cash providers for Scottish rugby, would have been none too pleased. If that was the case then I can understand the dilemma. That is why I think the whole cash thing has, even yet, not been thought through properly and why I think that when the SRU were giving us their blessing to appoint our own agents and to trawl for cash before the World Cup, they certainly had not fully considered the implications.

There is a further problem in defining just who the team 'belongs' to. In a supposedly amateur game does the team 'belong' to the SRU or are the individual players (within the confines of what would be reasonably expected of them as representatives of their country) free agents, able to do virtually as they please? That's a tricky question and one to which I don't have a satisfactory answer. There is no doubt, though, that there were individuals within the SRU who had their eyes opened to the possibilities when Proscot were working on the players' behalf. They recognised that, maybe, the players were marketable in their own right and they saw the players slipping out of SRU control.

The whole experience left me quite disillusioned. At the end of the World Cup tournament after battling our way through to fourth place and after the most intensely commercialised competition the rugby world has ever seen, the 26 members of the Scottish World Cup squad made £368.80 apiece. Outwith rugby, not all squad members were equally placed financially. Of course, we all like to have just that bit more and I'm not denying that there is certainly an attraction in earning extra money which could go towards a family holiday or whatever. However, I have taken much satisfaction from being able to divert substantial sums from whatever I have 'earned' from my rugby, through speeches and personal appearances, to immensely worthwhile causes like the Royal Hospital for Sick Children in Edinburgh. That currently stands at between £3,000 and £4,000. However, other squad members were less fortunately placed and it would have been reasonable had they been able to benefit in a financial sense from the massive commitment which they gave to the squad and to the game, throughout the World Cup and beyond. When our counterparts in the other home unions tell what they earned during their World Cup campaigns – reportedly £6,000 per man in England – it is even more galling to ponder our lost opportunity.

If I am to look on the bright side then I must say that at least we got something out of it and that, hopefully, we have blazed a trail for those who will come after us.

The lowest point in the whole affair, for me at any rate, came in January 1992, just before the start of that season's Five Nations' Championship. The SRU called a meeting at Murrayfield to be attended by all the players and by Scotland's IRFB members Ken Smith and Gordon Masson and committee man Freddie McLeod. The atmosphere was dreadful. It was a mixture of Spanish Inquisition and a class of delinquent pupils being hauled up before the headmaster.

They informed us that there were to be a number of changes. They were going to set up a players' Trust Fund and all commercial deals would be channelled through Murrayfield. Henceforth we would have no more need of agents. I must say I was stunned. I had assumed, wrongly, that we had established a good working relationship with the union and that we were managing to work something out to our mutual benefit.

I have thought about the whole thing quite deeply since and I am convinced that the SRU saw their commercial control of the playing squad slipping away. Proscot had been trying to market the squad almost as a separate entity and, undoubtedly, the SRU perceived dangers in that. What it came down to, again, was the fundamental question of who did the squad belong to?

The SRU said that from there on in, Murrayfield would administer the commercial needs of the players, and to enable that to happen they would require every member of the team to sign a code of conduct, or a 'participation agreement' as it was euphemistically termed. By this time the meeting was becoming quite heavy. You will all have to sign, they said, before you become eligible to play for Scotland against England. The Calcutta Cup match was to take place in just a fortnight's time. In effect the SRU were imposing a contract on the players and they were looking for signatures against the threat of non-selection for a game which was almost upon us.

Their treatment of the players was appalling. It was rude and high-handed and I certainly wasn't going to sign there and then. To have been issued with a contract in such a manner was, I considered, outrageous behaviour. I took it home with me and asked my lawyer to cast his professional eye over it on the players' behalf. I certainly would never have signed such a document in the course of my work without first taking professional advice and I saw no reason why we should be obliged to do so in these circumstances either. We didn't sign it before the Calcutta Cup game as the SRU had demanded as the document seemed to be weighted very heavily in the union's favour. In fact it wasn't signed until that season's Five Nations' Championship was almost over. I wouldn't go so far as to say that these off-stage negotiations acted as a distraction and adversely affected our performance during the Championship but they certainly didn't help.

The code of conduct, headed 'Scottish Rugby Participation Agreement', sets out the obligations of the SRU towards the players and vice-versa. It covers such innocuous matters as the provision of blazers, ties, playing kit, match tickets, post-match banquets and receptions and puts in writing the wide-ranging powers enjoyed by the team manager. It goes on to specify the players' responsibilities regarding cooperation with the SRU's commercial sponsors and charges the signatories to do all within their power to promote the game and its image, the SRU and its interests.

Additionally, the code lays down strict guidelines as to who is permitted to speak to the media and when. It also codifies the formation of the Scottish Rugby International Squad Trust established by the SRU to obtain monies for the benefit of the Scotland rugby union squad from contracts of appearance or communication and other arrangements from which material benefit may be received as permitted under IRFB regulations. Players are not permitted to engage in commercial activities other than those sanctioned by the Trust.

The code also, in the manner of the catch-all Official Secrets' Act, declares that a player should not disclose any privileged or confidential information obtained through his connection with the game. Perhaps, by merely outlining the code's main provisions I have perpetrated a heinous sin. Despite the unavoidable legal jargon employed in the Code and the rather unfortunate feudal nature of the relationship which it portrays as existing between the players and the SRU, I think that if we had to have a Code, and the SRU were intent on imposing one, then it is as good as we could have got. More importantly, I am a firm backer of the Trust concept. Because the trustees cannot be beneficiaries, the players' interests are looked after by Iain Milne along with three trustees appointed by the SRU.

The rather sad legacy of the entire episode was a feeling of dreadful mistrust between the players and the hierarchy. I feel sure that everyone involved will agree that we had established what all parties felt to be a superb relationship between the players and officialdom. However, at a stroke, with their imposition of the code of conduct, the SRU destroyed that and in its place, certainly in the short term, came a rather sour atmosphere of distrust. It struck me that some team officials simply didn't trust the players and their motives. As I've said, there seemed to be a feeling that control of the team was slipping away from Murrayfield and the code of conduct was the rather draconian solution which officialdom decided would redress the status quo.

Shortly after my retirement I received a personal letter from SRU secretary Bill Hogg. In view of all that had gone before, with respect to the painful negotiations which I have just outlined, I was most touched by its tone and its contents. He thanked me on the union's behalf for 'all that I had given and all that I had achieved for Scottish rugby' since my first Cap against the French in 1986.

He added: 'All in Scottish rugby and all in Scotland are disappointed that you are retiring although we can well appreciate your family and business commitments and are only too grateful for the tremendous service which you have given over seven years at a most successful time for Scottish rugby when there has been required ever more commitment from the players due to the world cups; and when the technical standards of the game have steadily increased at Scotland national level, due to the commitment and skills of the players, the coaches, the medics and the management.'

More pertinently, he went on: 'You have obviously, of course, as captain been the spokesman for the National Squad. Obviously the views of the Squad and the Committee do not always agree but you have always very fairly represented the players' views in the most important discussions which have taken place and on which I can reassure you again, despite what some members of the press say, that no member of the Committee holds anything whatsoever against you for so doing. It is always right and best that a spokesman states clearly the views of those whom he is representing.'

Bill continued by expressing thanks for my efforts on the Australian tour and ended by hoping that I would 'return to rugby sooner rather than later through coaching or, dare I say it, Committee work'.

I'm sure that last reference to 'Committee work' was written by Bill with his tongue fixed very firmly in his cheek. Nevertheless, I was greatly heartened by the letter and touched that he should have taken the trouble to write to me.

Ten or 15 years from now, I am sure, we will look back and wonder what all of the fuss was about. There is little doubt that during the negotiations in Scotland all concerned acted in good faith. Each of us did what we considered to be in the best interests of the game. I am convinced, though, that by the turn of the century, legitimate financial reward will be commonplace throughout rugby union. The IRFB have now accepted that money is inextricably linked with the game. Even the longest journey begins with a single step and so far as financial recompense for rugby union players is concerned that single step has now been taken. Currently, the Board has covered its embarrassment with the fig-leaf of 'communication for reward' and the façade of payment for non-rugby related activities. It will simply be a matter of time before the top players go back to signing 'under the counter' deals for boot endorsement and the like. To prevent this, the authorities will have to ensure that the players are sufficiently well recompensed that they do not have to rush off and conduct clandestine negotiations with boot and kit manufacturers. Even when this is done I don't see anyone getting super-rich playing this game. However, I do feel that we stand at the crossroads and if the correct decisions are taken now then we can take a healthy and expanding game into the 21st century.

Sooner rather than later the game will have to decide what it wants. In the world of commerce there ain't any such thing as a free lunch. Accordingly, if the game's administrators decide that they wish the sport to develop and expand in a truly significant manner and that to do this it will take financial advantage of the commercial concerns wishing to become associated with the game, then there will be a price to be paid.

There are those within the game who see their cosy little worlds being upset by the appearance on the horizon of commercially motivated sponsors. But if the game is happy to take the sponsors' money then it must recognise also that most of those who wish to offer commercial backing do not do so because they are altruistic philanthropists. They will want to see a fair commercial return on their investment. The sponsor will want his pound of flesh, and the trick is to satisfy his justifiable demands while at the same time preventing the commercial hoopla which could turn the game into a jamboree of tacky excesses and commercial bad taste. Serious negotiations will have to take place between commercial interests and the various Unions. As the game moves into the 21st century, and bearing in mind the increased commercial pressures which it will find itself under, I am not convinced that the cumbersome committee structure with which most Unions are currently saddled is the ideal format for the efficient administration of what have become, effectively, multi-million pound businesses.

My dealings have been almost exclusively with the SRU but I have no doubt that the other Unions are much the same. They are very strange beasts indeed. They are run by committees and the fundamental constitution dictates that they are run by the clubs. Over the years the SRU's stewardship of Scottish rugby has been, if not always benign, then mostly beneficial. The international rugby grounds at firstly Inverleith and then Murrayfield, where ongoing developments will make it one of the most modern rugby stadia in the world, are evidence of this. However, like it or not, on a day-to-day basis – and not necessarily on the major strategic issues like the expenditure of huge sums of money on stadium development – we are living in a world where communication has become almost instant. The commercial sector operates on a basis of virtually instant electronic communication by fax or electronic mailbox. Commercial decisions are made quickly and without fuss. That is the world into which rugby has found itself pitched. An organisation run by committees and where major decisions are dependent on a predetermined committee cycle is, perhaps, not really in a position to compete with the sharks which sometimes lurk in the commercial shallows.

The SRU secretary is now termed 'chief executive'. He is, nevertheless, still a servant of the committee structure. What is required is for high-powered professional people to be given the authority to take decisions on the Union's behalf without constant reference to the committee. In essence, the Union should be run like a business where the chief executive is just that, the principal executive officer who is entrusted to run the business but who, at the end of the day, is answerable to his board of directors and shareholders.

This approach should be adopted throughout the structure of the Union. The marketing and promotional arm of the SRU should be greatly expanded. Despite the best efforts of those involved I still feel that not enough was done to capitalise on Scotland's 1990 Grand Slam success. Similarly, during the 1991 World Cup, we still tended to hide our light under a barrowload of bushels. We now have rugby development officers throughout the country and this is an extremely worthwhile venture but what I am advocating here is a slick and ongoing marketing exercise designed to take rugby into people's living-rooms by means of professionally done TV and newspaper advertising.

In 1990 when Scotland toured New Zealand as European champions our eyes were opened as to how switched-on the NZ authorities are to the promotional possibilities of marketing and advertising. They ran a series of TV ads with superbly edited shots from our Five Nations' games with the voice-over that the 'Men from the Mountains' had come to New Zealand to challenge the All Blacks. Similar marketing campaigns also exist in Australia with promotional campaigns for the Wallabies. During our 1992 tour there we saw how seriously the Aussies were committed to promotion of the game, with match-day cheerleaders, glossy TV ads and general razzmatazz. Rugby is the national sport in New Zealand but it doesn't occupy such a privileged position just by accident. The NZ rugby authorities work hard at keeping it there. During the run-up to the two Tests the TV advertising campaigns were stepped up with well-shot film of the All Blacks putting in some big hits and all to the signature tune of Thin Lizzie's *The Boys are Back in Town*. Traditionalists might sneer and say that this isn't the kind of image that we want portrayed but there's no doubt that it is extremely effective in terms of keeping the game to the forefront of public consciousness. Rugby in New Zealand is the number one sport and everybody concerned with the game out there is working hard to make absolutely sure that it stays there.

Promotional and marketing activity which focuses on international matches would, I am sure, have a knock-on effect throughout the game. I know that Murrayfield is consistently sold-out and that seats are constantly at a premium, but a properly thought-through marketing campaign could be to the benefit of the sport as a whole. Certainly I'm sure that professional marketing or PR people could turn the District Championship, for instance, into a much more worthwhile and exciting event than it is just now. It is a real 'chicken and egg' situation but I remain firmly convinced that a professionally organised and ongoing marketing campaign which seriously raised the profile of the game in Scotland could only be to the benefit of the sport as a whole.

When I was at Bath I got a great buzz from playing in front of 10,000 people each weekend. You knew when you were slogging it out on the training paddock that at the end of each week there was something really worthwhile in store. In 1896, writing in *The Field* magazine, Dr H. H. Almond, the famous headmaster of Loretto School, near Edinburgh, declared that rugby was for the players and that the preferences of spectators should be treated as a 'very unimportant matter'. The same Dr Almond, who was an umpire at the first Scotland v England match in 1871, wrote too, that idle spectators should not be permitted to watch school rugby games as 'the very sight of loungers' took the spirit out of players. Spectating, he added, was the greatest of all rugby footballing dangers.

Despite the fact that crusty old Dr Almond was writing nearly 100 years ago, I feel that his views find favour even yet with some of the more regressive elements within the game. We have been most remiss in our failure to attract spectators. Apart from the obvious financial benefits which would accrue from getting a lot more 'bums on seats', the enhanced atmosphere which more spectators would provide could only be good for the standard and nature of the game itself. Most club matches in Scotland are played in front of a mere handful of onlookers. Think how much more of a special event Saturday match days would be if we could guarantee that thousands, and not just dozens or hundreds, of spectators were turning out for crucial club games. In spectating and general interest terms, rugby comes in a very poor second after football in Scotland but there is no reason why we should accept that. Sure, it will take time and, no doubt, money and the overturning of entrenched attitudes, but aggressive marketing of the game would, I am sure, pay handsome dividends in the medium and long terms.

More spectators will ultimately mean more players. I am constantly and pleasantly surprised that with 27,000 active rugby players we in Scotland are able to compete with any degree of success at all at International level. We are the real minnows of the game. They have 300,000 players to choose from in England. Even in Japan there are 90,000 playing the game regularly. Compared to England and Wales, the standards of club rugby in Scotland are pretty poor.

The way to progress and to improve the general standard is to emulate the New Zealand system and have your better than average players turning out for their districts, or provinces, on a more regular basis. Much more should be made of the District Championship here in Scotland and efforts should be made to establish regular fixtures with the district or provincial sides from other Five Nations countries and with the top English, Welsh and even French club sides. Sadly, there is no way that even our top Scottish club sides could compete with Harlequins, Wasps, Bath and the rest. However, if games with the Scottish districts could be slotted into their already busy fixture lists then I am sure that they would be highly attractive and competitive matches. In the short term it might be more feasible to organise a Scotland and Ireland inter-provincial championship. That would be of benefit to both countries. We should be striving to put our game on an equal footing with that in the southern hemisphere. In New Zealand the top players will take part in, say, 26 games in a season. They will play a few games for their clubs and then move on to provincial rugby, Ranfurly Shield games and Internationals. They are, though, playing consistently high-grade rugby. In those circumstances it is virtually impossible not to improve the all-round standard of play.

Since returning from the Australian tour in the summer of 1992 I've become convinced that we must follow the lead being given in that country with regard to the development of young players. By means of a 'scouting' system in schools and clubs, promising youngsters are picked out and taken under the wing of the ARFU. A less finely tuned system operates here in Scotland but I would like to see it developed along the lines of the Aussie set-up where the game's future stars are given personal fitness régimes to follow from a very early age. I have worked out in the gym since my late teens but it was all very un-scientific. In Australia, youngsters of a similar age and who are nurtured by the ARFU are given personal programmes to follow and are given every encouragement to stick to that programme and blossom as a result. The Institute of Sport in Canberra is heavily involved in the development of future Aussie rugby stars. Phil Kearns, the Wallaby hooker, is a current player who is playing proof to the worth of a scientific approach to the physiological side of the game.

Players in the southern hemisphere play much less rugby than we do in Europe. That, too, means that the All Blacks and the Australians – at least those who don't spend their summers in Italy or France – are generally much fresher than their northern hemisphere counterparts. At Bath, we had 56 fixtures to fulfil in a season. Throughout September and October there would be games every Saturday and Wednesday. By November the matches would be on Saturdays only and then in December you would have to start adding on Divisional games and in January through to March it would be the Cup and until April there would be Saturday and midweek games again. That's a lot of rugby for your top players.

The situation is not so bad in Scotland. In many respects the Scottish fixture system has a lot to commend it, with the League games and the Inter-District Championship, the Trial and then the Five Nations' Championship. There is a progressive stepping up of the pace. I would like to see, though, a full two months of district games through-out, say November and December. I would scrap the traditional January Trial at Murrayfield. There are so few players in Scotland who have a genuine chance of making the national side that I really don't think it is necessary for the selectors to have to see them in a one-off Trial match. If these players were participating in an extended District programme then the selectors would have ample opportunity to see all of the contenders participating in a higher grade of rugby.

A Cup final in early May would be the perfect way to bring down the curtain on the domestic season. In my experience there is little to equal Cup rugby as a means of sharpening the appetite. There are no second chances in Cup games. You are either still in or you are out. It concentrates the mind wonderfully. I would play it from January to

March, intermingled with the Five Nations' Championship. The Scottish Leagues would still operate from the beginning of the season until, maybe, November when the top players would leave their clubs for their Districts. The Leagues could then continue without them or not as the case may be. The top players would then return to their clubs in January for the start of the Cup competition. Such a structure would maintain the intensity of competition for your more talented players who could put that to good use during the International season and such a season would also satisfy spectators who would be guaranteed high-grade rugby on virtually every weekend of the season.

If you are still with me after what seems, on reflection, to have been rather a serious sermon then, first of all, many thanks for sticking with it. Secondly, no apologies. The future of the game is a serious business. There are important issues at stake and far-reaching decisions to be made.

I am deeply grateful for the opportunities that rugby has afforded me. Similarly, it has been an honour and a privilege to play for Scotland. Every time that I pulled a Scotland jersey over my head I was aware of the responsibilities that action entailed and of the fact that there were thousands of blokes who would have sold their grannies into slavery for the chance to swop places with me. And, despite the commercial trials and tribulations of my final season, I would do it all again tomorrow.

I have never wanted to make money from playing the game. If that had been my aim then I would have accepted the offer to turn professional with Widnes in 1990, I would have gone to South Africa in 1989 and I would have pocketed the speaking and personal appearance fees that I diverted towards the Sick Kids' Hospital in Edinburgh.

What I have strived to achieve was an equitable agreement which would have recompensed the players for the enormous amounts of time, energy and commitment that International squad members must now devote to their amateur sport. We would all do it for nothing. Of course we would. Basically we are no different to the hundreds of players who have worn that blue jersey since the first International match at Raeburn Place in 1871. Times change, attitudes change and the world around us changes. Rugby must change too. But the change should be on rugby's terms not on anyone else's. My great fear is that the non-progressive forces within the game will hold out until outside interests force change upon them. That way the ultimate loser will be the game itself. And none of us, I am sure, wants that.

CHAPTER 12

COACHES AND CAPTAINS

IT HAS become a rather glib truism in rugby to say that the single factor which links all successful coaches is that they have had at their disposal great players. That is true, certainly, but it is not the whole truth. At International level, the great coaches possess the ability to turn honest, journeymen players into individuals who can hold their own with the world's best and so produce consistently victorious teams.

As a demonstration that this is indeed the case, one need look no further than at Scottish rugby and at the achievements of the national team throughout the Eighties and Nineties. If one considers the rugby-playing resources that are available to us in Scotland then, with the exception of Ireland, we lag far behind the other Home countries. Naturally, because we lose out in the numbers game, we are not going to turn up as many genuinely world-class players as do our Five Nations' competitors.

It's often said that at any given time here in Scotland we will have, maybe, 25 players who are capable of coming into the International side. Of those, probably, no more than a handful could be considered world-class or would be seen as being worthy of automatic selection for the British Lions. In terms of playing personnel the past decade has been no better or worse than many others in the history of the game in Scotland.

Yet, since 1984 we have won two Grand Slams, taken the All Blacks to the wire on their own patch and reached the semi-finals of a World Cup. I would suggest that a large slice of the credit for these quite remarkable achievements must lie with the coaching personnel

217

that we have been blessed with throughout this period. They have been responsible for moulding teams generally containing, at most, four or five world-class players into superbly well-drilled and effective units.

The name of Jim Telfer, of course, springs immediately to mind in this regard. He was principal coach to the 1984 Grand Slam-winning side and subsequently was persuaded out of International retirement by a deputation of senior players like Fin Calder and Iain Milne. He did just that and became an ever-present face on the Scottish coaching scene until his final retiral after the 1991 World Cup.

However, Jim was not alone. We have been immensely fortunate in Scotland to have been able to call upon a series of coaches right out of the top drawer. Derrick Grant was hewn from the same block of uncompromising Border granite as Telfer. Derrick followed Jim as principal coach and latterly both stayed on to school the forwards under the overall stewardship of Ian McGeechan. He was assisted in his work with the backs by the former Stewart's-Melville and Scotland scrum-half, Dougie Morgan. All were superb International players in their own right and all were British Lions. Perhaps it isn't absolutely necessary for a coach to have actually played at the highest level but it certainly helps. A coach's task is made so much more difficult, even in just relating to what the players go through, if he has not personally 'been there'. Very often there really isn't a satisfactory substitute for personal experience.

Scottish coaches, certainly in the time that I was involved with the squad, prepared their sides to win. It was drummed into the players time and again that it wasn't enough just to have got into the Scottish side. The coaches judged success or failure on results. During my final season we won games that even five or six years ago we would have lost – most notably during my final Murrayfield appearance against France when, against all the odds, we won 10–6. I am sure that previously nine times out of ten Scottish sides would have lost that game. We won because we were mentally attuned to winning. Basically, we refused to be beaten. By virtue of the mental preparation that they provide for a side, coaches have a lot to do with such a frame of mind.

Coaches, too, bring organisation to a side. Geech set great store by the fact that he didn't much care about the number on a player's back. Obviously at set-piece situations we each had a specific job to do, but thereafter he made sure that every single member of the team, from 1 to 15, could, within reason, do one another's jobs. The number on the back became insignificant. All forwards had to get about the park and put in cover tackles and all backs had to be capable of operating as auxiliary flankers until such time as the cavalry had arrived. The concept was one of total rugby.

Leaving aside the coaching that I received at school and at Scottish Schoolboy level, I was first exposed to the concept of 'grown-up' coaching at Exeter University although even there, with a number of PE students in the side, we did a lot of it ourselves. Jeff Reece, a former Cambridge Blue who had gone on to play club rugby in Wales, was my first coach there. He was a former St Luke's College student who was doing post-graduate work at the University. Then we had George Squire, another former St Luke's student who, like Jeff, was carrying out post-grad work. At school I had trained virtually every day and it was at Exeter that I got into the routine of twice-weekly training sessions and games at the weekend, and sometimes in midweek as well.

Despite the fact that we did have recognised coaches at Exeter it wasn't until I had been recruited by Bath that I saw just what an influence a good coaching set-up can have on a team. Jack Rowell, David Robson and Tom Hudson were the coaching triumvirate at the Recreation Ground. Jack was a well-respected local businessman, David was a chartered accountant and Tom was director of physical education at Bath University. Basically, Tom looked after the fitness work and he would be in charge of the Monday night session. On Wednesdays David would oversee scrummage and set-piece work and Jack would look after the lineouts and the team runs at the end of the night. The club was fortunate at that time to have John Horton at fly-half and he was such an influential figure that he more or less looked after the backs.

Jack, who has gone on to coach England 'B', was a first-rate man manager. When I first went to the club, three of us – Gareth Chilcott, Richard Lee and myself – were all vying for two front-row places. Jack was desperately keen that we should all stay at Bath and he worked out a rota system which would allow us all to play. It was to his credit that the system more or less worked and none of us felt obliged to quit the club.

Jack had an extremely talented array of players at his disposal and with Roger Spurrell as captain and Johnny Horton calling the shots behind the scrum he was astute enough to realise that he didn't have to do much other than fine-tuning. He was never as specific as a McGeechan or a Telfer in terms of what he required from his side but he did pull the whole thing together and, in that type of club situation, showed the worth of having at the helm a high-powered businessman who was first and foremost a man-manager.

Jack was always very positive in his handling of the team. He would hold team meetings on the mornings of big games. If we were travelling to an away fixture then we would stop *en route* at a hotel for an early lunch and Jack would go over the game ahead. By and large he would tell us that we were an awful lot better than the opposition and that, accordingly, we would win. He would stress how important it was for the club that we continued to progress and so on. He was a good motivator without being a tub-thumper. Jack would go out of his way to accentuate the positive. He would stress how much better we were as individual players than that day's opposition. His approach wasn't universal – I would find out later that Jim Telfer didn't quite adopt the same attitude.

Generally, Jim would seek to impress upon his forwards just how utterly inadequate they were. The intention was to make you want to go out and prove him wrong. If Jack Rowell used the carrot and stick method then Jim was more inclined to the stick and more stick approach. His record, of course, speaks for itself and I hesitate to criticise him, however mildly. But I can't help feeling that this blanket approach to those under his charge was at times counter-productive. The eight forwards in any pack are eight individuals. They all react and respond to different stimuli. I know that some guys in the team under Jim's command just used to switch off. If you tell one guy that he is utterly useless and that if there was someone better available then he wouldn't be in the side then, to some players, that is a devastating indictment of their playing prowess. Strange as it may seem to the outsider, some of those whom I played alongside for Scotland didn't have much self-confidence. If they were told time and again that they were just there on sufferance, even as a motivational ploy as Jim intended it, then after a while they might well have begun to believe it.

Latterly, it got to the stage where everybody feared Jim Telfer's team-talks more than the game. I believe that quite often they were damaging so far as some of the milder souls in the team were concerned. Derek White was one of those who would more often than not find himself in the firing line. Jim, who had been a British Lion back-row man in his own right, probably saw Derek – despite his array of Scotland Caps – as having great untapped potential. He gave Derek a dreadfully hard time at training sessions. There was more than a hint of truth in Derek's oft-quoted remark that he didn't know whether he was more scared to tell his wife that he was going to another Scotland squad session or to inform Jim Telfer that he wasn't.

Paul Burnell, Damian Cronin and, from time to time, Kenny Milne, were others who also felt the rough edge of Jim's tongue. Kenny will say that he plays his best rugby when he feels under threat and when he has just been told by the coach that he is a useless individual. However, I'm not so sure. Kenny, too, is a bit of a gentle soul and I feel he is a 'confidence' player and one who needs to be told that he is appreciated. Kenny played well during the 1992 Five Nations' championship. He was confident about the things that he was doing, the lineout calls and all the rest of it. He never felt particularly confident when Jim was in charge.

These are all negative aspects of Jim's coaching style. The positive side was that he was utterly devoted to the Scottish cause. He was frighteningly single-minded in his pursuit of what he considered to be Scottish rugby's best interests. With two Grand Slams and two club championships with Melrose under his belt, he has an unassailable position as one the world's top coaches. He thought incredibly deeply about the game and, I think, after his less than successful spell as coach to the 1983 British Lions in New Zealand, he compensated by developing a strategic and tactical blueprint for Scottish International rugby which has lasted us more or less intact until the present day. Scottish rugby has a lot to thank Jim Telfer for and a large number of players who have 'suffered' under his regime will tell you that they are much better players for it.

With Scotland, Jim was not one of those fortunate coaches who prospered because they had a dressing-room full of world-class players with which to work. He, and all the Scottish coaches who have followed him, really have had to mould efficient and winning units from resources which, man for man, were often deficient when compared with those of our International rivals. He had the ability to take a player of average ability and to get much, much more out of him. He was a stickler for correct technique and 'body position' became almost a mantra for Scottish forwards. He more than any other individual was responsible for developing Scottish forward play throughout the 1980s and into the 1990s.

Jim was followed as principal coach by Derrick Grant. Derrick, from Hawick, as opposed to Jim's Melrose, was cast very much from the same mould as Jim. Both had been do-or-die back-row forwards in their playing days and both were dedicated to the cause almost to the point of tunnel vision. Derrick, though, was not quite so aggressive in his manner as Jim and, for my money, was perhaps the better communicator of the two. Derrick coached the 'B' side when I was first selected for it and then went on to coach the 'big' side before I made my breakthrough in 1986. All told I had six years under Derrick's tutelage. I was always very impressed by Derrick and his approach. He communicated with the players in a way which Jim never did. He wasn't by any means a soft touch, far from it, but he seemed to have an instinctive knack of being able to say the right things at the right time and to bolster fading confidence among individuals when it was required.

He was also tremendously good at assessing situations and individuals. He was able to gauge how sessions and whole trips were going. He was, in short, a very fine man-manager. He could administer bollockings with the best of them and certainly didn't treat fools gladly, if at all. I had my first taste of Scottish touring with the 1987 World Cup squad in New Zealand when Derrick was in charge. He was also first-rate during the 1990 New Zealand Tour when I feel the team played the best rugby of any Scottish side that I have been associated with.

Derrick was more relaxed on that 1990 Tour than at any other time and his contribution to the trip was immense. So far as the forwards were concerned it was probably true that Jim had laid the groundwork during the preceding season and Derrick was fine-tuning. The Scottish philosophy right through the Telfer–Grant, McGeechan–Morgan, Dixon–Johnston era has been one of total involvement – of recognition that every member of the team must be able to do more than just fulfil his basic function. Forwards had to be able to do more than just scrummage, ruck, maul and jump. They had to be able to give and take a pass and to be able to beat men and all of the rest of it. Generally speaking, Scottish players are able to do that and, by and large, to do it pretty well.

This quest for 'total rugby' has been so refined within the Scotland set-up that we now have flip-charts depicting various match situations in different parts of the ground. We might flip to a lineout in our own 22 and a back will be asked where he expects the ball to be thrown to and what type of ball he might expect it to be. A forward will then be asked what type of move he would expect the backs to work off that ball and where he should be running to. The answer could be a ball off the top with the contact point at outside centre and the ball to be moved even wider from there and for Gavin Hastings to come into the line. What we have tried to do is to develop an awareness throughout the team as to what is likely to happen next and to generate improved understanding between forwards and backs.

There is a school of thought within rugby coaching circles that forwards' coaches merely have to possess a big enough stick with which to beat the players over the head every time a repetitive drill is fouled up. Sooner or later, the argument goes, the players will have the skill under tuition beaten into them.

There is an element of truth in this. Generally speaking, forwards' coaches tend to be rather old-fashioned, martinet characters whereas backs' coaches or principal coaches tend to have to think more deeply about the game as a whole. They have to consider lines of running and defensive patterns. There is so much involved: which areas are to be attacked, how defences are to be committed, how the ball carriers and the dummy-runners will perform. Generally speaking, that overall strategic role calls for much greater finesse than the rather more brutal attributes necessary for a coach who is to devote his time entirely to the forwards.

Ian McGeechan, both with Scotland and the Lions, has proved himself to be a past master at the big strategic picture. With Geech and Jim, Derrick, and Dougie Morgan, we have been almost uniquely well-served in the coaching department. There has been a continuity in the Scotland coaching set-up which has made us the envy of many other nations. As one principal coach has stepped down, more often than not because the job was simply proving to be too time-consuming, one of the deputies has taken over as front-runner and the retiring encumbent has re-joined the team in a secondary capacity. It is a system which has worked extremely well and has produced tangible results.

As I relate elsewhere, my International career and Geech's coaching career have been intertwined since my earliest 'B' International days. He is the coach that I have been closest to over the years and the one that I have found it easiest to relate to. His methods are different again to those of Jim and Derrick. Ian is a very relaxed, thoughtful individual. Players don't fear him in the way that many did Jim Telfer. However, they would move mountains in order not to let Geech down. He is well liked and universally respected for what he achieved as a player and is now similarly liked and respected in his coaching capacity as well.

Geech, Telfer, Grant and Morgan were complementary characters. Jim and Derrick have already retired from the International scene and they will be a great loss. Moreover, it can only be a matter of time before Geech, too, decides to call it a day. His dedication to the game is absolutely all-consuming. He spends hours at his video recorder, editing and re-editing passages of play from past International matches so that he is better able to improve our performance and plan the downfall of our International opponents. As a strategic and tactical thinker I have never come across anyone who comes close to even emulating Ian, let alone surpassing him. Our 1990 Grand Slam defeat of England was as much a victory for the strategic and tactical planning of Geech and his fellow backroom boys as it was for the blokes who actually put their master plan into operation on the park. Ian is also a superb communicator and this is an area of his coaching that does not get the praise it deserves. He knows when to speak and when it is best to leave things unsaid. He is not by any means a tub-thumper but this, I think, makes his evocations to the players even more effective.

Geech was in his element on the Lions' tour to Australia in 1989, and again when he coached the World squad in New Zealand for the 1992 NZRFU centenary Test series. On both occasions he knew that he was in charge of any number of world-class players and he acted accordingly in order to bring out the best from those players. He was assisted in Australia by Roger Uttley who looked after the forwards. Roger, who was a player absolutely out of the top-drawer, is, I feel, one of those coaches referred to at the outset who have benefited enormously from having lots of top-class players under their control. It is certainly true that on a man-to-man basis England teams are invariably of better quality than their Scottish counterparts. Accordingly, it is much to the credit of the Scottish coaches over the years that we have, largely, been able to compete with our Sassenach rivals.

Dougie Morgan, whom I first encountered as a coach with the Edinburgh District side in 1987, is a first-class operator and one, I am sure, destined for greater things. He was an abrasive scrum-half in his playing days and that abrasiveness has endured into his coaching. He is equally at home taking forwards or backs and is pretty tactically astute as well. He combines the best of Telfer, Grant and McGeechan and I am certain that if he wants to then he will go right to the top in the Scottish International coaching set-up.

What all of these people have in common is that they have been achievers in a playing sense. The players have to be able to look at the coach and to know that he has been through it all; that he appreciates their fears and is privy to the aspirations of an International rugby player. It is vital that they should respect the coach for his reputation as a player as well as his leadership, or he will not be able to hold their attention – unless the coach is an almost unique human being blessed with superhuman charisma. In France it seems to be different. They have had a string of well respected former international players – Jacques Fouroux, Daniel Dubroca, Pierre Berbizier – but in a coaching sense they don't seem to be able to get it together. The French are such an enigmatic bunch anyway that perhaps their experience doesn't translate to Anglo-Saxon rugby. However, in spite of the French experience and the fact that Dick Best, Richie Dixon and Alan Davies now coach England, Scotland and Wales without full International playing honours behind them, I remain convinced that the International coach will find his task much easier if he has that personal playing experience to fall back upon.

Defences are so well organised these days that coaches spend a lot of their time formulating moves which will create the space which is invariably necessary before a try will result. Former International players, from the Fifties and Sixties, are sometimes critical of the way the game is played nowadays. They say that in their day the players looked for spaces to run into while in the modern game players seem to spend all of their time looking for someone to run into so that a ruck or maul can be set up. Well, the answer is that defences are now so well organised that it is almost impossible to make headway from set-piece situations. This is so even when the coaches have worked hard on producing a super-duper, never seen before move. International teams are now so well drilled defensively that you are really looking at second, or even third phase possession before you can get across the gain-line. The name of the game is getting your runners into space and to achieve that you have to commit their defenders to the tackle and, effectively, take them out of the game. Almost without exception that cannot be done at the set-piece, which is why it is true that modern rugby players do spend a lot of their time looking for someone to run into.

There have been players like Andy Irvine or Jim Renwick, for instance, who have possessed that God-given ability to prise open defences by virtue of the sheer class of their running. In the modern game Jerry Guscott is another who has that wraith-like ability to glide through openings which lesser mortals wouldn't even have recognised as such. However, players like those appear only once in a blue moon and the rest of us have to rely upon rehearsed moves to achieve the same ends.

Just as coaches have to win the respect of their players, captains, too, have to have that respect before they can hope to function properly. Roger Spurrell, my first captain at Bath, was an inspiration in this regard. Roger was a larger than life character in everything that he did and while he was skipper at Bath his troops would have followed him to the ends of the earth. On the field of play he was a very, very hard man. He had an unruly mop of curly, blond hair and, like Jean-Pierre Rives, he was instantly recognisable about the pitch.

Roger led from the front and the entire club revolved around him. When I think of Roger now, after all those years, the memories come flooding back and I realise that he utilised the Jim Telfer method of psyching people up. He would generally rubbish certain players who would then go and play their hearts out in order to prove him wrong and win their way back into his esteem. Roger could read his players like a book and he was good at getting the best out of his team-mates. He became a folk-hero in Bath when he captained the side and when he took the club to the John Player final at Twickenham virtually the entire population of Bath went too – and they were delighted all to be part of Spurrell's Army.

When I broke through into the Scotland team in 1986 the skipper was Colin Deans. He had just been appointed but he was a well-respected, world-class player who had been on a British Lions' tour – not as it turned out a particularly happy one for him – and had, generally, achieved a great deal within the game. Colin made a point, on the morning of the match, of going around each of the players individually. He would call in to see them in their rooms. He was a fantastic player who set a great example both on and off the pitch. He was a delight to play alongside and as a hooker one of the fastest strikers of a ball that I have ever seen. He also had the ability to adapt his hooking style to suit the needs of the moment and if either of his props found themselves in momentary difficulty then he was skilful enough to compensate and still get in a good strike at the ball. He also took the art of throwing in at the lineout on to a new plane. It was before my time, but going back to the 1984 Grand Slam, the manner in which he used to find David Leslie at the tail of the lineout was poetry in motion.

The next man to lead Scotland was Kelso's Gary Callander. Gary was unfortunate in that his best years were spent on the bench understudying Colin. Gary, too, was a fine hooker and, as skipper, a great thinker about the game. He had a fantastic rugby brain. Possibly Gary was too much of a poacher turned gamekeeper to really make his mark as a Scottish captain. He had sat on the bench so many times, and had been a member of the squad for so long, that he had been able to enjoy the pre- and post-match atmosphere without the tensions and pressures that the actual team members felt.

After Colin's retirement, though, when he was in the side, and what is more captaining it, the other members of the team couldn't forget his seasons on the bench and the good times off it. Gary thought very deeply about the game and accordingly he has turned his hand to coaching. I wouldn't be at all surprised if he goes on to make a big name for himself in this sphere.

Fin Calder took over from Gary. Again, like Roger Spurrell, Fin was a really charismatic character. Fin talks ten to the dozen at the best of times. As captain it became almost impossible to shut him up! He was a great man for getting a bit of volume into the dressing-room preparation before an International match. To carry it off you have to be a bit of a showman and Fin was that alright. He got a real buzz from International weekends. He was almost hyperactive, popping up here, there and everywhere, attending to this, that and the next thing. Also, he was another man who led from the front. His biggest test came during the 1989 Lions' Tour to Australia where he had to use all of his man-management and leadership skills to drag the Tour back from that first Test defeat.

All three of them, in their different ways, were first-rate Scottish captains and very hard acts to follow. I thought very deeply about my captaincy role, especially so in the week leading up to a game. I would think about the mental preparation and about what I was going to say to the guys and when. You had to gauge it just right. You would have to be conscious always of the mood of the party and to determine whether a particular moment was the best time to sit the guys down for a chat about the game to come, or whether it was better just to have let matters take their course for now. The job, in addition to making the decisions on the park, is to keep the team stimulated and to keep each individual focused on what his job is going to be.

It's said of coaches that the most difficult area for them to work in is the four inches above the players' eyes. The same is true for the captain and especially so for an International captain who has to walk that very fine line between remaining 'one of the boys' and retaining the respect of the players and yet still having the capability to crack the whip when it is required. In those circumstances I suppose it is inevitable to a certain extent that the captain will become slightly detached from the players. You do have other responsibilities such as dealing with the media and liaising with the coaches and the management.

However, I thought it important that the captain should remain very much part of the team, which is why I never favoured the previously held practice of the captain rooming on his own during Five Nations' weekends.

I think it is important, too, that the captain should set certain standards. This is particularly important during a Tour when you are abroad in a closed community with a bunch of guys who, apart from anything else, represent, maybe, a ten-year age differential. In those circumstances it is important that the captain provides a lead and that the teenagers in the party are encouraged to follow the lead given by the old hands and not vice-versa. There are times on Tour when it is appropriate to let your hair down and times when it is not. It is important that the captain makes sure that the players know just when it is appropriate and when it is not.

So far as the on-field duties of the captain are concerned I suppose you could say that he is there to make sure that the game plan drawn up by the coaches is put into practice. The captain has to have sufficient nous, though, to appreciate when things are going wrong and to have the experience and the confidence to change the tactics in mid-match.

Elsewhere I have told of the lineout codes we used to fox England in the 1990 Grand Slam match. As captain and a forward it was my job to compose the various codes and signals that we used on the touchline. There was a feeling that the codes were becoming just too complicated and so for the 1991 World Cup and the following Five Nations' championship we reverted to the use of visual signals as the mainstay of our touchline codes. In addition we had a number of pre-determined sequences of lineouts.

If I called, for instance, 'Sequence A', then the blokes would know that the next three lineouts would conform to an arranged pattern with the ball to be thrown to a pre-determined individual and with a pre-arranged number of forwards in the line. These 'sequence' lineouts had the benefit of saving time and keeping the opposition on the hop.

The main codes, though, were visual. During the 1992 Five Nations' competition, if I stood with my hands on cloth (i.e. with my palms on shorts or shirt) then the ball was to be thrown to the front of the line. If my hands were resting on skin then Kenny Milne would know to direct his throw towards the middle of the line. Hands off indicated a ball to the tail of the line and clenched fists meant the ball was going over the top.

In order to further confuse the opposition, the visual codes were augmented by numbers, colours and fruits. This would indicate the type of ball and the identity of the catcher. For instance, any fruit was a two-man line. A colour would mean that the ball was going to Derek White or Neil Edwards at the front of the line. Any number meant Doddie Weir would be the recipient.

The lineout code possibilities are virtually endless. Another that we used was the subtracted difference between the first or last pairs of numbers in a four-digit sequence. The four numbers would be prefaced by a letter which indicated whether it was to be the first or last pairs of numbers that were to be subtracted. Still with me? The subtracted numbers would always be five, four, three, two or one. These indicated a ball to me at the front of the line, a ball to the number two jumper, a ball over the top, a ball to the number eight at the tail of the line and, finally, an orthodox ball to the middle of the line jumper.

There is so much going on in an International match that it is vital that the guys give 100 per cent concentration all of the time. When Fin Calder, John Jeffrey and Derek White made up our back-row unit they were such a class act that we capitalised on their prowess. By the time of the World Cup in 1991 we had no fewer than 19 pre-planned back-row moves. Depending on where the scrummage was and what the circumstances were I might ask Fin if there was anything on. He would then call the move.

Before their retirals after the World Cup Fin and JJ took a great deal of the on-field load from my shoulders. They were such fine players and had been around for such a long time that we were generally at one as to what might be required in a given situation.

Behind the scrum Craig Chalmers would call the shots for the backs from fly-half. They, too, had their pre-planned moves and a variety of defensive alignments – one on one, one out, drift and so on – so you can see that even with the game being played at a frantic pace and the crowd going wild there is still a tremendous amount going on to occupy the old grey matter.

The captain also has an important part to play on match-day during the build-up to the game. If there were new Caps in the side then, taking a leaf from Colin Deans's book, I would go and see them in their hotel rooms on the morning of the game. It's important that first-timers are made to feel a part of the set-up. It's important, too, to ensure that their nerves don't get the better of them. Latterly for home games the Scotland side used the Dalmahoy Hotel and Country Club on the outskirts of Edinburgh. During the Saturday morning, after a long-ish lie-in I would get the blokes outside for a gentle stroll around the grounds. We would take a few rugby balls with us and maybe go through a few lineouts or back-row moves. More than anything we did so just to prevent the mind from wandering and to ease the tension. It served, too, to start getting everybody focused on the task ahead.

Generally, we would hold a team meeting around 11.15 with an early lunch at 11.30. By this time many of the guys would be getting quite twitchy and eating was a bit of a chore. I would make do with an omelette and a chocolate bar. That would be it until after the game.

One of the innovations which I brought in as captain was to get the team changed into playing kit at the hotel before the bus journey to the ground. It always struck me as a dreadful waste of time to get changed out of tracksuits into blazers and slacks for the trip to the ground where you would then have to get changed once again into shirt, shorts, boots and so on. Now we travel to the ground in our playing kit and Scotland shell-suits and this gets the boys into 'match mode' at an earlier and more beneficial time.

Once we were at the ground then I found the going easier. By far the hardest part of any International day was the hanging around. Once you were at the ground, though, you really did feel that the show was on the road. Before the kick-off the dressing-room is off-limits to all but the team, coaching and medical personnel and the team manager. Once the door is closed then the captain comes into his own.

The coaches will have said their piece at the hotel. In the dressing-room the captain will do most of the talking. The coaches will circulate among the team with personal words of encouragement and advice to a few individuals. I tended to take control at this stage and tried to get the boys really concentrating on the game. I wanted to get them tuned into what they would be doing. I got them to visualise the first scrummage, the first kick, the first lineout. Forwards would visualise the physical confrontations and the big hits to come. I wanted the players to have a positive picture in their minds of what was going to happen.

It was important, too, that the players talked to each other. Communication is all-important. We would go out and have the team photograph taken and then, if we were at Murrayfield, come back inside to the warm-up room under the stand. This enabled the team to work up a bit of a sweat. Then it would be back to the dressing-room to get the boots on. By this time kick-off was only ten minutes away and I would make a conscious effort to tone down the atmosphere which invariably by this time would be getting rather frenetic. I would gather the team around and, again, get them to paint mental pictures of what it was they were going to achieve. I would make sure that the dressing-room clock was showing the exact time so that I could coordinate the build-up right up until the kick-off.

At Murrayfield, it used to be the tradition that the SRU president would call in to see the players before the game. This tended to act as a distraction, though. The captain and the coaches would have been working with the team to achieve the right atmosphere and then when the president appeared it was as if a needle had been pushed into a balloon. The atmosphere was just deflated. I'm sure that no feelings were hurt or feathers ruffled when the practice was discontinued. There is plenty of time for the president to see the players after the game when, hopefully, there would be a victory to celebrate.

That is the match-day routine of a Scottish skipper. Captaincy is not everyone's cup of tea, but I have to admit that I really relished the responsibility. It gave an added dimension to my years with the Scotland team. I shall miss it.

CHAPTER 13

A RUGBY MISCELLANY

Icing on the Cake

RUGBY HAS BEEN a way of life for me now for over 20 years. I've no doubt that for quite a few autumns to come when I would normally be looking out the boots from the deepest recesses of the cupboard then I shall begin to suffer from withdrawal symptoms. Elsewhere in this book I hope that I have been able to share with the reader the major events in my rugby life. All the experiences which have fallen into readily definable categories are dealt with in these sections. What follows next is a *pot pourri* of rugby-related memories.

Selection for Scotland and my appointment as Scottish captain opened doors which might otherwise have remained tightly closed. Sometimes these doors led simply to more rugby, as in the case of my participation with a World XV in New Zealand or with the Barbarians or at the Hong Kong Sevens. Other doors opened out on to immensely worthwhile charity work and still more led directly to Wimbledon, or 10 Downing Street or a round of golf with Nick Faldo. The common denominator is that rugby either directly or indirectly allowed me to broaden my horizons and to have a bit of fun into the bargain.

In no particular order, then, what follows is a brief resumé of these extra-curricular activities – the icing on the cake.

TEST VICTORY IN NEW ZEALAND
I had waited a long time for a Test match win in New Zealand. It finally came in the Spring of 1992. Sadly, that much sought-after victory over the All Blacks didn't come in a Scotland shirt but as part of a World XV drawn together to celebrate the centenary of the NZRFU.

The taking of an All Black scalp would, of course, have been all the sweeter had it come as the result of a Scottish victory but any kind of Test win in the land of the silver fern is to be savoured. And savour it we did. There were quite a few vastly experienced players in the World squad to whom victory in New Zealand was a first-time experience and we celebrated long into the Christchurch night.

The World Squad, managed by Brian Lochore and coached by our own Ian McGeechan and the Australian Bob Templeton, was a gathering of rugby talent from a' the airts. As originally selected, only Gavin Hastings and myself were included from Scotland. However, due to injuries and non-availabilities, Derek White and Andy Nicol, who had made his Five Nations' debut only that season in place of the injured Gary Armstrong, were added to the party.

The timing of the trip made it especially interesting. New Zealand rugby, despite their third place finish in the 1991 World Cup, was going through something of a crisis. The All Blacks had gone to the World Cup as champions and to the highly demanding New Zealand public third place might as well have equalled 33rd place. Coaches Alex Wyllie and John Hart paid the ultimate price when they were replaced by Laurie Mains. World Cup skipper Gary Whetton suffered, too, as he didn't even make the final All Black Trials. His omission from the side would have interesting results for us as our mini-Tour progressed.

I was interested, too, to meet the South Africans who were included in the squad. The political climate is even more changeable than the British weather but for the first time in my playing career it looked virtually certain that the Springboks would emerge from their sporting exile. I was keen to see how the cream of their playing talent would shape up when exposed to the world game at its highest level. From what we had seen on our television sets the domestic game in South Africa seemed to be in a very healthy state but, even in South Africa, there is a huge difference between the domestic product and what is required at International level, a contention which was borne out when the Springboks were gallant losers to both New Zealand and Australia in the late summer of 1992.

The South Africans, Naas Botha, André Joubert, Michael Knoetze, Jannie Classens, Pieter Hendricks and Uli Schmidt were, I think, quite taken aback by the scope and intensity of the training sessions run by Ian and Bob. In fact the hooker Uli Schmidt was so impressed that he took constant notes so that he could take Geech and Tempo's drills back home with him.

Just from speaking to the South Africans it became clear that their isolation from world competition really has affected their game. Backs and forwards, apparently, rarely train together. Their philosophy seems to be very much one of 'backs is backs and forwards is forwards and never the twain shall meet'. In the rest of the world it is now generally accepted that it doesn't really matter what number you carry on your back. If you arrive first at the breakdown point then you immediately assume the role of auxiliary flanker. You get in there and either protect and secure the ball or you try to rip it clear from the opposition. This was a philosophy quite alien to the South African threequarters who seemed to think that they employed forwards to carry out these chores for them. They appeared to consider, also, that the forwards existed merely to retail them the ball and for very little else besides. My impression was that at home they were still playing a game based around a heavy pack and a ball-winning, open-side flanker, which on the world stage is ten to 15 years out of date.

This was an attitude which cost us dearly in the second Test when, to put it bluntly, some of the South African threequarters in the World side were extremely loth to get their sleeves rolled up and tackle.

The All Blacks are a fairly intimidating sight when they're running straight at you. This is especially true of somebody like Va'aiga Tuigamala, their left winger. The only way to stop them is to go for the feet. You can't tackle them above the waist because they're generally so strong that they'll just brush you aside. However, if you take them by the pins then they can't go anywhere without their legs and they'll come crashing down. It does, though, take a certain steadiness of nerve to stand your ground as 15 stones of All Black on the hoof thunders down upon you with boots flailing and studs glinting in the sunlight.

The Springbok fly-half Naas Botha is looked upon as a superstar back home in South Africa and he was quite obviously the leader of the South African contingent on our New Zealand trip. Whatever Naas said went with the others. Rather annoyingly, too, they would converse with each other in Afrikaans despite the fact that they all spoke perfectly good English and that Afrikaans wasn't one of the languages in which the rest of the party were particularly proficient.

I'm rather ashamed to admit that once we had seen Naas playing we took to calling him the traffic policeman in view of his eagerness to wave the opposition through. The England centre Jerry Guscott who was also on the trip says that Naas is the only fly-half he has ever seen pulling people out of rucks to stand in front of him so that he doesn't have to make the tackle! Naas may be a legend back home on the veldt but, in my opinion, and certainly on the evidence of his performances in the World squad, he has a long way to go before he has mastered the skills that we would expect of an International fly-half these days.

It became pretty obvious when we were doing the contact drills during the first week of our trip that the South Africans are some way behind the rest of the world when it comes to tackling by the three-quarters. This is something that they really will have to work on as they end their years of International exile. It is purely a technical thing and I am sure that they will get it right. If they don't, then they will regret it, of that I am certain.

In addition to the South Africans we had Scotsmen, Englishmen, Frenchmen, Australians, Western Samoans, and lone representatives from Japan, Canada and Argentina. We all got on like a house on fire. The South Africans were rather cliquey and to some extent kept themselves to themselves. However, even allowing for that, the atmosphere within the party was first-rate and we looked upon the whole exercise not as an extended holiday but as a genuine Test campaign.

There was never any suggestion that the New Zealand RFU wanted a Barbarians, carnival-type Test series. They wanted genuine, hard International rugby and that was what we provided.

We opened our Tour with a warm-up game at Timaru which we won by 70-odd points. It was really just a means of running the air-miles out of legs and letting the squad members get to know each other on the pitch. The Wallaby skipper Nick Farr-Jones, who was scheduled to captain the world side, wasn't due to arrive from Australia until well into the first week and so until his arrival I was made captain.

Unfortunately for Nick, he had injured an ankle before leaving Australia and therefore wasn't fit to take his place in the opening Test at Christchurch. The effect of this was that I was made captain for the opening encounter with the All Blacks and young Andy Nicol came into the side at scrum-half in place of Nick. It really had been an amazing season for Andy. He had made his Scotland debut straight from the second division side Dundee High School FP after injury to Gary Armstrong. His club, coached by the former Scotland flanker David Leslie, has now won promotion to the Scottish First Division. Andy had played outstandingly at the base of the Scottish scrum throughout the Five Nations' Championship and now, there he was about to make his debut with a World XV against the All Blacks in Christchurch.

Both Andy and Gary are superb players. It would be great to have them both in any side. The eventual destination of the Scotland number nine shirt is going to involve some long and hard deliberations by the selectors. It's a real tester. I'm glad that I won't be involved!

There were a number of new faces in the All Blacks side for the Lancaster Park game which the NZRFU marketing men were calling with perhaps just a hint of hyperbole 'The Clash of the Century'. Our side, in the main, consisted of 15 seasoned internationalists: Gavin Hastings (Scotland), Michael Knoetze (South Africa), Tim Horan (Australia), Jerry Guscott (England), Pieter Hendriks (South Africa), Didier Cambarabero (France), Andy Nicol (Scotland), David Sole (Scotland), captain, Phil Kearns (Australia), Peter Fatialofa (Western Samoa), Marc Cecillon (France), Olivier Roumat (France), Gord Mackinnon (Canada), Derek White (Scotland) and Willie Ofahengaue (Australia).

We won 28-14 and that just wasn't part of the All Black script. We had come to their centenary party and had pinched the presents. Unusually, the New Zealanders made a lot of errors. However, to a large extent they were forced into making mistakes because of our commitment. At one point we were 25-6 ahead. The Kiwis scored a couple of late tries and I got the guys together and said: 'Look, we're not going to throw this away now, are we?'

The look of horror on their faces indicated that 'No, we most certainly are not.' We really put in the tackles. It was hard stuff. I took a bit of a shoe-ing in the rucks courtesy of one Richard Loe and for days afterwards my torso resembled a London Underground map. However, it was worth it. To win a Test match in New Zealand is a huge achievement. Despite their fall from grace in the World Cup the All Blacks are still one of the great sides and to beat them on their own paddock takes some doing.

The scale of our achievement was underlined by the observation by Ian McGeechan that in his career as a 32-times capped Scotland player and as a two-times British Lion and as a coach of several years' standing he had only once – with the 1977 Lions – been involved with a side which had beaten the All Blacks. We felt good and after the game we had a Happy Hour which lasted for considerably longer than that.

The second Test followed four days later in Wellington. The New Zealand selectors had really wielded the axe. Out went long-time stars Grant Fox and John Kirwan. Scrum-half Graeme Bachop also got the chop. Four new caps were brought into the side we were to meet at Athletic Park. Our team was: André Joubert (South Africa), Yoshihito Yoshida (Japan), Jerry Guscott (England), Janie Classens (South Africa), Pieter Hendricks (South Africa), Naas Botha (South Africa), Nick Farr-Jones (Australia), captain, Federico Mendez (Argentina), Uli Schmidt (South Africa), Ewan McKenzie (Australia), John Eales (Australia), Olivier Roumat (France), Apollo Perelini (Western Samoa), Brendan Nasser (Australia), and Marc Cecillon (France).

I watched from the bench and it became clear early on that the New Zealanders were desperately keen to square the series. It soon transpired, too, that our defence left a lot to be desired with certain individuals posted missing on more than one occasion. Against the All Blacks you cannot afford to miss one tackle and the final scoreline of 54-26 tells its own tale.

Our cause was further hindered by the dismissal of Olivier Roumat. The big Frenchman received his marching orders from the New Zealand referee David Bishop when Olivier kicked Sean Fitzpatrick. Bishop, who had been involved in the Parc Des Princes controversy during the World Cup when he was alleged to have been manhandled by the French coach Daniel Dubroca, really had no alternative. However, as is almost always the case in these matters it wasn't so clear-cut as it appeared. Sean had swung a left hook at the big Frenchman. It had caught him on the chin and knocked him backwards. As he was falling Olivier had retaliated with his foot. Not very clever, true. But a spur of the moment kind of thing. The referee was right on the spot and there was no doubt in his mind that Roumat had to go. I don't think there was any doubt in Olivier's mind either but he was desperately disappointed. We were all choked for him. The atmosphere in the squad was absolutely first-rate. By this time it was no longer 26 blokes from nine different countries. We really did feel like a proper touring party.

If Olivier's sending-off was the low point of the second Test then the undoubted highlight for me was a spectacular try by the Japanese winger Yoshihito Yoshido. Japanese was one of the languages in which we were as a squad not particularly proficient. Nevertheless, little Yoshihito was one of the stars of the trip. By a very effective combination of sign language and mime he was into absolutely everything. His try followed a chip ahead by Jerry Guscott. He touched down under the posts after a death-defying full-length dive. He took the ball at about knee height and crashed over for one of the most spectacular tries that I have ever seen.

We suffered a couple of crucial injuries in the game. Jerry Guscott and John Eales both sustained shoulder damage. With Roumat now out of the reckoning for the deciding third Test this meant that our lock-forward situation was critical. The position was resolved with an invitation to Gary Whetton. Gary, who had captained the All Blacks during their World Cup campaign and who had been discarded as the price of failure, agreed to come into the side for the third Test at Eden Park, Auckland.

Come the Test, which we lost 26-15, I think we were lacking in certain areas. Perhaps we won enough ball but we didn't do enough with it. If we had the same back line as in the first Test then it might have been different but as it was we had Naas Botha in at fly-half and Janie Claassen at outside centre. Good player though he was, Janie wasn't in the same class as Jerry Guscott. And especially a Jerry Guscott with Tim Horan alongside him. Horan was a revelation. He gives the man outside him so much time and room and Guscott with time and space to play with is a devastating attacking commodity.

There was, though, a try for the best known piano-shifter in International rugby. Peter Fatialofa, Western Samoa's World Cup captain, emerged from the bottom of a ruck on the Kiwi line with the ball in his hands and a try to his credit. Fats was one of the characters of the party, for all the world like a well-tanned Gareth Chilcott and believe me there can be no higher endorsement than that!

THE BARBARIANS

Even in these days of rampant commercialism I still consider that one of the most coveted honours that can come the way of any rugby player is an invitation to turn out for the Barbarians. Founded in 1890 by one Percy Carpmael during an oyster and Guinness supper in Bradford, the Baa-Baas are still all about friendship and attacking rugby. I received my initial invitation to join the club in 1986. Unfortunately, I sustained some severe facial damage while playing for Bath. It ruled me out of three Scottish Internationals and also meant that I had to postpone my membership of rugby's most exclusive rugby club.

The following season I received an invitation to turn out for them in a midweek evening fixture against Newport. This time I was hale and hearty and able to take Geoff Windsor-Lewis up on the offer. Subsequently I played for the Baa-Baas against Australia and New Zealand and also twice more against Newport. My Baa-Baas career has also encompassed games for them against Bristol, Cardiff and East Midlands (twice). I've skippered the club on three occasions – against the Kiwis in 1989, during the Easter tour to Wales in 1991 and against the East Midlands in 1992.

The club games involving the Barbarians are treated very much as a relaxing afternoon's entertainment for both the players and for the large crowds which the Barbarians invariably attract. In the games against International opposition, though, there is obviously more at stake and the tendency in recent years has been to treat them that bit more seriously. Certainly when I captained the side against the All Blacks I treated the occasion very much as a serious match and not just a fun run-around.

However, lest it be said that I don't enter into the Barbarians' spirit, against Cardiff in 1991 and against East Midlands in 1992 I imposed a £2 fine on anyone who kicked to touch outside our own 22. I also awarded my old adversary Jeff Probyn the opportunity to have a kick at goal. I'm delighted to be able to report that Jeff slotted the ball sweetly between the uprights and was, therefore, able to maintain his 100 per cent goal-kicking record in first-class matches!

LES BARBARIANS FRANÇAIS

In 1988 I was invited to turn out for the French Barbarians in Mont-de-Marsan against the touring New Zealand Maoris. Andy Irvine and Iain Milne are the only other Scots that I know of who have been honoured with an invitation to play for the French Baa-Baas so I was in good company. I consider myself to be a bit of a Francophile. (I certainly like their wine!) Therefore I was delighted to accept. The Scots and the French have always got on well together. I always make a point of speaking to them in their own language which, I think, they appreciate. The French side now even stick around at Murrayfield for a beer after the game which until relatively recently they never did. We were beaten by the Maoris who had a fantastic side. They had Steve McDowell and Hika Reid in the front row; Marty Brooke was in the second row and in the back-row were Eric Rush, Buck Shelford and Zin Zan Brooke.

I must have done OK in 1988 because in 1990 I was invited back to play for the French Baa-Baas against the All Blacks under floodlights at Agen. That was a good French side. Philippe Dintrans was hooking, Cadieu was in the second row, while Benazzi and Cabannes were in the back row. Charvet and Lafond were among the backs and Pierre Berbizier was captain. Sadly, we lost the game but après-match entertainment was superb. The French, as in so many other things but particularly so in matters culinary, are so civilised. Whereas UK teams just go from the stadium to the hotel where immediately there begins a round of receptions before the official dinner, the French, knowing full well that a night of hard drinking lies ahead, prepare themselves accordingly.

The first thing that the French do when they come off the pitch is to get some food inside them. Be it bacon and eggs, as it was on the first occasion I played for them, or the *foie gras* and cheese that was on offer in Agen, the team immediately goes to a room set aside for the purpose where they can put a lining on their stomachs. This also, by the way, explains why so many French teams are late for the start of the official after-match functions! It is, though, a first-rate idea and one which UK teams should think about emulating.

After we had taken on board our *foie gras* and cheese we went off to the official banquet and then on to a bar in Agen. Strangely, my French gets more and more proficient in direct relation to the amount of alcohol I've consumed. At least I think it does. By the end of the evening the entire bar was given over to the singing of Scottish and French songs and Pierre Berbizier was delivering a passable imitation of the bagpipes. A superb night and a practical demonstration of how the attractions of the game and the special appeal of the Baa-Baas are universally understood and enjoyed.

THE HONG KONG SEVENS

The Hong Kong Sevens has a mystique and an allure all of its own. However, I'm sad to say that in 1991 when Scotland were invited to enter a national side for the first time, Happy Valley, where the event takes place, most assuredly didn't live up to its name. As Max Boyce might say, I should know, I was there!

A squad of nine – Tony Stanger, Scott Nichol, Scott Hastings, Craig Chalmers, Greig Oliver, John Jeffrey, Derek White, Ronnie Kirkpatrick and myself – were chosen by the SRU with JJ, who had been there four times before with invitation sides, doubling up as captain and coach.

In hindsight, of course, the entire adventure should have been approached much more professionally. There is no criticism implied or intended. It was just that because of the demands of the Championship season we had not put in the necessary work to have made a decent fist of our invitation.

Despite the fact that the sevens game originated in Scotland – at Melrose where in 1883 Ned Haig, a local butcher, dreamt it up as a fund-raising venture – we had been left far behind when it came to the type of power-play that now takes place on the International seven-a-sides circuit. In the Southern Hemisphere they take it all desperately seriously and the Kiwis actually hold seven-a-side trials before selecting their team to take part in the prestigious Hong Kong event. Of course, we know that now. We should probably have known it beforehand too, but when the nine of us arrived there, straight after our Five Nations' match against Ireland and with just a couple of days in which to get used to the radically altered disciplines of the abbreviated game we were like lambs to the slaughter. When we took part in a training session with the American Eagles the day after our arrival in Hong Kong that was the first time that we had played any seven-a-side rugby for an entire season, and some of us hadn't played sevens for an awful lot longer than that.

You can get away with that type of preparation if you have a set of forwards who can win ball allied to scorching pace in the threequarters. It has to be, though, the kind of searing pace possessed by the likes of Harlequins' speedster Andy Harriman, or New Zealand's Eric Rush or even Ayr's Derek Stark. Pace is the absolute be-all and end-all of the seven-a-side game. Unfortunately, we didn't have that kind of presence in our line-up. If you don't have that kind of pace then you can make up for it to a limited extent by enlightened team-work but that blend of togetherness only comes with prolonged practice and that was another commodity we were short on.

Privately, we had set ourselves the target of getting to the semi-finals. In the circumstances we reckoned that if we could have achieved that then we would have done well. Sadly, it was not to be.

We played Sri Lanka in our opening tie and the Selkirk centre Scott Nichol ran in for a hat-trick of tries in a 28-6 win. I picked up an ankle injury and had to go off to the hospital for a precautionary X-ray so missed the next tie against the Soviet Bears which was won 20-6; nothing showed up on the ankle X-ray and I was just about OK for our quarter-final tie against Canada the following day.

Basically, the Canadians were better than we were. No excuses, they simply outplayed us. They won 24-4 and deserved their victory. We felt that we had let down the huge Caledonian contingent in Hong Kong – many of them expatriates who, like expats everywhere, become a thousand times more Scottish than they ever were in Scotland – and we took a great deal of stick back home.

Perhaps our contribution to the tournament was best summed up during the competitors' parade when, resplendent in our kilts, we turned in unison, flipped up the kilts, and performed a collective 'moon' towards the trackside spectators. Unfortunately, the photographs of nine naked Scottish backsides winged their way around the world and appeared in newspapers and magazines back home. Frozen forever in glorious technicolour it didn't look like the good idea it had seemed at the time. Allied to our poor performance in the event itself, our 'moon' didn't go down especially well back in Scotland. We each received letters of rebuke from the SRU president Charlie Stewart. You learn to regret these things but what is done can't be undone. The sight of nine naked backsides was, however, the perfect metaphor for the way that we had played!

A ROUND WITH NICK FALDO

Now that I've retired I still intend to keep reasonably fit through tennis, ski-ing and keeping on my regular weight-training programme. Golf, though, will become my first choice of game. I've always played, off and on, and now that I have the time I intend to take it up much more seriously. I've got a set of clubs courtesy of the old-established Ben Sayers club-making firm in North Berwick, Scotland. I just hope I can do them justice.

Another of the bonus events which came my way by dint of being the Scottish rugby skipper – and perhaps, too, because United Distillers are my employers – was an invitation to take part in the annual Bell's Scottish Pro-am golf competition over the famous King's Course at Gleneagles in Perthshire.

My partner was Nick Faldo and I can tell you I have never been more nervous in my life. You can forget about the nerves before our Grand Slam match against England or before the third Test decider with the Lions in Australia. This was the real thing. Sweating palms, shaking hands, the lot. Standing on the first tee with 500 people and Nick Faldo looking on, my legs near enough turned to jelly.

At these prestige events, just like in the Open, there is a tee-side commentator whose job it is to announce over the PA who is the next player to go.

'On tee, Nick Faldo,' he says. Whereupon Nick steps forward and with the greatest of ease strikes a mighty blow and his ball disappears out of sight straight down the centre of the fairway.

'On tee, David Sole,' says the announcer. As I stepped forward to address the ball my hands and knees were shaking so much it was all that I could do to get into something approaching the proper stance. Think positive, I kept repeating to myself. After a couple of practice swings I offered up a silent prayer that I wouldn't make a complete mess of it. To my great relief, although I didn't connect as sweetly as I might have done, I at least got the ball off the tee and down the fairway. I can't begin to tell you how relieved I was. Each to his own, I suppose, but I really do hand it to those professional golfers who have to go through that every day of their working lives.

AN AUDIENCE WITH MRS T

Choices, choices. What was one to do? Before the Grand Slam decider against England in 1990 two invitations arrived chez Sole in Edinburgh. One was to attend a reception hosted by the Thatchers at 10 Downing Street and the other, which arrived just days before the game, was to appear on BBC TV's *Wogan Show*. Both events were to take place on the Monday immediately following the match. Sorry, Terry, but it wasn't really that much of a contest.

Jane and I decided that we might never get the chance again and that we were quite keen to meet Mrs Thatcher. We also wanted to see behind the world's most famous front door. Subsequently I discovered that England skipper Will Carling had received the same double invitation but had opted for Terry rather than the Thatchers.

During the week of the game Wogan's office called to say that Will was going to be appearing and that they would really like me to go along as well. (Left unsaid was what they obviously meant: We'd better have Sole along too just in case his lot win!) I said I was very sorry but we had already accepted an invitation to a reception at 10 Downing Street and it wasn't possible to do both. John Jeffrey and Ian McGeechan upheld Scottish honour on the *Wogan Show* while Jane and I sampled the delights of Downing Street. We flew down to London from Edinburgh with JJ. On our arrival at Heathrow we got an indication of the relative importance of the two events! As was only to be expected, Jane and myself had to find our own way to Downing Street but the BBC had laid on a limo for JJ. We hitched a lift with John and the BBC driver dropped us off at Downing Street after he had deposited JJ at TV Centre.

The reception was interesting and enjoyable. The first thing that immediately strikes one on going through the front door is just how big the PM's official London residence is inside. Mrs Thatcher and Denis were personally greeting all of those who had been invited, and very gracious they were too. There was, though, a bizarre and embarrassing moment when it was our turn to be introduced.

As we shook hands Denis the rugby buff and one-time referee said to me: 'Bad luck about Saturday, old boy.'

Whereupon, quick as a flash, Mrs Thatcher intervened to say: 'No, no, Denis. This is David Sole, not Will Carling. The Scots won.' Downward glances and embarrassed shuffling of feet all around.

I've met the former Prime Minister on a number of occasions. She always struck me as being amazingly self-assured, intimidating even. Within moments of arriving in a company she would more or less have taken control and would be running the show. A truly formidable lady.

There was a real cross-section of folk from all walks of life at the reception. In addition to the various captains of industry and a representative spinkling from the ranks of the statutory 'Great and the Good', among the other guests whose presence caught my eye were the cricketers Sir Len Hutton and Cyril Washbrook; the javelin thrower Steve Backley and various Commonwealth Games gold medallists; the cast of *Coronation Street* and last, but by no means least, dear old Cilla Black. It was, by any standards, a mixed bunch.

CHARITY WORK

After our 1990 championship win when the entire Scottish nation seemed to be in the grip of Grand Slam fever, the squad cut a record of *Flower of Scotland* with Ronnie Browne of The Corries. It was a unique experience and one that we all enjoyed but I don't think any of us got rich on the proceeds! Another spin-off from the Grand Slam did, however, pay dividends. The whisky distillers Glenmorangie produced a special one-off Grand Slam Dram which was sold in aid of the former West of Scotland player David Millar who sadly damaged his spine while playing rugby in New Zealand and who is now confined to a wheelchair. David's appeal fund benefited, I am told, to the tune of some £20,000 from the Grand Slam Dram exercise.

The fact that I have been able to capitalise for charity on whatever 'fame' has come my way as a result of my involvement with Scottish rugby has been one of the most pleasurable spin-offs to accrue from my rugby life.

I became heavily involved with the appeal raised by the Royal Hospital for Sick Children in Edinburgh. I was one of a number of 'celebrities' who appeared on fund-raising TV commercials and on billboard hoardings. Additionally, I decided to donate any speaking or public appearances fees to the Sick Kids' Appeal. My employer, United Distillers, kindly agreed to match, pound-for-pound, whatever I raised and to date I think we have, between us, raised some £4,000 for this eminently worthwhile cause.

Similarly, I've become involved with appeals for sufferers from Muscular Dystrophy and, most recently, became a trustee of a new medical charity called Flower of Scotland which seeks to combat Scotland's horrendous heart and lung disease record. Scotland tops the world league table in terms of heart and lung disease and much of this is attributed to bad diet and a sedentary life-style. The Flower of Scotland Trust is currently in its very early stages but once we have it up and running it will fulfil the twin functions of education and fund-raising. It has been decided that the three existing medical charities which will benefit from our fund-raising efforts will be the British Heart Foundation, Cancer Research and the Chest, Heart and Stroke Association.

Whenever I become involved in these causes I like to go along and see for myself just what is entailed. It is on occasions like these, on visits to hospitals and medical establishments, that one realises just how incredibly lucky one has been. Myself and my family have all been blessed with good health and for that we are eternally grateful. It sounds dreadfully corny but I do consider it a privilege to do whatever I can to help others less fortunate than ourselves.

This was brought home to me in particularly poignant fashion when I was invited to go along to a Marie Curie centre for the terminally ill at Stobhill in Glasgow. The invitation arrived shortly after the Grand Slam match. I accepted but have to admit that I had not been looking forward to the visit and had put it off for quite a few months.

Eventually, Jane and the children accompanied me and far from being a trying or upsetting experience it was, in its way, very satisfying and uplifting.

That visit to the hospice was a real eye-opener. The patients and the staff were very special people. The terminally ill residents were mainly old folk and it was humbling to see the real delight that they got from our having gone along. Gemma, our youngest, was a particular hit. One very frail old gent was in bed with his family around him. Gemma walked across and beamed a huge grin. He smiled back. His entire face lit up and his family said it was the first time that he had smiled in months. Sometimes when you are playing competitive sport to a high level it can become claustrophobic. You tend to focus so hard on your sport that tunnel vision sets in. Our experience at that hospice in Glasgow and the work that I've done with the Sick Kids' hospital really puts rugby into perspective and, as I've said, makes you appreciate just how fortunate you have been to have your health and to have lived such a rewarding life.

Throw in a *Jim'll Fix It*, a hat-trick of David Coleman's *A Question of Sport* (in which incidentally I have never appeared on the winning side and as an old 'has been' I doubt if I ever will), plus one or two other odds and ends and that more or less sums up the life of a Scottish rugby captain. Through the many highs and occasional lows it's been a real ball. I wouldn't have missed it for the world.

CAREER STATISTICS

SCOTTISH SCHOOLS (Season 1979–80)

	F	A
French Schools (Braidholm, Glasgow)	6	10
Welsh Schools (Murrayfield)	6	13
English Schools (Nuneaton)	13	11

UNIVERSITY AND CLUB RUGBY

Exeter University (1980–83): Appeared twice in Universities' Athletic Union final at Twickenham (1982 and 1983). Runners-up on both occasions.

Bath FC (1983–87): John Player Cup winners' medal 1987.

Edinburgh Academicals (1987–92): Runners-up McEwan's Division One championship, 1992.

ENGLISH COUNTIES and SCOTTISH DISTRICTS

Devon (1984): two appearances.

Somerset (1985): one appearance.

Anglo-Scots (1983–87): Debut against Lancashire. Eighteen appearances in total.

Edinburgh (1987–92): Eighteen appearances, including five as captain.
Champions 1988 and 1989.

SCOTLAND 'B'

	F	A
1983–84		
Ireland (The Greenyards)	22	13
France (Albi)	13	10
1984–85		
Ireland (Galway)†	20	23
France (Murrayfield)	21	12
1985–86		
Italy (Old Anniesland)	9	0

†Denotes try

SCOTLAND

Tours and World Cups, 1987 and 1991, appear separately

	F	A
1985–86		
France, Murrayfield	18	17
Wales, Cardiff	15	22
1986–87		
Ireland, Murrayfield	16	12
France, Paris	22	28
Wales, Murrayfield	21	15
England, Twickenham	12	21
1987–88		
Ireland, Dublin	18	22
France, Murrayfield	23	12
Wales, Cardiff	20	25
England, Murrayfield	6	9
1988–89		
Australia, Murrayfield	13	32
Wales, Murrayfield	23	7
England, Twickenham	12	12

Ireland, Murrayfield	37	21
France, Paris	3	19

1989–90

Fiji*, Murrayfield	38	17
Romania*†, Murrayfield	32	0
Ireland*, Dublin	13	10
France*, Murrayfield	21	0
Wales*, Cardiff	13	9
England*, Murrayfield	13	7

1990–91

Argentina*, Murrayfield	49	3
France*, Paris	9	15
Wales*, Murrayfield	32	12
England*, Twickenham	12	21
Ireland*, Murrayfield	28	25

1991–92

England*, Murrayfield	7	25
Ireland*, Dublin	18	10
France*, Murrayfield	10	6
Wales*, Cardiff	12	15

Non-Cap internationals:
1986–87

Japan, Murrayfield	33	18
Spain, Murrayfield	25	7

1987–88

France, Netherdale	15	12

1991–92

Romania*, Bucharest	12	18
Barbarians*, Murrayfield	16	16

*Denotes captain
†Denotes try

Scotland career record: Capped 44 times. Twenty-five appearances as captain, overtaking Ian McLauchlan's previous record of 19 during game against England in 1992. Fourteen victories as captain.

BARBARIANS

Nine appearances for the Baa-Baas (1987–92). Captained the side against All Blacks (1989); during Easter tour to Wales (1991) and against East Midlands (1992).

FRENCH BARBARIANS

Two appearances: against the NZ Maoris at Mont-de-Marsan (1988) and against the All Blacks (Agen) 1990.

WORLD CUP 1987

Fullbacks: A. G. Hastings (Watsonians), P. W. Dods (Gala).

Threequarters: G. R. T. Baird (Kelso), M. D. F. Duncan (West of Scotland), I. Tukalo (Selkirk), S. Hastings (Watsonians), K. W. Robertson (Melrose), A. V. Tait (Kelso).

Half-backs: J. Y. Rutherford (Selkirk), R. Cramb (Harlequins)*, D. S. Wyllie (Stewart's-Melville FP), R. J. Laidlaw (Jed-Forest), G. H. Oliver (Hawick).

Forwards: C. T. Deans (Hawick), captain, D. M. B. Sole (Bath), N. A. Rowan (Boroughmuir), I. G. Milne (Heriot's FP), A. K. Brewster (Stewart's-Melville FP), J. F. Richardson (Edinburgh Acads), J. R. E. Campbell-Lamerton (London Scottish), D. B. White (Gala), A. J. Tomes (Hawick), D. J. Turnbull (Hawick), F. Calder (Stewart's-Melville FP), J. Jeffrey (Kelso), I. A. M. Paxton (Selkirk).

*Replacement for J. Y. Rutherford (Selkirk).

Manager: R. D. S. Munro.

Coaches: Derrick Grant and Ian McGeechan.

Medical staff: Dr Clark Sharpe and Mr David McLean.

Pool Four runners-up. Lost 3–30 to New Zealand in quarter-final.

	F	A
France, Christchurch*	20	20
Zimbabwe, Wellington*	60	21
Romania, Dunedin*	55	28

Quarter final:
New Zealand, Wellington*   3   30

*Denotes games played in.

THE 1989 BRITISH LIONS IN AUSTRALIA

Fullbacks: P. W. Dods (Gala), A. G. Hastings (London Scottish).

Threequarters: J. A. Devereux (Bridgend), J. C. Evans (Llanelli), J. C. Guscott (Bath), M. R. Hall (Cambridge University and Bridgend), S. Hastings (Watsonians), B. J. Mullin (London Irish), C. Oti (Wasps), R. Underwood (Leicester and RAF).

Half-backs: C. R. Andrews* (Wasps), C. M. Chalmers (Melrose), A. Clement* (Swansea), P. M. Dean (St Mary's College), G. Armstrong (Jed-Forest), R. N. Jones (Swansea).

Forwards: P. J. Ackford (Harlequins), F. Calder, captain (Stewart's-Melville FP), G. J. Chilcott (Bath), W. A. Dooley (Preston Grasshoppers), M. Griffiths (Bridgend), J. Jeffrey (Kelso), D. G. Lenihan (Cork Constitution), B. C. Moore (Nottingham), R. L. Norster (Cardiff), D. Richards (Leicester), R. A. Robinson (Bath), S. J. Smith (Ballymena), D. M. B. Sole (Edinburgh Academicals), M. C. Teague (Gloucester), D. B. White (London Scottish), D. Young (Cardiff).

*Replacements.

Manager: D. C. T. Rowlands (Wales).

Coaches: I. R. McGeechan (Scotland) and R. M. Uttley (England).

Medical staff: Dr B. Gilfeather and K. Murphy (both RFU).

Tour record: Played 12   Won 11   Lost 1   Drawn 0

	F	A
Western Australia*	44	0
Australia 'B'	23	18
Queensland*	19	15
Queensland 'B'	30	6
New South Wales*	23	21
New South Wales 'B'*†‡	39	19
First Test*	12	30
ACT§	41	25
Second Test*	19	12

Third Test*	19	18
NSW Country XV	72	13
Anzacs*†	19	15

*Denotes games played in
†Denotes captaincy
‡Denotes try
§Denotes replacement

SCOTLAND TOUR PARTY IN NEW ZEALAND, 1990

Fullbacks: P. W. Dods (Gala), A. G. Hastings (London Scottish).

Threequarters: A. Moore (Edinburgh Academicals), S. T. G. Porter (Malone), A. G. Stanger (Hawick), I. Tukalo (Selkirk), S. Hastings (Watsonians), S. R. P. Lineen (Boroughmuir), A. C. Redpath (Melrose), A. G. Shiel (Melrose).

Half-backs: C. M. Chalmers (Melrose), D. S. Wyllie (Stewart's-Melville FP), G. Armstrong (Jed-Forest), G. H. Oliver (Hawick).

Forwards: A. K. Brewster (Stewart's-Melville FP), A. P. Burnell (London Scottish), I. G. Milne (Heriot's FP), D. M. B. Sole (Edinburgh Academicals), captain, J. Allan (Edinburgh Academicals), K. S. Milne (Heriot's FP), D. F. Cronin (Bath), C. A. Gray (Nottingham), J. F. Richardson (Edinburgh Academicals), G. W. Weir (Melrose), G. A. E. Buchanan-Smith (Heriot's FP), F. Calder (Stewart's-Melville FP), J. Jeffrey (Kelso), D. J. Turnbull (Hawick), G. R. Marshall (Selkirk), D. B. White (London Scottish).

Manager: D. S. Paterson.

Coaches: I. R. McGeechan and D. Grant.

Tour record: Played 8   Won 5   Lost 2   Drawn 1

	F	A
Poverty Bay – East Coast*	45	0
Wellington*	16	16
Nelson Bays – Marlborough	23	6
Canterbury*	21	12
Southland	45	12
First Test*†	16	31

Manawatu	19	4
Second Test*	18	21

*Denotes games played in
†Denotes try

WORLD CUP 1991

Fullbacks: A. G. Hastings (Watsonians), P. W. Dods (Gala).

Threequarters: A. G. Stanger (Hawick), I. Tukalo (Selkirk), S. R. P. Lineen (Boroughmuir), M. Moncrieff (Gala), A. G. Shiel (Melrose), S. Hastings (Watsonians).

Half-backs: C. M. Chalmers (Melrose), D. S. Wyllie (Stewart's-Melville FP), G. Armstrong (Jed-Forest), G. H. Oliver (Hawick).

Forwards: D. M. B. Sole (Edinburgh Academicals), captain, A. P. Burnell (London Scottish), A. G. J. Watt (Glasgow High-Kelvinside), D. F. Milne (Heriot's FP), K. S. Milne (Heriot's FP), J. Allan (Edinburgh Academicals), D. F. Cronin (Bath), G. W. Weir (Melrose), C. A. Gray (Nottingham), F. Calder (Stewart's-Melville FP), J. Jeffrey (Kelso), D. J. Turnbull (Hawick), G. R. Marshall (Selkirk), D. B. White (London Scottish).

Manager: D. S. Paterson.

Coaches: I. R. McGeechan, J. W. Telfer, D. Grant, D. W. Morgan.

Medical staff: Dr Donald Macleod, Dr J. P. Robson, Mr David McLean.

Pool two winners. Quarter-final winners against Western Samoa. Defeated in semi-final against England. Defeated in third-place play-off against New Zealand.

Pool matches:

	F	A
Japan,*† Murrayfield	47	9
Zimbabwe, Murrayfield	51	12
Ireland,* Murrayfield	24	15
Quarter final:		
Western Samoa,* Murrayfield	28	6

Semi-final:
England,* Murrayfield   6   9

Third place play-off:
New Zealand,* Cardiff   6   13

*Denotes played in
†Denotes replaced hurt after 75 minutes

SCOTLAND TOUR PARTY IN AUSTRALIA, 1992

Fullbacks: A. G. Hastings (Watsonians), P. W. Dods (Gala).

Threequarters: D. C. Bain (Melrose), A. G. Shiel (Melrose), K. M. Logan (Stirling County), S. R. P. Lineen (Boroughmuir), S. Hastings (Watsonians), D. A. Stark (Ayr).

Half-backs: C. M. Chalmers (Melrose), D. B. Millard (London Scottish), A. D. Nicol (Dundee HSFP), G. P. J. Townsend (Gala).

Forwards: P. M. Jones (Gloucester), D. M. B. Sole (Edinburgh Academicals), captain, A. G. J. Watt (Glasgow High-Kelvinside), P. H. Wright (Boroughmuir), I. Corcoran (Gala), K. S. Milne (Heriot's FP), M. W. Scott (Dunfermline),* D. F. Cronin (London Scottish), N. G. B. Edwards (Harlequins), C. A. Gray (Nottingham), G. W. Weir (Melrose), S. J. Reid (Boroughmuir), C. D. Hogg (Melrose), A. E. D. Macdonald (Heriot's FP),† D. J. McIvor (Edinburgh Academicals), J. Robertson (Heriot's FP), I. R. Smith (Gloucester), R. I. Wainwright (Edinburgh Academicals).

*Replacement for K. S. Milne.
†Replacement for S. J. Reid.

Manager: C. Ritchie.
Assistant manager: D. W. Arneil.

Coaches: J. R. Dixon and D. I. Johnston.

Tour record: Played 8   Won 2   Lost 4   Drawn 2

	F	A
Northern Territory Invitation XV	16	17
Queensland*	15	15
Emerging Wallabies*†	24	24

New South Wales	15	35
New South Wales Country Origin	26	10
First Test*	12	27
Queensland Country Origin	29	12
Second Test*‡	13	37

*Denotes games played in
†Denotes replacement
‡Denotes try